THE HOLY QUR'ĀN

Translations of Selected Verses

OTHER BOOKS BY MARTIN LINGS
AVAILABLE FROM
THE ISLAMIC TEXTS SOCIETY

◆

Muhammad: His Life Based on the Earliest Sources

A Sufi Saint of the Twentieth Century:
Shaikh Aḥmad al-ʿAlawī

Sufi Poems: A Mediaeval Anthology

The Book of Certainty: the Sufi Doctrine of
Faith, Vision and Gnosis

What is Sufism?

THE HOLY QUR'ĀN

Translations of Selected Verses

Martin Lings

THE ROYAL AAL AL-BAYT INSTITUTE
FOR ISLAMIC THOUGHT

THE ISLAMIC TEXTS SOCIETY

Copyright © Royal Aal al-Bayt Institute for Islamic Thought 2007

This first edition published 2007 by
The Royal Aal al-Bayt Institute for Islamic Thought &
The Islamic Texts Society
22A Brooklands Avenue,
Cambridge, CB2 8DQ, UK

ISBN: 978 1 903682 52 4 hardback
ISBN: 978 1 903682 53 1 paper

*All rights reserved. No part of this publication
may be reproduced, stored in a retrieval system,
or transmitted in any form or by any means, electronic,
mechanical, photocopying, recording, or otherwise,
without the prior written permission of the Publisher.*

British Library Cataloguing-in-Publication Data.
A catalogue record for this book is
available from the British Library.

Cover design copyright © The Islamic Texts Society

Cover illustration detail Moroccan Qur'ān, 975 AH/1568 AD.
British Library Or. MS 1405, f. 400.
Copyright © The British Library Board.

Printed in Turkey by Mega Printing.

Contents

List of Sources with Abbreviations. xi
Preface. xiii
Translations. 1
   Al-Fātiḥah (I). 2
     (verses 1-7)
   Al-Baqarah (II). 4
     (verses 1-5, 8, 11-12, 14, 25-26, 30, 34-35, 37-38, 60-61, 74, 109, 115, 135, 143-144, 152-157, 185-186, 193, 198, 203, 214, 217, 245, 249, 253, 260, 269, 285-286)
   Āl-ʿImrān (III). 18
     (verses 19, 33, 36-37, 40, 42, 59-61, 96, 110, 118, 120, 137-139, 142-144, 159, 169, 173, 191, 195)
   An-Nisāʾ (IV). 26
     (verses 31, 43, 69, 80, 94-95, 130, 142, 156-157, 171, 174)
   Al-Māʾidah (V). 30
     (verses 3, 5, 12, 24, 48, 54, 69, 82-83, 114)
   Al-Anʿām (VI). 38
     (verses 29, 52, 54, 59, 75-79, 91, 103, 122, 125, 154)
   Al-Aʿrāf (VII). 44
     (verses 43, 46, 55-56, 127, 143-144, 156-157, 172, 180, 187)
   Al-Anfāl (VIII). 50
     (verses 1-2, 9, 12, 17, 24, 39, 57-58, 61-63, 67, 69-70)
   At-Tawbah (IX). 54
     (verses 25-28, 33, 36, 40, 60, 72, 80, 84, 103, 115, 118)
   Yūnus (X). 60
     (verses 5, 7, 24-25, 47)

Hūd (XI)... 62
(verses 7, 17, 37, 56, 105-108)
Yūsuf (XII)... 66
(verses 18, 31, 53, 76, 84, 92)
Ar-Ra'd (XIII)... 68
(verses 12-13, 17, 28, 39)
Ibrāhīm (XIV)... 70
(verses 24-26, 37)
Al-Ḥijr (XV)... 72
(verses 21, 23, 29, 42, 47)
An-Naḥl (XVI)... 72
(verses 13, 42, 78, 126)
Al-Isrā' (XVII)... 74
(verses 1, 21, 41, 44, 55, 60, 65, 79, 81, 85, 95, 110)
Al-Kahf (XVIII)... 78
(verses 23-24, 28, 60, 65-70, 109)
Maryam (XIX)... 80
(verses 16-21, 40)
Ṭā Hā (XX)... 82
(verses 11-12, 14, 26-27, 32, 41, 109, 111, 114, 120)
Al-Anbiyā' (XXI)... 84
(verses 16, 23, 30, 35, 78-79, 91, 104, 107)
Al-Ḥajj (XXII)... 86
(verses 26-27, 39-40, 46-47, 74)
Al-Mu'minūn (XXIII)... 88
(verse 115)
An-Nūr (XXIV)... 90
(verses 11, 15-17, 22, 35, 37, 39, 42)
Al-Furqān (XXV)... 96
(verses 1, 15-16, 21-22, 48-50, 53-54, 61-62, 70)
Ash-Shu'arā' (XXVI)... 98
(verses 192-194, 214-215)
An-Naml (XXVII)... 100
(verses 7-8, 29-30, 38-44)

Contents

Al-Qaṣaṣ (XXVIII) 104
(verses 56, 68, 71-73, 85, 88)
Al-ʿAnkabūt (XXIX) 106
(verses 43, 45, 64, 69)
Ar-Rūm (XXX) 108
(verses 4, 7-8, 21, 30)
Luqmān (XXXI) 110
(verses 15, 27)
As-Sajdah (XXXII) 110
(verses 16-17)
Al-Aḥzāb (XXXIII) 112
(verses 9-11, 21-23, 28-29, 35, 37, 40, 53, 56, 72)
Sabā' (XXXIV) 118
(verse 9)
Fāṭir (XXXV) 118
(verse 15)
Yā Sīn (XXXVI) 120
(verses 1-11, 13, 22, 26-27, 36-42, 55-58, 78-79, 82-83)
Aṣ-Ṣāffāt (XXXVII) 126
(verses 28, 177)
Ṣād (XXXVIII) 126
(verses 35, 67, 75)
Az-Zumar (XXXIX) 128
(verses 23, 53-54, 67)
Ghāfir (XL) 130
(verses 16, 44, 60, 78)
Fuṣṣilat (XLI) 132
(verses 30-32, 35, 37, 53)
Ash-Shūrā (XLII) 134
(verses 11, 52-53)
Az-Zukhruf (XLIII) 134
(verse 84)

THE HOLY QUR'ĀN: SELECTED VERSES

Ad-Dukhān (XLIV)............ 136
  (verse 38)
Al-Aḥqāf (XLVI)............. 136
  (verse 3)
Muḥammad (XLVII)............ 136
  (verse 38)
Al-Fatḥ (XLVIII)............ 138
  (verses 1-2, 4-5, 10, 18, 21, 27)
Al-Ḥujurāt (XLIX)........... 142
  (verse 14)
Qāf (L)..................... 142
  (verses 16, 37)
Adh-Dhāriyāt (LI)........... 144
  (verses 50, 55-56)
Aṭ-Ṭūr (LII)................ 144
  (verses 48-49)
An-Najm (LIII).............. 146
  (verses 13-18, 42)
Al-Qamar (LIV).............. 146
  (verse 55)
Ar-Raḥmān (LV).............. 148
  (verses 1-78)
Al-Wāqiʿah (LVI)............ 160
  (verses 10-11, 13-14, 25-26, 38-41, 77-80, 85)
Al-Ḥadīd (LVII)............. 164
  (verses 3-4, 11, 16)
Al-Ḥashr (LIX).............. 166
  (verses 8, 14, 21)
Al-Mumtaḥanah (LX).......... 168
  (verse 7)
Aṣ-Ṣaff (LXI)............... 168
  (verses 4, 9)
Al-Munāfiqūn (LXIII)........ 168
  (verse 9)

At-Taḥrīm (LXVI). 170
   (verses 1, 4-5, 10-12)
Al-Qalam (LXVIII). 174
   (verses 1-4)
Al-Jinn (LXXII). 174
   (verses 1-2)
Al-Muzzammil (LXXIII). 176
   (verses 1-5, 8-10, 17, 19-20)
Al-Muddaththir (LXXIV). 180
   (verses 1-5, 8-10)
Al-Qiyāmah (LXXV). 180
   (verse 2)
Al-Insān (LXXVI). 182
   (verses 5-6, 26, 29)
Al-Mursalāt (LXXVII). 182
   (verses 35-36)
An-Nabaʾ (LXXVIII). 184
   (verses 10-11)
ʿAbasa (LXXX). 184
   (verses 1-2, 5-10)
Al-Muṭaffifīn (LXXXIII). 186
   (verses 7, 13-14, 18, 21, 25-28)
Al-Burūj (LXXXV). 186
   (verse 22)
Aṭ-Ṭāriq (LXXXVI). 188
   (verse 17)
Al-Ghāshiyah (LXXXVIII). 188
   (verses 17-20)
Al-Fajr (LXXXIX). 188
   (verses 27-30)
Aḍ-Ḍuḥā (XCIII). 190
   (verses 1-11)
Ash-Sharḥ (XCIV). 192
   (verses 1, 5)

At-Tīn (xcv). 192
   (verses 1-8)
Al-ʿAlaq (xcvi). 194
   (verses 1-5, 19)
Al-Qadr (xcvii). 194
   (verses 1-5)
Al-Qāriʿah (ci). 196
   (verses 4-5)
Al-ʿAṣr (ciii). 196
   (verses 1-3)
Al-Fīl (cv). 198
   (verses 1-5)
Quraysh (cvi). 198
   (verses 1-4)
Al-Kāfirūn (cix). 200
   (verses 1-6)
Al-Ikhlāṣ (cxii). 200
   (verses 1-4)
Al-Falaq (cxiii). 202
   (verses 1-5)
An-Nās (cxiv). 202
   (verses 1-6)
Appendix: Ninety-Nine Beautiful Names of God . . 205
Index. 213

List of Sources in Chronological Order with Abbreviations[1]

BOOKS

[BC] : *The Book of Certainty*, Rider, London, 1952; revised and expanded edn. Islamic Texts Society, Cambridge, 1992.

[SS] : *A Moslem Saint of the Twentieth Century*, Allen & Unwin, London, 1961; 3rd edn., as *A Sufi Saint of the Twentieth Century*, Islamic Texts Society, Cambridge, 1993.

[WS] : *What is Sufism?*, George Allen & Unwin, London, 1975; 2nd edn. Islamic Texts Society, Cambridge, 1993.

[QACI] : *The Quranic Art of Calligraphy and Illumination*, World of Islam Festival Trust, London, 1976.

[M] : *Muhammad: His Life Based on the Earliest Sources*, George Allen & Unwin and The Islamic Texts Society, London, 1983; 2nd edn. Islamic Texts Society, Cambridge, 1991.

[SA] : *Symbol and Archetype*, Quinta Essentia, Cambridge, 1991.

[SP] : *Sufi Poems*, Islamic Texts Society, Cambridge, 2004.

[Mec.] : *Mecca*, Archetype, Cambridge, 2004.

[RS] : *Return to the Spirit*, Fons Vitae, Kentucky, 2005.

[SQCI] : *Splendours of Qur'ān Calligraphy and Illumination*, Thesaurus Islamicus Foundation, Vaduz, 2005.

ARTICLES

[ICCT] : 'The Islamic and Christian Conceptions of the March of Time', *The Islamic Quarterly*, vol. 1, no. 4, 1954.

[PI] : 'Proofs of Islam', Islamic Cultural Centre, London, 1954.

---

[1] Where reference has been made to a later editon, both editions have been included.

[OS]	:	'The Origins of Sufism', *The Islamic Quarterly*, vol. III, no. 1, 1956.
[S]	:	'Sufism', *Religion in the Middle East*, ed. A. J. Arberry, Cambridge University Press, Cambridge, 1969.
[SCR-SA]	:	'Sufi Answers to Questions On Ultimate Reality', *Studies in Comparative Religions*, Summer/Autumn, 1979.
[NOS]	:	'The Nature and Origin of Sufism', *Islamic Spirituality: Foundations*, Routledge & Kegan Paul, London, 1987.
[MP]	:	'Mystical Poetry', *The Cambridge History of Arabic Literature: Abbasid Belles-Lettres*, Cambridge University Press, Cambridge, 1990.

LECTURES

[L-HOD]	:	Human Origins and Destinies According to the Great Religions of the World.
[L-II]	:	An Introduction to Islam.
[L-MPP]	:	Metaphysics and the Perennial Philosophy.
[L-QD]	:	The Qur'ānic Doctrine of the Afterlife.
[L-QOS]	:	The Qur'ānic Origins of Sufism.
[L-UQ]	:	The Universality of the Qur'ān.

UNPUBLISHED MATERIAL

[PT]	:	Private Talks
[UM]	:	Unpublished Material, 1938–2005

Preface

IN 2004, the Royal Aal al-Bayt Institute for Islamic Thought of Jordan commissioned Dr Martin Lings, Shaykh Abū Bakr Sirāj ad-Dīn, to translate the Qur'ān into English. Unfortunately, this work had not advanced very far when Dr Lings passed away on 12 May 2005. The Institute was graciously granted access by Dr Lings' widow to his unpublished papers, and permission to put together and publish a collection of all the translations that exist in Dr Lings' books, articles, lectures and private and unpublished papers.

The task of collating this material was undertaken by Mr Aftab Ahmed, American University of Sharjah, who has been familiar with the work of Dr Lings for many years. The Publishers wish to express their gratitude to Mr Ahmed for his complete dedication and unstinting support. A list of all sources used with abbreviations is included; it must be noted that this does not include all of Dr Lings' publications but only those in which Qur'ānic verses were found. The list is in chronological order with unpublished material [UM] last as it was not possible to date this. The Arabic verses of the Qur'ān have been placed on facing pages to the English translations. The Sūra-Chapter headings have not been translated as we could not find translations for all of them in the writings. The headings, therefore, appear only in transliteration; and in this, we have followed Dr Lings' preferred system which is more phonetic than alphabetic.

Dr Lings' published manuscripts were always published exactly as they were received by the publisher and were never edited. Therefore, out of respect for Dr Lings, we have reproduced the translations from the different works as they appear in the originals without any editing. The reader may therefore find in this work some variations which may appear as inconsistencies. This is inevitable given that we have collated material from several books and unedited private papers written over a number of decades. The original works are of course completely consistent in themselves, the problem arises only because we have brought together extracts from different writings. We are thinking in particular of the transliteration of Arabic words. Readers will note that a word may be transliterated differently in different places. An interesting feature here is to see how the transliteration of Arabic words has evolved over Dr Lings' lifetime and the increased integration of Arabic terms into the English language. For example, the word Qur'ān itself appears as: Koran, Qoran, Quran, Qur'an and Qur'ān.

Dr Lings often translated the same verse in different ways; we have included all the variations in chronological order. The only exception to this ordering is when the earlier translations were only partial translations. In these cases, we have placed the full translation at the top, followed by all the others in chronological order. This was particularly necessary when a verse continued on the following page as the Arabic would then not have matched the English. We believe that this is the first time ever that multiple translations of the same verses from the Qur'ān have appeared together in one book. The different translations of a single verse are a wonderful illustration of the possible interpretations of the original Arabic as the sacred language can never have a single definitive translation. The repetition of verse after verse with seemingly unimportant variations might strike some readers as unnecessary. The effect of reading these translations, however, is not at all unrelated to the mystery of

Preface

rhythm which, as Dr Lings explains in *Sufi Saint of the Twentieth Century*, acts 'as a bridge from the perpetual fluctuation of this world or, more particularly, of the soul, to the Immutability of the Infinite World of the Divine Peace.'[1] Thus the different translations of a single verse other than being of interest to students of Arabic and of translation who will appreciate the often inspired turns of phrases crafted by Dr Lings, and other than their interest to Qur'ānic scholars who will appreciate the successful solutions given to some difficult passages, the multiple translations have in a way the interiorizing effect of ritual repetition. It could not be otherwise, since reading this book is sharing in the intimate lifelong relationship of a saintly man with his Scripture, a relation in which there is no real repetition due to the depth and mystery of the Sacred Text and where every instance of the same word has a uniqueness and utter unrepeatability deriving directly from the Divine Infinitude.

We have deliberately cited the entire text of the Arabic verses translated here even when there are only partial translations of the verses. For we believe that whilst it is one thing to quote parts of verses of the Holy Qur'ān—that is, parts of verses whose meaning can stand alone and which do not contradict the meanings of the complete verse—in the context of religious instruction or scholarship, it is altogether another to publish a whole book full of incomplete verses of the Holy Qur'ān. Moreover, citing whole verses in Arabic gives the reader better insight into the English translations themselves and into their accuracy. All ellipses in the English translation have been marked in the text in order to faithfully reflect the difference with the Arabic.

---

[1] *A Sufi Saint of the Twentieth Century: Shaikh Aḥmad al-ʿAlawī, his Spiritual Heritage and Legacy*, Islamic Texts Society, Cambridge, 1993, p. 158. See also *ibid*., p. 92.

THE HOLY QUR'ĀN: SELECTED VERSES

We would also like to alert readers to the following: Due to the fact that the Arabic verses are longer than the English translations and because in some cases we have several translations of the one verse, we have been obliged to make a number of compromises with the layout. Firstly, on the English pages, we would have preferred a smaller line spacing between the translations of the same verse and a wider one between the different verses in order to make each new verse clearer; this was not possible and we were obliged to have the same line spacing throughout. Readers should therefore refer regularly to the verse numbers. Secondly, on the Arabic pages we were obliged to follow on some of the verses in order to be able to match the layout with the English. This has been kept to an absolute minimum and only where the verses follow each other numerically. Thirdly, some of the translations are very short, at times only of one or two Arabic words. We have preferred to retain these as we felt that they are of value from the point of view of translation. Finally, due to the missing verses in a large number of the Sūrahs, this work cannot be used in the usual way for the recitation of Qur'ān; it is intended as a supplement to this recitation and not a replacement.

At the end of *The Holy Qur'ān: Translations of Selected Verses*, we have included an appendix of the Ninety-nine Beautiful Names of God with as many translations of the Names as could be found in the writings of Dr Lings. We have also included an index which we hope will work as a short concordance.

In his article 'Proofs of Islam', Dr Lings calls the Qur'ān 'the greatest proof of Islam,' and he says, 'As a man approaches Islam, he soon comes face to face with the *Basmalah* and the *Ḥamdalah*, with the *Sūrat al-Fātiḥah* and the *Sūrat al-Ikhlāṣ*, and first of all there is the *Shahādah* itself with its marvellous form, its dazzling clarity and its mystery of

Preface

infinite implications. All these Quranic outposts bear the print of the Absolute; they are as gates, which invite and compel one to enter more deeply into the Holy Book.'[1] We would like to end with a further quotation from the above article, 'It is sometimes a good, as it were, to take stock of our treasures, to count up some of our reasons for saying *al-Ḥamduli'Llāh*.'[2] *Al-Ḥamduli'Llāh*, therefore, for the Holy Qur'ān; for all that helps in deepening our understanding of it; and for the life, example and writings of Shaykh Abū Bakr Sirāj ad-Dīn, *raḍiya Allāh ʿanhu*.

The Publishers
11 Ṣafar 1428/1 March 2007

---

[1] 'Proofs of Islam', Islamic Cultural Centre, London, 1954, p. 8.
[2] *Ibid.*, p. 1.

THE HOLY QUR'ĀN
Translations of Selected Verses

THE HOLY QUR'ĀN: SELECTED VERSES

Al-Fātiḥah (I)

1. In the Name of God, the Clement, the Merciful. [UM]
1. In the Name of God, the Infinitely Good, the Ever-Merciful. [UM]
1. In the Name of God, the All-Merciful, the Merciful. [SS]
1. In the Name of God, the Infinitely Good, the All-Merciful. [M] [SQCI]
1. In the Name of God, the Infinitely Good, the Boundlessly Merciful. [SA]
2. Praise be to God, the Lord of the worlds. [SS] [M]
3. The Infinitely Good, the All-Merciful. [M]
4. Owner of the Day of Judgement. [UM]
4. Master of the day of judgement. [M]
5. Thee we worship and from Thee we seek help. [UM]
5. It is Thee we adore, and it is in Thee we seek refuge. [UM]
5. Thee we worship, and in Thee we seek help. [M]
6. Lead us on the straight path. [UM]
6. Guide us upon the way of Transcendence. [UM]
6. Lead us along the straight path. [OS] [SS]
6. Guide us up the ascending path. [WS] [RS]
6. Guide us upon the straight path. [M] [SA]
7. The Path of those to whom Thou accordest Thy Grace, not of those who incur Thy wrath, nor of those who go astray. [UM]
7. Those upon whom is Thy Grace, not those upon whom is Thy Wrath, nor those who go astray. [UM]
7. The way of those on whom Thy Grace is not those who deserve anger nor those who are astray. [UM]
7. The path of those on whom Thy grace is, not those on whom Thine anger is, nor those who are astray. [M]

(١) سُورَةُ ٱلْفَاتِحَةِ

بِسْمِ ٱللَّهِ ٱلرَّحْمَٰنِ ٱلرَّحِيمِ ۝

ٱلْحَمْدُ لِلَّهِ رَبِّ ٱلْعَٰلَمِينَ ۝

ٱلرَّحْمَٰنِ ٱلرَّحِيمِ ۝

مَٰلِكِ يَوْمِ ٱلدِّينِ ۝

إِيَّاكَ نَعْبُدُ وَإِيَّاكَ نَسْتَعِينُ ۝

ٱهْدِنَا ٱلصِّرَٰطَ ٱلْمُسْتَقِيمَ ۝

صِرَٰطَ ٱلَّذِينَ أَنْعَمْتَ عَلَيْهِمْ غَيْرِ ٱلْمَغْضُوبِ عَلَيْهِمْ وَلَا ٱلضَّآلِّينَ ۝

Al-Baqarah (II)

In the Name of God, the Infinitely Good, the Ever-Merciful

1. Alif-Lām-Mīm. [WS] [M]
2. That, beyond doubt, is the book—a guidance for the pious. [WS]
2. This beyond doubt is the Book, a guidance unto the God-fearing. [M]
3. Who believe in the Unseen and perform the prayer and give of that which We have bestowed upon them. [M]
4. And who believe in that which is revealed unto thee and in that which was revealed before thee, and who are certain of the hereafter. [M]
5. These are they who follow guidance from their Lord and these are they who shall prosper. [M]
8. And of men there are some who say: We believe in God and in the last day, yet they are not believers. [M]
11. And when it is said to them: 'Cause not corruption in the land,' they say: 'We are nothing if not reformers.' [SS]
12. Nay, unknown to themselves they are workers of corruption. [SS]
14. When they meet those who believe they say: we believe. And when they go apart unto their satans, they say: Verily we are with you; we did but mock. [M]
25. Give glad tidings unto those who believe and do deeds of piety that verily they shall have gardens of Paradise watered by flowing rivers. Whenever they are given to eat of one of the fruits thereof they say: This is that which we were given aforetime, and they were given a likeness of it... [RS][L-QD]
25. ...whensoever they are fed therein with a fruit, they shall say: 'This is that wherewith we were fed aforetime;' and they shall be given the like thereof... [UM]

(٢) سُورَةُ ٱلْبَقَرَةِ
بِسْمِ ٱللَّهِ ٱلرَّحْمَٰنِ ٱلرَّحِيمِ

الٓمٓ ۝

ذَٰلِكَ ٱلْكِتَٰبُ لَا رَيْبَ ۛ فِيهِ ۛ هُدًى لِّلْمُتَّقِينَ ۝

ٱلَّذِينَ يُؤْمِنُونَ بِٱلْغَيْبِ وَيُقِيمُونَ ٱلصَّلَوٰةَ وَمِمَّا رَزَقْنَٰهُمْ يُنفِقُونَ ۝

وَٱلَّذِينَ يُؤْمِنُونَ بِمَآ أُنزِلَ إِلَيْكَ وَمَآ أُنزِلَ مِن قَبْلِكَ وَبِٱلْءَاخِرَةِ هُمْ يُوقِنُونَ ۝

أُو۟لَٰٓئِكَ عَلَىٰ هُدًى مِّن رَّبِّهِمْ ۖ وَأُو۟لَٰٓئِكَ هُمُ ٱلْمُفْلِحُونَ ۝

وَمِنَ ٱلنَّاسِ مَن يَقُولُ ءَامَنَّا بِٱللَّهِ وَبِٱلْيَوْمِ ٱلْءَاخِرِ وَمَا هُم بِمُؤْمِنِينَ ۝

وَإِذَا قِيلَ لَهُمْ لَا تُفْسِدُوا۟ فِى ٱلْأَرْضِ قَالُوٓا۟ إِنَّمَا نَحْنُ مُصْلِحُونَ ۝

أَلَآ إِنَّهُمْ هُمُ ٱلْمُفْسِدُونَ وَلَٰكِن لَّا يَشْعُرُونَ ۝

وَإِذَا لَقُوا۟ ٱلَّذِينَ ءَامَنُوا۟ قَالُوٓا۟ ءَامَنَّا وَإِذَا خَلَوْا۟ إِلَىٰ شَيَٰطِينِهِمْ قَالُوٓا۟ إِنَّا مَعَكُمْ إِنَّمَا نَحْنُ مُسْتَهْزِءُونَ ۝

وَبَشِّرِ ٱلَّذِينَ ءَامَنُوا۟ وَعَمِلُوا۟ ٱلصَّٰلِحَٰتِ أَنَّ لَهُمْ جَنَّٰتٍ تَجْرِى مِن تَحْتِهَا ٱلْأَنْهَٰرُ ۖ كُلَّمَا رُزِقُوا۟ مِنْهَا مِن ثَمَرَةٍ رِّزْقًا ۙ قَالُوا۟ هَٰذَا ٱلَّذِى رُزِقْنَا مِن قَبْلُ ۖ

25. ...whensoever they are given to eat of the fruits of the garden, they say: 'This is that which was given us aforetime;' and it was given them in a likeness thereof... [BC]

26. Verily God disdaineth not to cite as symbol even a gnat or something smaller... [BC]

30. ...verily I am about to make on earth a viceregent... [BC]

34. And when We said unto the angels: 'Make prostration before Adam,' they prostrated themselves all save Iblis... [BC]

35. And We said: 'O Adam, dwell thou and thy wife in the Paradise... And come not nigh this tree, for then would ye be transgressors.' [BC]

37. Then Adam received words from his Lord, Who relented towards him. Verily He is the Relenting, the Merciful. [BC]

37. Then Adam received words from his Lord, Who relented unto him. Verily He is the Ever-Relenting, the All-Merciful. [RS][L-QD]

38. We said: 'Go fallen hence, all of you together. Yet assuredly will I send unto you a guidance, and whosoever shall follow My guidance, no fear shall come upon them, neither shall they grieve.' [BC]

38. ...there shall come unto you from Me a guidance, and whoso followeth My guidance no harm shall come upon them neither shall they grieve. [RS][L-QD]

وَأُتُوا بِهِۦ مُتَشَٰبِهًاۖ وَلَهُمْ فِيهَآ أَزْوَٰجٌ مُّطَهَّرَةٌۖ وَهُمْ فِيهَا خَٰلِدُونَ ۝

إِنَّ ٱللَّهَ لَا يَسْتَحْىِۦٓ أَن يَضْرِبَ مَثَلًا مَّا بَعُوضَةً فَمَا فَوْقَهَاۚ فَأَمَّا ٱلَّذِينَ ءَامَنُوا۟ فَيَعْلَمُونَ أَنَّهُ ٱلْحَقُّ مِن رَّبِّهِمْۖ وَأَمَّا ٱلَّذِينَ كَفَرُوا۟ فَيَقُولُونَ مَاذَآ أَرَادَ ٱللَّهُ بِهَٰذَا مَثَلًاۘ يُضِلُّ بِهِۦ كَثِيرًا وَيَهْدِى بِهِۦ كَثِيرًاۚ وَمَا يُضِلُّ بِهِۦٓ إِلَّا ٱلْفَٰسِقِينَ ۝

وَإِذْ قَالَ رَبُّكَ لِلْمَلَٰٓئِكَةِ إِنِّى جَاعِلٌ فِى ٱلْأَرْضِ خَلِيفَةًۖ قَالُوٓا۟ أَتَجْعَلُ فِيهَا مَن يُفْسِدُ فِيهَا وَيَسْفِكُ ٱلدِّمَآءَ وَنَحْنُ نُسَبِّحُ بِحَمْدِكَ وَنُقَدِّسُ لَكَۖ قَالَ إِنِّىٓ أَعْلَمُ مَا لَا تَعْلَمُونَ ۝

وَإِذْ قُلْنَا لِلْمَلَٰٓئِكَةِ ٱسْجُدُوا۟ لِءَادَمَ فَسَجَدُوٓا۟ إِلَّآ إِبْلِيسَ أَبَىٰ وَٱسْتَكْبَرَ وَكَانَ مِنَ ٱلْكَٰفِرِينَ ۝

وَقُلْنَا يَٰٓـَٔادَمُ ٱسْكُنْ أَنتَ وَزَوْجُكَ ٱلْجَنَّةَ وَكُلَا مِنْهَا رَغَدًا حَيْثُ شِئْتُمَا وَلَا تَقْرَبَا هَٰذِهِ ٱلشَّجَرَةَ فَتَكُونَا مِنَ ٱلظَّٰلِمِينَ ۝

فَتَلَقَّىٰٓ ءَادَمُ مِن رَّبِّهِۦ كَلِمَٰتٍ فَتَابَ عَلَيْهِۚ إِنَّهُۥ هُوَ ٱلتَّوَّابُ ٱلرَّحِيمُ ۝

قُلْنَا ٱهْبِطُوا۟ مِنْهَا جَمِيعًاۖ فَإِمَّا يَأْتِيَنَّكُم مِّنِّى هُدًى فَمَن تَبِعَ هُدَاىَ فَلَا خَوْفٌ عَلَيْهِمْ وَلَا هُمْ يَحْزَنُونَ ۝

60. And when Moses asked for water for his people, and We said: 'Strike with thy staff the rock,' and there gushed forth from it twelve springs, everyone knew his drinking place... [SA]

61. ...not content with one food...prefer to take what is inferior in exchange for the superior... [SS]

74. Then even after that your hearts grew hard so that they were like rocks or even harder, for verily there are rocks from which rivers gush forth, and there are rocks which split asunder so that water floweth from them... [SA]

74. ...as hard as stones or even harder... [SS]

109. Many of the people of the Book long to bring you back into disbelief after your belief through envy that is in their souls... [M]

115. Unto God are the East and the West, and whithersoever ye turn, there is the Face of God. Verily God is Infinitely Vast, Infinitely Knowing. [NOS]

115. ...wheresoever ye turn, there is the Face of God... [OS] [SS] [S] [QACI] [MP] [M] [SQCI]

115. ...wheresoever ye turn, there is the Face of God. Verily God is the Infinitely Vast, the Infinitely Knowing. [WS]

115. ...wheresoever ye turn, there is the Face of God. Verily God is Vast, All-Knowing. [SA]

115. ...wheresoever ye turn, there is the Face of God. Verily God is Infinitely Vast, the All-Knowing. [PT]

وَإِذِ ٱسْتَسْقَىٰ مُوسَىٰ لِقَوْمِهِۦ فَقُلْنَا ٱضْرِب بِّعَصَاكَ ٱلْحَجَرَ ۖ فَٱنفَجَرَتْ مِنْهُ ٱثْنَتَا عَشْرَةَ عَيْنًا ۖ قَدْ عَلِمَ كُلُّ أُنَاسٍ مَّشْرَبَهُمْ ۖ كُلُوا۟ وَٱشْرَبُوا۟ مِن رِّزْقِ ٱللَّهِ وَلَا تَعْثَوْا۟ فِى ٱلْأَرْضِ مُفْسِدِينَ ۝

وَإِذْ قُلْتُمْ يَٰمُوسَىٰ لَن نَّصْبِرَ عَلَىٰ طَعَامٍ وَٰحِدٍ فَٱدْعُ لَنَا رَبَّكَ يُخْرِجْ لَنَا مِمَّا تُنۢبِتُ ٱلْأَرْضُ مِنۢ بَقْلِهَا وَقِثَّآئِهَا وَفُومِهَا وَعَدَسِهَا وَبَصَلِهَا ۖ قَالَ أَتَسْتَبْدِلُونَ ٱلَّذِى هُوَ أَدْنَىٰ بِٱلَّذِى هُوَ خَيْرٌ ۚ ٱهْبِطُوا۟ مِصْرًا فَإِنَّ لَكُم مَّا سَأَلْتُمْ ۗ وَضُرِبَتْ عَلَيْهِمُ ٱلذِّلَّةُ وَٱلْمَسْكَنَةُ وَبَآءُو بِغَضَبٍ مِّنَ ٱللَّهِ ۗ ذَٰلِكَ بِأَنَّهُمْ كَانُوا۟ يَكْفُرُونَ بِـَٔايَٰتِ ٱللَّهِ وَيَقْتُلُونَ ٱلنَّبِيِّـۧنَ بِغَيْرِ ٱلْحَقِّ ۗ ذَٰلِكَ بِمَا عَصَوا۟ وَّكَانُوا۟ يَعْتَدُونَ ۝

ثُمَّ قَسَتْ قُلُوبُكُم مِّنۢ بَعْدِ ذَٰلِكَ فَهِىَ كَٱلْحِجَارَةِ أَوْ أَشَدُّ قَسْوَةً ۚ وَإِنَّ مِنَ ٱلْحِجَارَةِ لَمَا يَتَفَجَّرُ مِنْهُ ٱلْأَنْهَٰرُ ۚ وَإِنَّ مِنْهَا لَمَا يَشَّقَّقُ فَيَخْرُجُ مِنْهُ ٱلْمَآءُ ۚ وَإِنَّ مِنْهَا لَمَا يَهْبِطُ مِنْ خَشْيَةِ ٱللَّهِ ۗ وَمَا ٱللَّهُ بِغَٰفِلٍ عَمَّا تَعْمَلُونَ ۝

وَدَّ كَثِيرٌ مِّنْ أَهْلِ ٱلْكِتَٰبِ لَوْ يَرُدُّونَكُم مِّنۢ بَعْدِ إِيمَٰنِكُمْ كُفَّارًا حَسَدًا مِّنْ عِندِ أَنفُسِهِم مِّنۢ بَعْدِ مَا تَبَيَّنَ لَهُمُ ٱلْحَقُّ ۖ فَٱعْفُوا۟ وَٱصْفَحُوا۟ حَتَّىٰ يَأْتِىَ ٱللَّهُ بِأَمْرِهِۦٓ ۗ إِنَّ ٱللَّهَ عَلَىٰ كُلِّ شَىْءٍ قَدِيرٌ ۝

وَلِلَّهِ ٱلْمَشْرِقُ وَٱلْمَغْرِبُ ۚ فَأَيْنَمَا تُوَلُّوا۟ فَثَمَّ وَجْهُ ٱللَّهِ ۚ إِنَّ ٱللَّهَ وَٰسِعٌ عَلِيمٌ ۝

135. ...the religion of Abraham...[M]
143. We have made you a middle people...[WS]
143. We have appointed you a middle nation...[NOS]
144. We have seen the turning of thy face unto the sky; and now We shall turn thee a way that shall well please thee. So turn thou thy face towards the Inviolable Mosque; and wheresoever ye may be, turn ye your faces toward it...[M]
152. And remember Me; I will remember you...[UM]
152. Remember Me and I shall remember you...[UM]
153. O ye who believe, seek help of God in steadfastness and in prayer. Verily God is with the steadfast. [M]
154. And say not 'dead' of those who have been slain in God's path, for they are living, only ye perceive not. [M]
154. Count not those who have been slain in the way of God as dead. Nay they are living...[L-QD]
155. And We shall surely try you with something of fear and of hunger, and loss of goods and lives and harvesting. But give good tidings unto the steadfast. [M]
156. Who say when a blow befalleth them: Verily we are for God, and verily unto Him are we returning. [M]
156. ...verily we are for God and verily unto Him are we returning. [OS] [SS]
156. ...verily we are for God and verily unto Him we are returning. [WS]

وَقَالُوا۟ كُونُوا۟ هُودًا أَوْ نَصَـٰرَىٰ تَهْتَدُوا۟ ۗ قُلْ بَلْ مِلَّةَ إِبْرَٰهِـۧمَ حَنِيفًا ۖ وَمَا كَانَ مِنَ ٱلْمُشْرِكِينَ ۝

وَكَذَٰلِكَ جَعَلْنَـٰكُمْ أُمَّةً وَسَطًا لِّتَكُونُوا۟ شُهَدَآءَ عَلَى ٱلنَّاسِ وَيَكُونَ ٱلرَّسُولُ عَلَيْكُمْ شَهِيدًا ۗ وَمَا جَعَلْنَا ٱلْقِبْلَةَ ٱلَّتِى كُنتَ عَلَيْهَآ إِلَّا لِنَعْلَمَ مَن يَتَّبِعُ ٱلرَّسُولَ مِمَّن يَنقَلِبُ عَلَىٰ عَقِبَيْهِ ۚ وَإِن كَانَتْ لَكَبِيرَةً إِلَّا عَلَى ٱلَّذِينَ هَدَى ٱللَّهُ ۗ وَمَا كَانَ ٱللَّهُ لِيُضِيعَ إِيمَـٰنَكُمْ ۚ إِنَّ ٱللَّهَ بِٱلنَّاسِ لَرَءُوفٌ رَّحِيمٌ ۝

قَدْ نَرَىٰ تَقَلُّبَ وَجْهِكَ فِى ٱلسَّمَآءِ ۖ فَلَنُوَلِّيَنَّكَ قِبْلَةً تَرْضَىٰهَا ۚ فَوَلِّ وَجْهَكَ شَطْرَ ٱلْمَسْجِدِ ٱلْحَرَامِ ۚ وَحَيْثُ مَا كُنتُمْ فَوَلُّوا۟ وُجُوهَكُمْ شَطْرَهُۥ ۗ وَإِنَّ ٱلَّذِينَ أُوتُوا۟ ٱلْكِتَـٰبَ لَيَعْلَمُونَ أَنَّهُ ٱلْحَقُّ مِن رَّبِّهِمْ ۗ وَمَا ٱللَّهُ بِغَـٰفِلٍ عَمَّا يَعْمَلُونَ ۝

فَٱذْكُرُونِىٓ أَذْكُرْكُمْ وَٱشْكُرُوا۟ لِى وَلَا تَكْفُرُونِ ۝

يَـٰٓأَيُّهَا ٱلَّذِينَ ءَامَنُوا۟ ٱسْتَعِينُوا۟ بِٱلصَّبْرِ وَٱلصَّلَوٰةِ ۚ إِنَّ ٱللَّهَ مَعَ ٱلصَّـٰبِرِينَ ۝

وَلَا تَقُولُوا۟ لِمَن يُقْتَلُ فِى سَبِيلِ ٱللَّهِ أَمْوَٰتٌۢ ۚ بَلْ أَحْيَآءٌ وَلَـٰكِن لَّا تَشْعُرُونَ ۝

وَلَنَبْلُوَنَّكُم بِشَىْءٍ مِّنَ ٱلْخَوْفِ وَٱلْجُوعِ وَنَقْصٍ مِّنَ ٱلْأَمْوَٰلِ وَٱلْأَنفُسِ وَٱلثَّمَرَٰتِ ۗ وَبَشِّرِ ٱلصَّـٰبِرِينَ ۝

ٱلَّذِينَ إِذَآ أَصَـٰبَتْهُم مُّصِيبَةٌ قَالُوٓا۟ إِنَّا لِلَّهِ وَإِنَّآ إِلَيْهِ رَٰجِعُونَ ۝

157. On these are blessings from their Lord and mercy; and these are the rightly guided. [M]

185. ...God wishes for you ease; He does not wish for you the difficult... [UM]

186. If My slaves ask thee of Me, say I am Near. I answer the prayer of the pray-er when he prayeth Me... [S] [SA]

186. ...I answer the invocation of the invoker when he invoketh Me... [BC] [WS]

186. ...I answer the prayer of the pray-er when he prayeth Me... [SS]

193. Fight them until there is no longer any sedition, and religion is all for God... [BC]

198. ...remember God at the Holy Monument... [SS]

203. Remember God during the appointed days... [SS]

أُوْلَٰٓئِكَ عَلَيْهِمْ صَلَوَٰتٌ مِّن رَّبِّهِمْ وَرَحْمَةٌ ۖ وَأُوْلَٰٓئِكَ هُمُ ٱلْمُهْتَدُونَ ۝

شَهْرُ رَمَضَانَ ٱلَّذِىٓ أُنزِلَ فِيهِ ٱلْقُرْءَانُ هُدًى لِّلنَّاسِ وَبَيِّنَٰتٍ مِّنَ ٱلْهُدَىٰ وَٱلْفُرْقَانِ ۚ فَمَن شَهِدَ مِنكُمُ ٱلشَّهْرَ فَلْيَصُمْهُ ۖ وَمَن كَانَ مَرِيضًا أَوْ عَلَىٰ سَفَرٍ فَعِدَّةٌ مِّنْ أَيَّامٍ أُخَرَ ۗ يُرِيدُ ٱللَّهُ بِكُمُ ٱلْيُسْرَ وَلَا يُرِيدُ بِكُمُ ٱلْعُسْرَ وَلِتُكْمِلُواْ ٱلْعِدَّةَ وَلِتُكَبِّرُواْ ٱللَّهَ عَلَىٰ مَا هَدَىٰكُمْ وَلَعَلَّكُمْ تَشْكُرُونَ ۝

وَإِذَا سَأَلَكَ عِبَادِى عَنِّى فَإِنِّى قَرِيبٌ ۖ أُجِيبُ دَعْوَةَ ٱلدَّاعِ إِذَا دَعَانِ ۖ فَلْيَسْتَجِيبُواْ لِى وَلْيُؤْمِنُواْ بِى لَعَلَّهُمْ يَرْشُدُونَ ۝

وَقَٰتِلُوهُمْ حَتَّىٰ لَا تَكُونَ فِتْنَةٌ وَيَكُونَ ٱلدِّينُ لِلَّهِ ۖ فَإِنِ ٱنتَهَوْاْ فَلَا عُدْوَٰنَ إِلَّا عَلَى ٱلظَّٰلِمِينَ ۝

لَيْسَ عَلَيْكُمْ جُنَاحٌ أَن تَبْتَغُواْ فَضْلًا مِّن رَّبِّكُمْ ۚ فَإِذَآ أَفَضْتُم مِّنْ عَرَفَٰتٍ فَٱذْكُرُواْ ٱللَّهَ عِندَ ٱلْمَشْعَرِ ٱلْحَرَامِ ۖ وَٱذْكُرُوهُ كَمَا هَدَىٰكُمْ وَإِن كُنتُم مِّن قَبْلِهِۦ لَمِنَ ٱلضَّآلِّينَ ۝

وَٱذْكُرُواْ ٱللَّهَ فِىٓ أَيَّامٍ مَّعْدُودَٰتٍ ۚ فَمَن تَعَجَّلَ فِى يَوْمَيْنِ فَلَآ إِثْمَ عَلَيْهِ وَمَن تَأَخَّرَ فَلَآ إِثْمَ عَلَيْهِ ۚ لِمَنِ ٱتَّقَىٰ ۗ وَٱتَّقُواْ ٱللَّهَ وَٱعْلَمُوٓاْ أَنَّكُمْ إِلَيْهِ تُحْشَرُونَ ۝

214. Think ye to enter Paradise while yet there hath come unto you the like of what came unto those who passed away before you? Affliction smote them and injuries and they were made to quake until the Messenger of God said, and with him those who believed: When cometh the help of God? Lo, verily the help of God is nigh. [M]

217. They question thee about the sacred month and fighting therein. Say: to fight therein is a grave offence; but barring men from God's path and sacrilege against Him and the holy mosque and driving out His people therefrom are graver with God. And torturing is graver than killing... [M]

245. ...God it is who contracteth and expandeth... [SS]

249. ...how many a little band hath overcome a multitude by God's leave! And God is with the steadfast. [M]

أَمْ حَسِبْتُمْ أَن تَدْخُلُوا۟ ٱلْجَنَّةَ وَلَمَّا يَأْتِكُم مَّثَلُ ٱلَّذِينَ خَلَوْا۟ مِن قَبْلِكُم مَّسَّتْهُمُ ٱلْبَأْسَآءُ وَٱلضَّرَّآءُ وَزُلْزِلُوا۟ حَتَّىٰ يَقُولَ ٱلرَّسُولُ وَٱلَّذِينَ ءَامَنُوا۟ مَعَهُۥ مَتَىٰ نَصْرُ ٱللَّهِ ۗ أَلَآ إِنَّ نَصْرَ ٱللَّهِ قَرِيبٌ ۝

يَسْـَٔلُونَكَ عَنِ ٱلشَّهْرِ ٱلْحَرَامِ قِتَالٍ فِيهِ ۖ قُلْ قِتَالٌ فِيهِ كَبِيرٌ ۖ وَصَدٌّ عَن سَبِيلِ ٱللَّهِ وَكُفْرٌۢ بِهِۦ وَٱلْمَسْجِدِ ٱلْحَرَامِ وَإِخْرَاجُ أَهْلِهِۦ مِنْهُ أَكْبَرُ عِندَ ٱللَّهِ ۚ وَٱلْفِتْنَةُ أَكْبَرُ مِنَ ٱلْقَتْلِ ۗ وَلَا يَزَالُونَ يُقَاتِلُونَكُمْ حَتَّىٰ يَرُدُّوكُمْ عَن دِينِكُمْ إِنِ ٱسْتَطَاعُوا۟ ۚ وَمَن يَرْتَدِدْ مِنكُمْ عَن دِينِهِۦ فَيَمُتْ وَهُوَ كَافِرٌ فَأُو۟لَـٰٓئِكَ حَبِطَتْ أَعْمَـٰلُهُمْ فِى ٱلدُّنْيَا وَٱلْـَٔاخِرَةِ ۖ وَأُو۟لَـٰٓئِكَ أَصْحَـٰبُ ٱلنَّارِ ۖ هُمْ فِيهَا خَـٰلِدُونَ ۝

مَّن ذَا ٱلَّذِى يُقْرِضُ ٱللَّهَ قَرْضًا حَسَنًا فَيُضَـٰعِفَهُۥ لَهُۥٓ أَضْعَافًا كَثِيرَةً ۚ وَٱللَّهُ يَقْبِضُ وَيَبْصُۜطُ وَإِلَيْهِ تُرْجَعُونَ ۝

فَلَمَّا فَصَلَ طَالُوتُ بِٱلْجُنُودِ قَالَ إِنَّ ٱللَّهَ مُبْتَلِيكُم بِنَهَرٍ فَمَن شَرِبَ مِنْهُ فَلَيْسَ مِنِّى وَمَن لَّمْ يَطْعَمْهُ فَإِنَّهُۥ مِنِّىٓ إِلَّا مَنِ ٱغْتَرَفَ غُرْفَةًۢ بِيَدِهِۦ ۚ فَشَرِبُوا۟ مِنْهُ إِلَّا قَلِيلًا مِّنْهُمْ ۚ فَلَمَّا جَاوَزَهُۥ هُوَ وَٱلَّذِينَ ءَامَنُوا۟ مَعَهُۥ قَالُوا۟ لَا طَاقَةَ لَنَا ٱلْيَوْمَ بِجَالُوتَ وَجُنُودِهِۦ ۚ قَالَ ٱلَّذِينَ يَظُنُّونَ أَنَّهُم مُّلَـٰقُوا۟ ٱللَّهِ كَم مِّن فِئَةٍ قَلِيلَةٍ غَلَبَتْ فِئَةً كَثِيرَةًۢ بِإِذْنِ ٱللَّهِ ۗ وَٱللَّهُ مَعَ ٱلصَّـٰبِرِينَ ۝

253. ...God doth what He will. [RS]

260. ...Hast thou not faith? Yes, but [show me] so that my heart may be at rest... [WS]

269. He [Allah] giveth wisdom to whom He will; and He to whom wisdom hath been given hath received a great good... [UM]

285. The messenger believeth, and the faithful believe, in what hath been revealed unto him from his Lord. Each one believeth in God and His angels and His books and His messengers: we make no distinction between any of His messengers. And they say: we hear and we obey; grant us, Thou our Lord, Thy forgiveness; unto Thee is the ultimate becoming. [M]

285. ...they believe, all of them, in God and His Angels and His Books and His Messengers. And they say, 'We make no distinction between any of His Messengers.'... [RS] [L-II]

285. ...believe in God and his Angels and His Books and His Messengers. We make no distinction between His Messengers... [SS]

285. ...we make no distinction between any of His Apostles... [BC]

286. ...Our Lord, lay not upon us such a burden as Thou didst lay upon those before us! Our Lord, burden us not with that which is beyond our strength!... [ICCT]

تِلْكَ ٱلرُّسُلُ فَضَّلْنَا بَعْضَهُمْ عَلَىٰ بَعْضٍ ۘ مِّنْهُم مَّن كَلَّمَ ٱللَّهُ ۖ وَرَفَعَ بَعْضَهُمْ دَرَجَٰتٍ ۚ وَءَاتَيْنَا عِيسَى ٱبْنَ مَرْيَمَ ٱلْبَيِّنَٰتِ وَأَيَّدْنَٰهُ بِرُوحِ ٱلْقُدُسِ ۗ وَلَوْ شَآءَ ٱللَّهُ مَا ٱقْتَتَلَ ٱلَّذِينَ مِنۢ بَعْدِهِم مِّنۢ بَعْدِ مَا جَآءَتْهُمُ ٱلْبَيِّنَٰتُ وَلَٰكِنِ ٱخْتَلَفُوا۟ فَمِنْهُم مَّنْ ءَامَنَ وَمِنْهُم مَّن كَفَرَ ۚ وَلَوْ شَآءَ ٱللَّهُ مَا ٱقْتَتَلُوا۟ وَلَٰكِنَّ ٱللَّهَ يَفْعَلُ مَا يُرِيدُ ۝

وَإِذْ قَالَ إِبْرَٰهِـۧمُ رَبِّ أَرِنِى كَيْفَ تُحْىِ ٱلْمَوْتَىٰ ۖ قَالَ أَوَلَمْ تُؤْمِن ۖ قَالَ بَلَىٰ وَلَٰكِن لِّيَطْمَئِنَّ قَلْبِى ۖ قَالَ فَخُذْ أَرْبَعَةً مِّنَ ٱلطَّيْرِ فَصُرْهُنَّ إِلَيْكَ ثُمَّ ٱجْعَلْ عَلَىٰ كُلِّ جَبَلٍ مِّنْهُنَّ جُزْءًا ثُمَّ ٱدْعُهُنَّ يَأْتِينَكَ سَعْيًا ۚ وَٱعْلَمْ أَنَّ ٱللَّهَ عَزِيزٌ حَكِيمٌ ۝

يُؤْتِى ٱلْحِكْمَةَ مَن يَشَآءُ ۚ وَمَن يُؤْتَ ٱلْحِكْمَةَ فَقَدْ أُوتِىَ خَيْرًا كَثِيرًا ۗ وَمَا يَذَّكَّرُ إِلَّآ أُو۟لُوا۟ ٱلْأَلْبَٰبِ ۝

ءَامَنَ ٱلرَّسُولُ بِمَآ أُنزِلَ إِلَيْهِ مِن رَّبِّهِۦ وَٱلْمُؤْمِنُونَ ۚ كُلٌّ ءَامَنَ بِٱللَّهِ وَمَلَٰٓئِكَتِهِۦ وَكُتُبِهِۦ وَرُسُلِهِۦ لَا نُفَرِّقُ بَيْنَ أَحَدٍ مِّن رُّسُلِهِۦ ۚ وَقَالُوا۟ سَمِعْنَا وَأَطَعْنَا ۖ غُفْرَانَكَ رَبَّنَا وَإِلَيْكَ ٱلْمَصِيرُ ۝ لَا يُكَلِّفُ ٱللَّهُ نَفْسًا إِلَّا وُسْعَهَا ۚ لَهَا مَا كَسَبَتْ وَعَلَيْهَا مَا ٱكْتَسَبَتْ ۗ رَبَّنَا لَا تُؤَاخِذْنَآ إِن نَّسِينَآ أَوْ أَخْطَأْنَا ۚ رَبَّنَا وَلَا تَحْمِلْ عَلَيْنَآ إِصْرًا كَمَا حَمَلْتَهُۥ عَلَى ٱلَّذِينَ مِن قَبْلِنَا ۚ رَبَّنَا وَلَا تُحَمِّلْنَا مَا لَا طَاقَةَ لَنَا بِهِۦ ۖ وَٱعْفُ عَنَّا وَٱغْفِرْ لَنَا وَٱرْحَمْنَآ ۚ أَنتَ مَوْلَىٰنَا فَٱنصُرْنَا عَلَى ٱلْقَوْمِ ٱلْكَٰفِرِينَ ۝

Āl-ʿImrān (III)

In the Name of God, the Infinitely Good, the Ever-Merciful

19. Verily before God religion is submission... [BC]

19. And verily Religion with God is *islām*... [L-UQ]

33. Verily God chose Adam and Noah and the family of Abraham and the family of ʿImrān above all the worlds. [M]

36. ...and verily I have named her Maryam; and verily I place her, and her offspring, beneath Thy protection [O Lord] against Satan the stoned. [UM]

37. And her Lord accepted her [Maryam] with a fair acceptance, and made her to grow with a fair growing and entrusted her to Zachariah; whensoever Zachariah entered unto her in the sanctuary, he found that she had food; he said: O Maryam, whence hast thou this? She said: it is from God; verily God giveth his subsistence unto whom He will without reckoning. [UM]

37. ...each time that Zakariya entered unto her in the sanctuary he found near her the needed nourishment; he said: O Maryam, whence cometh unto thee this? She replied: This cometh from God; verily God giveth His sustenance to whom He will, without reckoning. [UM]

37. ...every time that Zachariah went unto her in the Miḥrāb...Verily, God giveth to whom He will, without reckoning. [UM]

37. ...verily, God giveth sustenance to whom He will, beyond all reckoning. [PT]

40. ...God does what He wills. [UM]

42. And when the angels said: O Maryam, God hath chosen thee and purified thee, and hath chosen thee above all the women of the world. [UM]

(٣) سُورَةُ آلِ عِمْرَانَ

بِسْمِ ٱللَّهِ ٱلرَّحْمَٰنِ ٱلرَّحِيمِ

إِنَّ ٱلدِّينَ عِندَ ٱللَّهِ ٱلْإِسْلَٰمُ ۗ وَمَا ٱخْتَلَفَ ٱلَّذِينَ أُوتُوا۟ ٱلْكِتَٰبَ إِلَّا مِنۢ بَعْدِ مَا جَآءَهُمُ ٱلْعِلْمُ بَغْيًۢا بَيْنَهُمْ ۗ وَمَن يَكْفُرْ بِـَٔايَٰتِ ٱللَّهِ فَإِنَّ ٱللَّهَ سَرِيعُ ٱلْحِسَابِ ۝

إِنَّ ٱللَّهَ ٱصْطَفَىٰٓ ءَادَمَ وَنُوحًا وَءَالَ إِبْرَٰهِيمَ وَءَالَ عِمْرَٰنَ عَلَى ٱلْعَٰلَمِينَ ۝

فَلَمَّا وَضَعَتْهَا قَالَتْ رَبِّ إِنِّى وَضَعْتُهَآ أُنثَىٰ وَٱللَّهُ أَعْلَمُ بِمَا وَضَعَتْ وَلَيْسَ ٱلذَّكَرُ كَٱلْأُنثَىٰ ۖ وَإِنِّى سَمَّيْتُهَا مَرْيَمَ وَإِنِّىٓ أُعِيذُهَا بِكَ وَذُرِّيَّتَهَا مِنَ ٱلشَّيْطَٰنِ ٱلرَّجِيمِ ۝

فَتَقَبَّلَهَا رَبُّهَا بِقَبُولٍ حَسَنٍ وَأَنۢبَتَهَا نَبَاتًا حَسَنًا وَكَفَّلَهَا زَكَرِيَّا ۖ كُلَّمَا دَخَلَ عَلَيْهَا زَكَرِيَّا ٱلْمِحْرَابَ وَجَدَ عِندَهَا رِزْقًا ۖ قَالَ يَٰمَرْيَمُ أَنَّىٰ لَكِ هَٰذَا ۖ قَالَتْ هُوَ مِنْ عِندِ ٱللَّهِ ۖ إِنَّ ٱللَّهَ يَرْزُقُ مَن يَشَآءُ بِغَيْرِ حِسَابٍ ۝

قَالَ رَبِّ أَنَّىٰ يَكُونُ لِى غُلَٰمٌ وَقَدْ بَلَغَنِىَ ٱلْكِبَرُ وَٱمْرَأَتِى عَاقِرٌ ۖ قَالَ كَذَٰلِكَ ٱللَّهُ يَفْعَلُ مَا يَشَآءُ ۝

وَإِذْ قَالَتِ ٱلْمَلَٰٓئِكَةُ يَٰمَرْيَمُ إِنَّ ٱللَّهَ ٱصْطَفَىٰكِ وَطَهَّرَكِ وَٱصْطَفَىٰكِ عَلَىٰ نِسَآءِ ٱلْعَٰلَمِينَ ۝

59. Verily the likeness of Jesus with God is as the likeness of Adam. He created him of dust, then said to him 'Be' and he was. [M]

60. This is the Truth from thy Lord, so be not of the doubters. [M]

61. And whoso contendeth with thee about him after the knowledge that hath reached thee, say: Come ye, and let us summon our sons and your sons, and our women and your women, and ourselves and yourselves. Then we will imprecate, putting God's curse on those who lie. [M]

96. Verily the first sanctuary established for men is the house at Baca, a blessed place and a guidance for all the world. [Mec.]

110. Ye are the best people that hath been brought forth [as a pattern] for mankind... [WS]

110. ... the best people ever brought forth as an example for men... [ICCT]

118. ... they will do all they can to ruin you, and they love to cause you trouble. Their hatred is clear from what their mouths utter, and what their breasts conceal is greater... [M]

120. If good befall you, it is evil in their eyes, and if evil befall you they rejoice thereat... [M]

إِنَّ مَثَلَ عِيسَىٰ عِندَ ٱللَّهِ كَمَثَلِ ءَادَمَ خَلَقَهُۥ مِن تُرَابٍ ثُمَّ قَالَ لَهُۥ كُن فَيَكُونُ ۝

ٱلْحَقُّ مِن رَّبِّكَ فَلَا تَكُن مِّنَ ٱلْمُمْتَرِينَ ۝

فَمَنْ حَآجَّكَ فِيهِ مِنۢ بَعْدِ مَا جَآءَكَ مِنَ ٱلْعِلْمِ فَقُلْ تَعَالَوْاْ نَدْعُ أَبْنَآءَنَا وَأَبْنَآءَكُمْ وَنِسَآءَنَا وَنِسَآءَكُمْ وَأَنفُسَنَا وَأَنفُسَكُمْ ثُمَّ نَبْتَهِلْ فَنَجْعَل لَّعْنَتَ ٱللَّهِ عَلَى ٱلْكَٰذِبِينَ ۝

إِنَّ أَوَّلَ بَيْتٍ وُضِعَ لِلنَّاسِ لَلَّذِى بِبَكَّةَ مُبَارَكًا وَهُدًى لِّلْعَٰلَمِينَ ۝

كُنتُمْ خَيْرَ أُمَّةٍ أُخْرِجَتْ لِلنَّاسِ تَأْمُرُونَ بِٱلْمَعْرُوفِ وَتَنْهَوْنَ عَنِ ٱلْمُنكَرِ وَتُؤْمِنُونَ بِٱللَّهِ وَلَوْ ءَامَنَ أَهْلُ ٱلْكِتَٰبِ لَكَانَ خَيْرًا لَّهُم مِّنْهُمُ ٱلْمُؤْمِنُونَ وَأَكْثَرُهُمُ ٱلْفَٰسِقُونَ ۝

يَٰٓأَيُّهَا ٱلَّذِينَ ءَامَنُوا۟ لَا تَتَّخِذُوا۟ بِطَانَةً مِّن دُونِكُمْ لَا يَأْلُونَكُمْ خَبَالًا وَدُّوا۟ مَا عَنِتُّمْ قَدْ بَدَتِ ٱلْبَغْضَآءُ مِنْ أَفْوَٰهِهِمْ وَمَا تُخْفِى صُدُورُهُمْ أَكْبَرُ قَدْ بَيَّنَّا لَكُمُ ٱلْءَايَٰتِ إِن كُنتُمْ تَعْقِلُونَ ۝

إِن تَمْسَسْكُمْ حَسَنَةٌ تَسُؤْهُمْ وَإِن تُصِبْكُمْ سَيِّئَةٌ يَفْرَحُوا۟ بِهَا وَإِن تَصْبِرُوا۟ وَتَتَّقُوا۟ لَا يَضُرُّكُمْ كَيْدُهُمْ شَيْـًٔا إِنَّ ٱللَّهَ بِمَا يَعْمَلُونَ مُحِيطٌ ۝

137. Ways of life have passed away before you. Travel in the land and see what was the end of those who belied God's messengers. [M]

138. This is a clear affirmation for mankind, and a guidance and an exhortation for the pious. [M]

139. Falter not nor grieve, for ye shall overcome them if ye are true believers. [M]

142. Deemed ye that ye would enter Paradise ere God knoweth those of you that truly strive and ere He knoweth the steadfast? [M]

143. Ye wished for death until ye met it; now ye have seen it face to face! [M]

144. Muḥammad is but a messenger, and messengers have passed away before him. If he die or be slain, will ye then turn upon your heels? Whoso turneth upon his heels will thereby do no hurt unto God; and God will reward the thankful. [M]

159. ...consult them about their affairs; and when thou art resolved, then trust in God... [M]

169. Count not those who have been slain in the way of God as dead. Nay they are living, from their Lord they receive sustenance. [RS]

قَدْ خَلَتْ مِن قَبْلِكُمْ سُنَنٌ فَسِيرُوا۟ فِى ٱلْأَرْضِ فَٱنظُرُوا۟ كَيْفَ كَانَ عَـٰقِبَةُ ٱلْمُكَذِّبِينَ ۝١٣٧

هَـٰذَا بَيَانٌ لِّلنَّاسِ وَهُدًى وَمَوْعِظَةٌ لِّلْمُتَّقِينَ ۝١٣٨

وَلَا تَهِنُوا۟ وَلَا تَحْزَنُوا۟ وَأَنتُمُ ٱلْأَعْلَوْنَ إِن كُنتُم مُّؤْمِنِينَ ۝١٣٩

أَمْ حَسِبْتُمْ أَن تَدْخُلُوا۟ ٱلْجَنَّةَ وَلَمَّا يَعْلَمِ ٱللَّهُ ٱلَّذِينَ جَـٰهَدُوا۟ مِنكُمْ وَيَعْلَمَ ٱلصَّـٰبِرِينَ ۝١٤٢

وَلَقَدْ كُنتُمْ تَمَنَّوْنَ ٱلْمَوْتَ مِن قَبْلِ أَن تَلْقَوْهُ فَقَدْ رَأَيْتُمُوهُ وَأَنتُمْ تَنظُرُونَ ۝١٤٣

وَمَا مُحَمَّدٌ إِلَّا رَسُولٌ قَدْ خَلَتْ مِن قَبْلِهِ ٱلرُّسُلُ أَفَإِي۟ن مَّاتَ أَوْ قُتِلَ ٱنقَلَبْتُمْ عَلَىٰٓ أَعْقَـٰبِكُمْ وَمَن يَنقَلِبْ عَلَىٰ عَقِبَيْهِ فَلَن يَضُرَّ ٱللَّهَ شَيْـًٔا وَسَيَجْزِى ٱللَّهُ ٱلشَّـٰكِرِينَ ۝١٤٤

فَبِمَا رَحْمَةٍ مِّنَ ٱللَّهِ لِنتَ لَهُمْ وَلَوْ كُنتَ فَظًّا غَلِيظَ ٱلْقَلْبِ لَٱنفَضُّوا۟ مِنْ حَوْلِكَ فَٱعْفُ عَنْهُمْ وَٱسْتَغْفِرْ لَهُمْ وَشَاوِرْهُمْ فِى ٱلْأَمْرِ فَإِذَا عَزَمْتَ فَتَوَكَّلْ عَلَى ٱللَّهِ إِنَّ ٱللَّهَ يُحِبُّ ٱلْمُتَوَكِّلِينَ ۝١٥٩

وَلَا تَحْسَبَنَّ ٱلَّذِينَ قُتِلُوا۟ فِى سَبِيلِ ٱللَّهِ أَمْوَٰتًۢا بَلْ أَحْيَآءٌ عِندَ رَبِّهِمْ يُرْزَقُونَ ۝١٦٩

173. ...God is our sufficiency, and supremely to be trusted is He. [M]

173. ...our sufficiency is God and excellent is He in whom we trust. [UM]

191. Who remember God standing and sitting and reclining upon their sides... [SS]

195. ...I will take away their faults and enable them to enter Paradise... [L-HOD]

ٱلَّذِينَ قَالَ لَهُمُ ٱلنَّاسُ إِنَّ ٱلنَّاسَ قَدْ جَمَعُوا۟ لَكُمْ فَٱخْشَوْهُمْ فَزَادَهُمْ إِيمَـٰنًا وَقَالُوا۟ حَسْبُنَا ٱللَّهُ وَنِعْمَ ٱلْوَكِيلُ ۝

ٱلَّذِينَ يَذْكُرُونَ ٱللَّهَ قِيَـٰمًا وَقُعُودًا وَعَلَىٰ جُنُوبِهِمْ وَيَتَفَكَّرُونَ فِى خَلْقِ ٱلسَّمَـٰوَٰتِ وَٱلْأَرْضِ رَبَّنَا مَا خَلَقْتَ هَـٰذَا بَـٰطِلًا سُبْحَـٰنَكَ فَقِنَا عَذَابَ ٱلنَّارِ ۝

فَٱسْتَجَابَ لَهُمْ رَبُّهُمْ أَنِّى لَا أُضِيعُ عَمَلَ عَـٰمِلٍ مِّنكُم مِّن ذَكَرٍ أَوْ أُنثَىٰ بَعْضُكُم مِّنۢ بَعْضٍ ۖ فَٱلَّذِينَ هَاجَرُوا۟ وَأُخْرِجُوا۟ مِن دِيَـٰرِهِمْ وَأُوذُوا۟ فِى سَبِيلِى وَقَـٰتَلُوا۟ وَقُتِلُوا۟ لَأُكَفِّرَنَّ عَنْهُمْ سَيِّـَٔاتِهِمْ وَلَأُدْخِلَنَّهُمْ جَنَّـٰتٍ تَجْرِى مِن تَحْتِهَا ٱلْأَنْهَـٰرُ ثَوَابًا مِّنْ عِندِ ٱللَّهِ ۗ وَٱللَّهُ عِندَهُۥ حُسْنُ ٱلثَّوَابِ ۝

An-Nisā' (IV)

In the Name of God, the Infinitely Good, the Ever-Merciful

31. If ye avoid the great sins ye are forbidden We will wipe out your faults and cause you to enter with a noble entry. [RS] [L-QD]

43. ... if ye find not water then purify yourselves with clean earth, wiping therewith your faces and hands... [M]

69. ... with those upon whom God hath lavished His favour, the Prophets and the Saints and the Martyrs and the Righteous, most excellent for communion are they. [SCR-SA]

69. ... with those upon whom God hath showered His favour, the prophets and the saints and the martyrs and the righteous, most excellent for communion are they. [M]

69. ... with those upon whom God hath showered His favour, the prophets and the sages and the martyrs and the righteous, most excellent for communion are they. [SA]

69. ... with the Prophets and the sages and the martyrs and the righteous; excellent are they in companionship. [PT]

69. ... with the Prophets and the sages and the martyrs and the righteous; excellent in companionship are they. [PT]

80. Whoso obeyeth the Apostle obeyeth God... [SS]

94. O ye who believe, when ye fight in the way of God, discriminate, nor say unto him who proffereth you peace: 'Thou are not a believer,' seeking the gains of this lower life, for with God are spoils in plenty. Thus were ye wont to be aforetime, but God hath sent down His Grace upon you. Therefore discriminate. Verily God is Informed of what ye do. [M]

(٤) سُورَةُ النِّسَاءِ

بِسْمِ اللَّهِ الرَّحْمَٰنِ الرَّحِيمِ

إِن تَجْتَنِبُوا كَبَائِرَ مَا تُنْهَوْنَ عَنْهُ نُكَفِّرْ عَنكُمْ سَيِّئَاتِكُمْ وَنُدْخِلْكُم مُّدْخَلًا كَرِيمًا ۝

يَٰٓأَيُّهَا ٱلَّذِينَ ءَامَنُوا لَا تَقْرَبُوا ٱلصَّلَوٰةَ وَأَنتُمْ سُكَارَىٰ حَتَّىٰ تَعْلَمُوا مَا تَقُولُونَ وَلَا جُنُبًا إِلَّا عَابِرِي سَبِيلٍ حَتَّىٰ تَغْتَسِلُوا ۚ وَإِن كُنتُم مَّرْضَىٰٓ أَوْ عَلَىٰ سَفَرٍ أَوْ جَآءَ أَحَدٌ مِّنكُم مِّنَ ٱلْغَآئِطِ أَوْ لَٰمَسْتُمُ ٱلنِّسَآءَ فَلَمْ تَجِدُوا مَآءً فَتَيَمَّمُوا صَعِيدًا طَيِّبًا فَٱمْسَحُوا بِوُجُوهِكُمْ وَأَيْدِيكُمْ ۗ إِنَّ ٱللَّهَ كَانَ عَفُوًّا غَفُورًا ۝

وَمَن يُطِعِ ٱللَّهَ وَٱلرَّسُولَ فَأُوْلَٰٓئِكَ مَعَ ٱلَّذِينَ أَنْعَمَ ٱللَّهُ عَلَيْهِم مِّنَ ٱلنَّبِيِّـۧنَ وَٱلصِّدِّيقِينَ وَٱلشُّهَدَآءِ وَٱلصَّٰلِحِينَ ۚ وَحَسُنَ أُوْلَٰٓئِكَ رَفِيقًا ۝

مَّن يُطِعِ ٱلرَّسُولَ فَقَدْ أَطَاعَ ٱللَّهَ ۖ وَمَن تَوَلَّىٰ فَمَآ أَرْسَلْنَٰكَ عَلَيْهِمْ حَفِيظًا ۝

يَٰٓأَيُّهَا ٱلَّذِينَ ءَامَنُوٓا إِذَا ضَرَبْتُمْ فِي سَبِيلِ ٱللَّهِ فَتَبَيَّنُوا وَلَا تَقُولُوا لِمَنْ أَلْقَىٰٓ إِلَيْكُمُ ٱلسَّلَٰمَ لَسْتَ مُؤْمِنًا تَبْتَغُونَ عَرَضَ ٱلْحَيَوٰةِ ٱلدُّنْيَا فَعِندَ ٱللَّهِ مَغَانِمُ كَثِيرَةٌ ۚ كَذَٰلِكَ كُنتُم مِّن قَبْلُ فَمَنَّ ٱللَّهُ عَلَيْكُمْ فَتَبَيَّنُوٓا ۚ إِنَّ ٱللَّهَ كَانَ بِمَا تَعْمَلُونَ خَبِيرًا ۝

95. The non-combatants amongst the believers, making exception for those afflicted with infirmity, and the combatants in the way of Allah, with their goods and their lives, are not equal; Allah hath placed the combatants with their goods and their lives a degree above the non-combatants; to each, Allah hath promised what is most fair; Allah hath placed the combatants above the non-combatants, with an immense reward. [UM]

95. ...those who fight in the way of Allah with their goods and lives... [UM]

95. ...unto both God hath promised good. But he hath favoured those who fight with an immense reward above those who stay behind. [WS]

130. If the two separate, God will enrich both out of His Abundance... [SS]

142. ...and they only remember God a little. [SS]

156. ...they uttered against Mary a tremendous calumny. [SS]

157. ...verily we have slain the Messiah Jesus the Son of Mary, the Messenger of God. And they did not slay him and they did not crucify him, but it seemed to them that they had done so... [RS]

157. ...[the Jews claim] 'We have killed the Messiah, Jesus the Son of Mary, the Messenger of God.' They killed him not, nor crucified him, but it seemed to them that they had done so... [L-UQ]

171. ...Jesus son of Mary is Messenger of God and His Word which he cast unto Mary and a Spirit from Him... [M]

171. ...His Word which he delivered unto Mary and as a spirit from Him... [SQCI]

171. ...the Word of God whom He cast Mary, and a Spirit from God... [L-UQ]

174. ...We have sent down to you a clear light. [QACI] [SQCI]

لَّا يَسْتَوِى ٱلْقَٰعِدُونَ مِنَ ٱلْمُؤْمِنِينَ غَيْرُ أُو۟لِى ٱلضَّرَرِ وَٱلْمُجَٰهِدُونَ فِى سَبِيلِ ٱللَّهِ بِأَمْوَٰلِهِمْ وَأَنفُسِهِمْ ۚ فَضَّلَ ٱللَّهُ ٱلْمُجَٰهِدِينَ بِأَمْوَٰلِهِمْ وَأَنفُسِهِمْ عَلَى ٱلْقَٰعِدِينَ دَرَجَةً ۚ وَكُلًّا وَعَدَ ٱللَّهُ ٱلْحُسْنَىٰ ۚ وَفَضَّلَ ٱللَّهُ ٱلْمُجَٰهِدِينَ عَلَى ٱلْقَٰعِدِينَ أَجْرًا عَظِيمًا ۝

وَإِن يَتَفَرَّقَا يُغْنِ ٱللَّهُ كُلًّا مِّن سَعَتِهِۦ ۚ وَكَانَ ٱللَّهُ وَٰسِعًا حَكِيمًا ۝ إِنَّ ٱلْمُنَٰفِقِينَ يُخَٰدِعُونَ ٱللَّهَ وَهُوَ خَٰدِعُهُمْ وَإِذَا قَامُوٓا۟ إِلَى ٱلصَّلَوٰةِ قَامُوا۟ كُسَالَىٰ يُرَآءُونَ ٱلنَّاسَ وَلَا يَذْكُرُونَ ٱللَّهَ إِلَّا قَلِيلًا ۝

وَبِكُفْرِهِمْ وَقَوْلِهِمْ عَلَىٰ مَرْيَمَ بُهْتَٰنًا عَظِيمًا ۝ وَقَوْلِهِمْ إِنَّا قَتَلْنَا ٱلْمَسِيحَ عِيسَى ٱبْنَ مَرْيَمَ رَسُولَ ٱللَّهِ وَمَا قَتَلُوهُ وَمَا صَلَبُوهُ وَلَٰكِن شُبِّهَ لَهُمْ ۚ وَإِنَّ ٱلَّذِينَ ٱخْتَلَفُوا۟ فِيهِ لَفِى شَكٍّ مِّنْهُ ۚ مَا لَهُم بِهِۦ مِنْ عِلْمٍ إِلَّا ٱتِّبَاعَ ٱلظَّنِّ ۚ وَمَا قَتَلُوهُ يَقِينًۢا ۝ يَٰٓأَهْلَ ٱلْكِتَٰبِ لَا تَغْلُوا۟ فِى دِينِكُمْ وَلَا تَقُولُوا۟ عَلَى ٱللَّهِ إِلَّا ٱلْحَقَّ ۚ إِنَّمَا ٱلْمَسِيحُ عِيسَى ٱبْنُ مَرْيَمَ رَسُولُ ٱللَّهِ وَكَلِمَتُهُۥٓ أَلْقَىٰهَآ إِلَىٰ مَرْيَمَ وَرُوحٌ مِّنْهُ ۖ فَـَٔامِنُوا۟ بِٱللَّهِ وَرُسُلِهِۦ ۖ وَلَا تَقُولُوا۟ ثَلَٰثَةٌ ۚ ٱنتَهُوا۟ خَيْرًا لَّكُمْ ۚ إِنَّمَا ٱللَّهُ إِلَٰهٌ وَٰحِدٌ ۖ سُبْحَٰنَهُۥٓ أَن يَكُونَ لَهُۥ وَلَدٌ ۘ لَّهُۥ مَا فِى ٱلسَّمَٰوَٰتِ وَمَا فِى ٱلْأَرْضِ ۗ وَكَفَىٰ بِٱللَّهِ وَكِيلًا ۝

يَٰٓأَيُّهَا ٱلنَّاسُ قَدْ جَآءَكُم بُرْهَٰنٌ مِّن رَّبِّكُمْ وَأَنزَلْنَآ إِلَيْكُمْ نُورًا مُّبِينًا ۝

Al-Mā'idah (V)

In the Name of God, the Infinitely Good, the Ever-Merciful

3. ...this day the disbelievers despair of prevailing against your religion, so fear them not, but fear Me! This day have I perfected for you your religion and fulfilled my favour unto you, and it hath been My good pleasure to choose Islam for you as your religion... [M]

5. ...the food [of those who have been given the Book] is lawful for you; your food is lawful for them... [L-UQ]

(٥) سُورَةُ المَائِدَةِ

بِسْمِ اللَّهِ الرَّحْمَٰنِ الرَّحِيمِ

حُرِّمَتْ عَلَيْكُمُ ٱلْمَيْتَةُ وَٱلدَّمُ وَلَحْمُ ٱلْخِنزِيرِ وَمَآ أُهِلَّ لِغَيْرِ ٱللَّهِ بِهِۦ وَٱلْمُنْخَنِقَةُ وَٱلْمَوْقُوذَةُ وَٱلْمُتَرَدِّيَةُ وَٱلنَّطِيحَةُ وَمَآ أَكَلَ ٱلسَّبُعُ إِلَّا مَا ذَكَّيْتُمْ وَمَا ذُبِحَ عَلَى ٱلنُّصُبِ وَأَن تَسْتَقْسِمُوا۟ بِٱلْأَزْلَٰمِ ذَٰلِكُمْ فِسْقٌ ٱلْيَوْمَ يَئِسَ ٱلَّذِينَ كَفَرُوا۟ مِن دِينِكُمْ فَلَا تَخْشَوْهُمْ وَٱخْشَوْنِ ٱلْيَوْمَ أَكْمَلْتُ لَكُمْ دِينَكُمْ وَأَتْمَمْتُ عَلَيْكُمْ نِعْمَتِى وَرَضِيتُ لَكُمُ ٱلْإِسْلَٰمَ دِينًا فَمَنِ ٱضْطُرَّ فِى مَخْمَصَةٍ غَيْرَ مُتَجَانِفٍ لِّإِثْمٍ فَإِنَّ ٱللَّهَ غَفُورٌ رَّحِيمٌ ۝

ٱلْيَوْمَ أُحِلَّ لَكُمُ ٱلطَّيِّبَٰتُ وَطَعَامُ ٱلَّذِينَ أُوتُوا۟ ٱلْكِتَٰبَ حِلٌّ لَّكُمْ وَطَعَامُكُمْ حِلٌّ لَّهُمْ وَٱلْمُحْصَنَٰتُ مِنَ ٱلْمُؤْمِنَٰتِ وَٱلْمُحْصَنَٰتُ مِنَ ٱلَّذِينَ أُوتُوا۟ ٱلْكِتَٰبَ مِن قَبْلِكُمْ إِذَآ ءَاتَيْتُمُوهُنَّ أُجُورَهُنَّ مُحْصِنِينَ غَيْرَ مُسَٰفِحِينَ وَلَا مُتَّخِذِىٓ أَخْدَانٍ وَمَن يَكْفُرْ بِٱلْإِيمَٰنِ فَقَدْ حَبِطَ عَمَلُهُۥ وَهُوَ فِى ٱلْءَاخِرَةِ مِنَ ٱلْخَٰسِرِينَ ۝

THE HOLY QUR'ĀN: SELECTED VERSES

12. ...Lo, I am with you... [SS]

24. ...go thou and thy Lord and fight; we shall sit here. [M]

48. And unto thee We have revealed the Book, the Scripture with the Truth confirming what was before it and a watcher over it... To each of you We have established a law and a way, and if God had wished, He would have made you one People. But [He has willed it otherwise] that He may put you to a fair test in what He has given you. So vie with one another in good works. Unto God ye will be brought back and He will inform you about that wherein ye differed. [L-UQ]

48. ...for each We have appointed a law and traced out a path, and if God had wished, verily He would have made you one people. But He hath made you as ye are that He may put you to the test in what He hath given you. So vie with one another in good works. Unto God ye will all be brought back and He will then tell you about those things wherein ye differed. [BC]

48. ...for each of you We have appointed a law and traced out a path, and if God had so willed, He would have made you one community... [SS]

48. ...for each We have appointed a law and a path, and if God had wished, He would have made you one people. But He hath made you as ye are that He may put you to the test in what He hath given you. So vie with one another in good works. Unto God ye will all be brought back and He will then tell you about those things wherein ye differed. [WS]

48. ...for each We have appointed a law and a path, and if God had wished, He could have made you one people... So vie with one another in good works. Unto God ye will all be brought back and He will then inform you about those things wherein ye differed. [M]

32

وَلَقَدْ أَخَذَ اللَّهُ مِيثَاقَ بَنِي إِسْرَاءِيلَ وَبَعَثْنَا مِنْهُمُ اثْنَيْ عَشَرَ نَقِيبًا ۖ وَقَالَ اللَّهُ إِنِّي مَعَكُمْ ۖ لَئِنْ أَقَمْتُمُ الصَّلَوٰةَ وَءَاتَيْتُمُ الزَّكَوٰةَ وَءَامَنتُم بِرُسُلِي وَعَزَّرْتُمُوهُمْ وَأَقْرَضْتُمُ اللَّهَ قَرْضًا حَسَنًا لَّأُكَفِّرَنَّ عَنكُمْ سَيِّـَٔاتِكُمْ وَلَأُدْخِلَنَّكُمْ جَنَّـٰتٍ تَجْرِى مِن تَحْتِهَا ٱلْأَنْهَـٰرُ ۚ فَمَن كَفَرَ بَعْدَ ذَٰلِكَ مِنكُمْ فَقَدْ ضَلَّ سَوَاءَ ٱلسَّبِيلِ ۞

قَالُوا۟ يَـٰمُوسَىٰٓ إِنَّا لَن نَّدْخُلَهَآ أَبَدًا مَّا دَامُوا۟ فِيهَا ۖ فَٱذْهَبْ أَنتَ وَرَبُّكَ فَقَـٰتِلَآ إِنَّا هَـٰهُنَا قَـٰعِدُونَ ۞

وَأَنزَلْنَآ إِلَيْكَ ٱلْكِتَـٰبَ بِٱلْحَقِّ مُصَدِّقًا لِّمَا بَيْنَ يَدَيْهِ مِنَ ٱلْكِتَـٰبِ وَمُهَيْمِنًا عَلَيْهِ ۖ فَٱحْكُم بَيْنَهُم بِمَآ أَنزَلَ ٱللَّهُ ۖ وَلَا تَتَّبِعْ أَهْوَاءَهُمْ عَمَّا جَاءَكَ مِنَ ٱلْحَقِّ ۚ لِكُلٍّ جَعَلْنَا مِنكُمْ شِرْعَةً وَمِنْهَاجًا ۚ وَلَوْ شَاءَ ٱللَّهُ لَجَعَلَكُمْ أُمَّةً وَٰحِدَةً وَلَـٰكِن لِّيَبْلُوَكُمْ فِى مَآ ءَاتَىٰكُمْ ۖ فَٱسْتَبِقُوا۟ ٱلْخَيْرَٰتِ ۚ إِلَى ٱللَّهِ مَرْجِعُكُمْ جَمِيعًا فَيُنَبِّئُكُم بِمَا كُنتُمْ فِيهِ تَخْتَلِفُونَ ۞

48. ...for each We have appointed a law and a path; and if God had wished He would have made you one people... So vie with one another in good works. Unto God is your return, all of you together, and He will then inform you of that wherein ye were at variance. [NOS]

48. ...for each of you We have appointed a law and a way. And if God had so willed, He would have made you one people. But (He hath willed it otherwise) that He may put you to the test in what He has given you. So vie with one another in good works. Unto God will ye be brought back and He will inform you about that wherein ye differed. [RS]

48. ...to each of you we have given a Law and traced out a path. And if God had wished He would have made you one people, but He did what He did that He might put you to a fair test in what He gave you. So vie with each other in good works... [PT]

54. ...this is God's Grace. He giveth It whom He will... [SS]

69. Verily they that believe, and those who are Jews, and the Sabaeans and the Christians—whomsoever believeth in God and the last day and acteth piously—there shall come no fear upon them, neither shall they grieve. [BC]

69. Verily the Faithful, and the Jews, and the Sabians and the Christians—whoso believeth in God and the Last Day and doeth deeds of piety—no fear shall come upon them, neither shall they grieve. [SS] [RS]

69. Verily the Faithful [Muslims], and the Jews, and the Christians and the Sabaeans—whoso hath faith in God and the Last Day and doeth deeds of piety—their meed is kept for them with their Lord, and no fear shall come upon them, neither shall they grieve. [IS]

وَأَنزَلْنَا إِلَيْكَ ٱلْكِتَٰبَ بِٱلْحَقِّ مُصَدِّقًا لِّمَا بَيْنَ يَدَيْهِ مِنَ ٱلْكِتَٰبِ وَمُهَيْمِنًا عَلَيْهِ ۖ فَٱحْكُم بَيْنَهُم بِمَا أَنزَلَ ٱللَّهُ ۖ وَلَا تَتَّبِعْ أَهْوَاءَهُمْ عَمَّا جَاءَكَ مِنَ ٱلْحَقِّ ۚ لِكُلٍّ جَعَلْنَا مِنكُمْ شِرْعَةً وَمِنْهَاجًا ۚ وَلَوْ شَاءَ ٱللَّهُ لَجَعَلَكُمْ أُمَّةً وَٰحِدَةً وَلَٰكِن لِّيَبْلُوَكُمْ فِى مَآ ءَاتَىٰكُمْ ۖ فَٱسْتَبِقُوا۟ ٱلْخَيْرَٰتِ ۚ إِلَى ٱللَّهِ مَرْجِعُكُمْ جَمِيعًا فَيُنَبِّئُكُم بِمَا كُنتُمْ فِيهِ تَخْتَلِفُونَ ۝

يَٰٓأَيُّهَا ٱلَّذِينَ ءَامَنُوا۟ مَن يَرْتَدَّ مِنكُمْ عَن دِينِهِ فَسَوْفَ يَأْتِى ٱللَّهُ بِقَوْمٍ يُحِبُّهُمْ وَيُحِبُّونَهُۥٓ أَذِلَّةٍ عَلَى ٱلْمُؤْمِنِينَ أَعِزَّةٍ عَلَى ٱلْكَٰفِرِينَ يُجَٰهِدُونَ فِى سَبِيلِ ٱللَّهِ وَلَا يَخَافُونَ لَوْمَةَ لَآئِمٍ ۚ ذَٰلِكَ فَضْلُ ٱللَّهِ يُؤْتِيهِ مَن يَشَاءُ ۚ وَٱللَّهُ وَٰسِعٌ عَلِيمٌ ۝

إِنَّ ٱلَّذِينَ ءَامَنُوا۟ وَٱلَّذِينَ هَادُوا۟ وَٱلصَّٰبِئُونَ وَٱلنَّصَٰرَىٰ مَنْ ءَامَنَ بِٱللَّهِ وَٱلْيَوْمِ ٱلْءَاخِرِ وَعَمِلَ صَٰلِحًا فَلَا خَوْفٌ عَلَيْهِمْ وَلَا هُمْ يَحْزَنُونَ ۝

69. Verily those who believe and those who are Jews and Sabeans and Christians, whosoever believeth in God and the Last Day and doeth good, no fear shall come upon them, neither shall they grieve. [L-UQ]

82. ...thou shalt find that the nearest in affection to believing Muslims are those who say: 'Verily we are Christians.' That is because they have amongst them priests and monks, and because they are not proud. [RS]

83. And when they hear that which hath been revealed unto the Messenger thou seest their eyes overflowing with tears at their recognition of the Truth. They say: 'Our Lord, we believe, so inscribe us amongst those who bear witness to the Truth.' [RS]

83. When they hear what hath been revealed unto the Prophet, thou seest their eyes overflow with tears from their recognition of the Truth... [SS]

114. ...O God, our Lord, send down to us a banquet from Heaven which will be a feast for the first of us and the last of us, and a sign from Thee... [SA]

114. ...a banquet of food from Heaven to be for us a feast, for the first of us and for the last of us, and a sign from Thee... [SQCI]

114. ...O God,... send down from Heaven a banquet which will be for the first and the last of us a sign... [L-UQ]

إِنَّ ٱلَّذِينَ ءَامَنُواْ وَٱلَّذِينَ هَادُواْ وَٱلصَّٰبِـُٔونَ وَٱلنَّصَٰرَىٰ مَنْ ءَامَنَ بِٱللَّهِ وَٱلْيَوْمِ ٱلْءَاخِرِ وَعَمِلَ صَٰلِحًا فَلَا خَوْفٌ عَلَيْهِمْ وَلَا هُمْ يَحْزَنُونَ ۝٦٩

لَتَجِدَنَّ أَشَدَّ ٱلنَّاسِ عَدَٰوَةً لِّلَّذِينَ ءَامَنُواْ ٱلْيَهُودَ وَٱلَّذِينَ أَشْرَكُواْ ۖ وَلَتَجِدَنَّ أَقْرَبَهُم مَّوَدَّةً لِّلَّذِينَ ءَامَنُواْ ٱلَّذِينَ قَالُوٓاْ إِنَّا نَصَٰرَىٰ ۚ ذَٰلِكَ بِأَنَّ مِنْهُمْ قِسِّيسِينَ وَرُهْبَانًا وَأَنَّهُمْ لَا يَسْتَكْبِرُونَ ۝٨٢

وَإِذَا سَمِعُواْ مَآ أُنزِلَ إِلَى ٱلرَّسُولِ تَرَىٰٓ أَعْيُنَهُمْ تَفِيضُ مِنَ ٱلدَّمْعِ مِمَّا عَرَفُواْ مِنَ ٱلْحَقِّ ۖ يَقُولُونَ رَبَّنَآ ءَامَنَّا فَٱكْتُبْنَا مَعَ ٱلشَّٰهِدِينَ ۝٨٣

قَالَ عِيسَى ٱبْنُ مَرْيَمَ ٱللَّهُمَّ رَبَّنَآ أَنزِلْ عَلَيْنَا مَآئِدَةً مِّنَ ٱلسَّمَآءِ تَكُونُ لَنَا عِيدًا لِّأَوَّلِنَا وَءَاخِرِنَا وَءَايَةً مِّنكَ ۖ وَٱرْزُقْنَا وَأَنتَ خَيْرُ ٱلرَّٰزِقِينَ ۝١١٤

Al-An'ām (VI)

In the Name of God, the Infinitely Good, the Ever-Merciful

29. ... there is naught but the life of this world and we shall not be raised. [M]

52. ... they seek His Face... [OS]

54. ... your Lord has prescribed for Himself Clemency... [UM]

59. And with Him are the keys of the unmanifest. None but He knoweth them; and He knoweth what is on land and sea; there falleth no leaf without His knowledge, nor any seed in the darkness of the earth, naught filled with sap nor any dry thing, but it is written in the Clear Book. [BC]

75. Thus did We show unto Abraham the dominion of the Heavens and of the earth that he might be of those possessing certainty. [BC] [SS]

76. When the night grew dark upon him he beheld a planet, and said: 'This is my Lord.' Then when it set, he said: 'I love not that which setteth.' [BC]

76. When the night grew dark upon him he beheld a planet, and said: 'This is my Lord.' Then when it set, he said: 'I love not things which set.' [SS]

(٦) سُورَةُ الْأَنْعَامِ

بِسْمِ اللَّهِ الرَّحْمَٰنِ الرَّحِيمِ

وَقَالُوا إِنْ هِيَ إِلَّا حَيَاتُنَا الدُّنْيَا وَمَا نَحْنُ بِمَبْعُوثِينَ ﴿٢٩﴾

وَلَا تَطْرُدِ الَّذِينَ يَدْعُونَ رَبَّهُم بِالْغَدَاةِ وَالْعَشِيِّ يُرِيدُونَ وَجْهَهُ ۖ مَا عَلَيْكَ مِنْ حِسَابِهِم مِّن شَيْءٍ وَمَا مِنْ حِسَابِكَ عَلَيْهِم مِّن شَيْءٍ فَتَطْرُدَهُمْ فَتَكُونَ مِنَ الظَّالِمِينَ ﴿٥٢﴾

وَإِذَا جَاءَكَ الَّذِينَ يُؤْمِنُونَ بِآيَاتِنَا فَقُلْ سَلَامٌ عَلَيْكُمْ ۖ كَتَبَ رَبُّكُمْ عَلَىٰ نَفْسِهِ الرَّحْمَةَ ۖ أَنَّهُ مَنْ عَمِلَ مِنكُمْ سُوءًا بِجَهَالَةٍ ثُمَّ تَابَ مِن بَعْدِهِ وَأَصْلَحَ فَأَنَّهُ غَفُورٌ رَّحِيمٌ ﴿٥٤﴾

وَعِندَهُ مَفَاتِحُ الْغَيْبِ لَا يَعْلَمُهَا إِلَّا هُوَ ۚ وَيَعْلَمُ مَا فِي الْبَرِّ وَالْبَحْرِ ۚ وَمَا تَسْقُطُ مِن وَرَقَةٍ إِلَّا يَعْلَمُهَا وَلَا حَبَّةٍ فِي ظُلُمَاتِ الْأَرْضِ وَلَا رَطْبٍ وَلَا يَابِسٍ إِلَّا فِي كِتَابٍ مُّبِينٍ ﴿٥٩﴾

وَكَذَٰلِكَ نُرِي إِبْرَاهِيمَ مَلَكُوتَ السَّمَاوَاتِ وَالْأَرْضِ وَلِيَكُونَ مِنَ الْمُوقِنِينَ ﴿٧٥﴾

فَلَمَّا جَنَّ عَلَيْهِ اللَّيْلُ رَأَىٰ كَوْكَبًا ۖ قَالَ هَٰذَا رَبِّي ۖ فَلَمَّا أَفَلَ قَالَ لَا أُحِبُّ الْآفِلِينَ ﴿٧٦﴾

77. And when he saw the moon uprising, he said: 'This is my Lord.' Then when it set, he said: 'Unless my Lord lead me, I must needs become one of the folk who have gone astray.' [BC] [SS]

78. And when he saw the sun uprising, he said: 'This is my Lord. This is greatest.' Then when it set, he said: 'O my people, verily I am innocent of all that ye set up beside God.' [BC]

78. And when he saw the sun uprising, he said: 'This is my Lord. This is greatest.' Then when it set, he said: 'O my people, verily I am innocent of all that ye place beside God.' [SS]

79. Verily I have turned my face towards Him who created the Heavens and the earth... [SS]

91. They esteem not God as He hath the right to be esteemed... [NOS]

91. They have not rated God at His true worth... [PT] [L-UQ]

91. ...say *Allāh*: and leave them to their idle prating. [SS]

91. ...say *Allāh*: then leave them to their idle talk. [WS]

91. ...say *Allāh*; then leave them to their vain discourse. [UM]

91. ...say *Allāh*; then leave them to their vain talk. [UM]

103. Their sight overtaketh Him not, but He overtaketh their sight and He is the All-Pervading All-Prevailing, the Infinitely Aware. [BC] [WS]

103. The sight overtaketh Him not, but He overtaketh the sight... [SS]

103. Men's sight cannot reach Him... [S]

122. Is he who was dead, and whom then We raised to life, setting for him a light whereby he might walk among men, like unto him who is as it were in darkness whence he cannot emerge... [BC]

فَلَمَّا رَءَا ٱلْقَمَرَ بَازِغًا قَالَ هَٰذَا رَبِّى ۖ فَلَمَّآ أَفَلَ قَالَ لَئِن لَّمْ يَهْدِنِى رَبِّى لَأَكُونَنَّ مِنَ ٱلْقَوْمِ ٱلضَّآلِّينَ ۝

فَلَمَّا رَءَا ٱلشَّمْسَ بَازِغَةً قَالَ هَٰذَا رَبِّى هَٰذَآ أَكْبَرُ ۖ فَلَمَّآ أَفَلَتْ قَالَ يَٰقَوْمِ إِنِّى بَرِىٓءٌ مِّمَّا تُشْرِكُونَ ۝

إِنِّى وَجَّهْتُ وَجْهِىَ لِلَّذِى فَطَرَ ٱلسَّمَٰوَٰتِ وَٱلْأَرْضَ حَنِيفًا ۖ وَمَآ أَنَا۠ مِنَ ٱلْمُشْرِكِينَ ۝

وَمَا قَدَرُوا۟ ٱللَّهَ حَقَّ قَدْرِهِۦٓ إِذْ قَالُوا۟ مَآ أَنزَلَ ٱللَّهُ عَلَىٰ بَشَرٍ مِّن شَىْءٍ ۗ قُلْ مَنْ أَنزَلَ ٱلْكِتَٰبَ ٱلَّذِى جَآءَ بِهِۦ مُوسَىٰ نُورًا وَهُدًى لِّلنَّاسِ ۖ تَجْعَلُونَهُۥ قَرَاطِيسَ تُبْدُونَهَا وَتُخْفُونَ كَثِيرًا ۖ وَعُلِّمْتُم مَّا لَمْ تَعْلَمُوٓا۟ أَنتُمْ وَلَآ ءَابَآؤُكُمْ ۖ قُلِ ٱللَّهُ ۖ ثُمَّ ذَرْهُمْ فِى خَوْضِهِمْ يَلْعَبُونَ ۝

لَّا تُدْرِكُهُ ٱلْأَبْصَٰرُ وَهُوَ يُدْرِكُ ٱلْأَبْصَٰرَ ۖ وَهُوَ ٱللَّطِيفُ ٱلْخَبِيرُ ۝

أَوَمَن كَانَ مَيْتًا فَأَحْيَيْنَٰهُ وَجَعَلْنَا لَهُۥ نُورًا يَمْشِى بِهِۦ فِى ٱلنَّاسِ كَمَن مَّثَلُهُۥ فِى ٱلظُّلُمَٰتِ لَيْسَ بِخَارِجٍ مِّنْهَا ۚ كَذَٰلِكَ زُيِّنَ لِلْكَٰفِرِينَ مَا كَانُوا۟ يَعْمَلُونَ ۝

122. …he who was dead and whom We have brought to life, making for him a light whereby he walketh among men… [WS]

122. Is he who was dead and whom We brought to life, setting for him a light whereby he walketh among men, like unto him who is in darkness whence he cannot emerge… [RS]

125. And whomsoever God wisheth to guide, He expandeth his breast unto submission. And whomsoever He wisheth to lead astray He contracteth his breast and maketh it narrow as if he were climbing heaven… [BC]

154. An exposition of everything… [M]

أَوَمَن كَانَ مَيْتًا فَأَحْيَيْنَهُ وَجَعَلْنَا لَهُ نُورًا يَمْشِى بِهِۦ فِى ٱلنَّاسِ كَمَن مَّثَلُهُۥ فِى ٱلظُّلُمَٰتِ لَيْسَ بِخَارِجٍ مِّنْهَا ۚ كَذَٰلِكَ زُيِّنَ لِلْكَٰفِرِينَ مَا كَانُوا۟ يَعْمَلُونَ ۝

فَمَن يُرِدِ ٱللَّهُ أَن يَهْدِيَهُۥ يَشْرَحْ صَدْرَهُۥ لِلْإِسْلَٰمِ ۖ وَمَن يُرِدْ أَن يُضِلَّهُۥ يَجْعَلْ صَدْرَهُۥ ضَيِّقًا حَرَجًا كَأَنَّمَا يَصَّعَّدُ فِى ٱلسَّمَآءِ ۚ كَذَٰلِكَ يَجْعَلُ ٱللَّهُ ٱلرِّجْسَ عَلَى ٱلَّذِينَ لَا يُؤْمِنُونَ ۝

ثُمَّ ءَاتَيْنَا مُوسَى ٱلْكِتَٰبَ تَمَامًا عَلَى ٱلَّذِىٓ أَحْسَنَ وَتَفْصِيلًا لِّكُلِّ شَىْءٍ وَهُدًى وَرَحْمَةً لَّعَلَّهُم بِلِقَآءِ رَبِّهِمْ يُؤْمِنُونَ ۝

Al-Aʿrāf (VII)

In the Name of God, the Infinitely Good, the Ever-Merciful

43. And we remove whatever there may be of rancour in their breasts... [M]

46. ...and on the heights are men...They call out to the people of Paradise. Peace be on you. They have not entered it yet, though they long to enter. [RS]

46. ...on the heights are men...They call up to the people of Paradise 'Peace be on you.' They have not entered it yet though they are eager to enter. [L-QD]

46. ...they have not yet entered Paradise, though they long to do so. [L-HOD]

55. Invoke your Lord with humility and in secret. He loveth not transgressors. [UM]

55. Call upon God in humility and in secret... [WS]

56. And cause not corruption upon the earth after its ordering; and invoke Him with fear and desire; truly the Mercy of God is nigh upon those who do good. [UM]

56. ...call upon Him in fear and in eager desire... [WS]

127. ...verily We stand over them Irresistible. [SS]

143. ...thou shalt not see Me. Gaze upon the mountain: if it stand firm in its place, then shalt thou see Me. And when

(٧) سُورَةُ الْأَعْرَافِ

بِسْمِ اللَّهِ الرَّحْمَٰنِ الرَّحِيمِ

وَنَزَعْنَا مَا فِي صُدُورِهِم مِّنْ غِلٍّ تَجْرِي مِن تَحْتِهِمُ الْأَنْهَارُ وَقَالُوا الْحَمْدُ لِلَّهِ الَّذِي هَدَانَا لِهَٰذَا وَمَا كُنَّا لِنَهْتَدِيَ لَوْلَا أَنْ هَدَانَا اللَّهُ لَقَدْ جَاءَتْ رُسُلُ رَبِّنَا بِالْحَقِّ وَنُودُوا أَن تِلْكُمُ الْجَنَّةُ أُورِثْتُمُوهَا بِمَا كُنتُمْ تَعْمَلُونَ ۝

وَبَيْنَهُمَا حِجَابٌ وَعَلَى الْأَعْرَافِ رِجَالٌ يَعْرِفُونَ كُلًّا بِسِيمَاهُمْ وَنَادَوْا أَصْحَابَ الْجَنَّةِ أَن سَلَامٌ عَلَيْكُمْ لَمْ يَدْخُلُوهَا وَهُمْ يَطْمَعُونَ ۝

ادْعُوا رَبَّكُمْ تَضَرُّعًا وَخُفْيَةً إِنَّهُ لَا يُحِبُّ الْمُعْتَدِينَ ۝

وَلَا تُفْسِدُوا فِي الْأَرْضِ بَعْدَ إِصْلَاحِهَا وَادْعُوهُ خَوْفًا وَطَمَعًا إِنَّ رَحْمَتَ اللَّهِ قَرِيبٌ مِّنَ الْمُحْسِنِينَ ۝

وَقَالَ الْمَلَأُ مِن قَوْمِ فِرْعَوْنَ أَتَذَرُ مُوسَىٰ وَقَوْمَهُ لِيُفْسِدُوا فِي الْأَرْضِ وَيَذَرَكَ وَآلِهَتَكَ قَالَ سَنُقَتِّلُ أَبْنَاءَهُمْ وَنَسْتَحْيِي نِسَاءَهُمْ وَإِنَّا فَوْقَهُمْ قَاهِرُونَ ۝

وَلَمَّا جَاءَ مُوسَىٰ لِمِيقَاتِنَا وَكَلَّمَهُ رَبُّهُ قَالَ رَبِّ أَرِنِي أَنظُرْ إِلَيْكَ قَالَ لَن تَرَانِي وَلَٰكِنِ انظُرْ إِلَى الْجَبَلِ فَإِنِ اسْتَقَرَّ مَكَانَهُ فَسَوْفَ تَرَانِي فَلَمَّا

His Lord manifested Himself unto the mountain... Moses fell down senseless... [SS]

144. ...O Moses I have chosen thee above all mankind by My messages and My speaking unto thee... [M]

156. ...My Mercy embraceth all things... [QACI] [SQCI]

156. ...I shall fate it as being for them that fear Me... [UM]

157. ...the unlettered Prophet... [QACI] [SQCI]

172. Remember when thy Lord took the seeds of the sons of Adam from their loins and made them bear witness against themselves, and said: 'Am I not your Lord?' They said: 'Yea, we testify.' This was lest ye should say on the day of Resurrection: 'Of this we were unaware.' [SS]

تَجَلَّىٰ رَبُّهُۥ لِلْجَبَلِ جَعَلَهُۥ دَكًّا وَخَرَّ مُوسَىٰ صَعِقًا ۚ فَلَمَّآ أَفَاقَ قَالَ سُبْحَٰنَكَ تُبْتُ إِلَيْكَ وَأَنَا۠ أَوَّلُ ٱلْمُؤْمِنِينَ ۝

قَالَ يَٰمُوسَىٰٓ إِنِّى ٱصْطَفَيْتُكَ عَلَى ٱلنَّاسِ بِرِسَٰلَٰتِى وَبِكَلَٰمِى فَخُذْ مَآ ءَاتَيْتُكَ وَكُن مِّنَ ٱلشَّٰكِرِينَ ۝

وَٱكْتُبْ لَنَا فِى هَٰذِهِ ٱلدُّنْيَا حَسَنَةً وَفِى ٱلْءَاخِرَةِ إِنَّا هُدْنَآ إِلَيْكَ ۚ قَالَ عَذَابِىٓ أُصِيبُ بِهِۦ مَنْ أَشَآءُ ۖ وَرَحْمَتِى وَسِعَتْ كُلَّ شَىْءٍ ۚ فَسَأَكْتُبُهَا لِلَّذِينَ يَتَّقُونَ وَيُؤْتُونَ ٱلزَّكَوٰةَ وَٱلَّذِينَ هُم بِـَٔايَٰتِنَا يُؤْمِنُونَ ۝

ٱلَّذِينَ يَتَّبِعُونَ ٱلرَّسُولَ ٱلنَّبِىَّ ٱلْأُمِّىَّ ٱلَّذِى يَجِدُونَهُۥ مَكْتُوبًا عِندَهُمْ فِى ٱلتَّوْرَىٰةِ وَٱلْإِنجِيلِ يَأْمُرُهُم بِٱلْمَعْرُوفِ وَيَنْهَىٰهُمْ عَنِ ٱلْمُنكَرِ وَيُحِلُّ لَهُمُ ٱلطَّيِّبَٰتِ وَيُحَرِّمُ عَلَيْهِمُ ٱلْخَبَٰٓئِثَ وَيَضَعُ عَنْهُمْ إِصْرَهُمْ وَٱلْأَغْلَٰلَ ٱلَّتِى كَانَتْ عَلَيْهِمْ ۚ فَٱلَّذِينَ ءَامَنُوا۟ بِهِۦ وَعَزَّرُوهُ وَنَصَرُوهُ وَٱتَّبَعُوا۟ ٱلنُّورَ ٱلَّذِىٓ أُنزِلَ مَعَهُۥٓ ۙ أُو۟لَٰٓئِكَ هُمُ ٱلْمُفْلِحُونَ ۝

وَإِذْ أَخَذَ رَبُّكَ مِنۢ بَنِىٓ ءَادَمَ مِن ظُهُورِهِمْ ذُرِّيَّتَهُمْ وَأَشْهَدَهُمْ عَلَىٰٓ أَنفُسِهِمْ أَلَسْتُ بِرَبِّكُمْ ۖ قَالُوا۟ بَلَىٰ ۛ شَهِدْنَآ ۛ أَن تَقُولُوا۟ يَوْمَ ٱلْقِيَٰمَةِ إِنَّا كُنَّا عَنْ هَٰذَا غَٰفِلِينَ ۝

180. God's are the most Beautiful Names, so call on Him by them... [OS]

180. And unto God belong the most beautiful names... [UM]

187. ...it weighs heavily in the womb of the heavens and the earth... [WS]

187. ...the heavens and the earth are pregnant with it... [M]

وَلِلَّهِ ٱلْأَسْمَاءُ ٱلْحُسْنَىٰ فَٱدْعُوهُ بِهَا ۖ وَذَرُوا۟ ٱلَّذِينَ يُلْحِدُونَ فِىٓ أَسْمَـٰٓئِهِۦ ۚ سَيُجْزَوْنَ مَا كَانُوا۟ يَعْمَلُونَ ۝

يَسْـَٔلُونَكَ عَنِ ٱلسَّاعَةِ أَيَّانَ مُرْسَىٰهَا ۖ قُلْ إِنَّمَا عِلْمُهَا عِندَ رَبِّى ۖ لَا يُجَلِّيهَا لِوَقْتِهَآ إِلَّا هُوَ ۚ ثَقُلَتْ فِى ٱلسَّمَـٰوَٰتِ وَٱلْأَرْضِ ۚ لَا تَأْتِيكُمْ إِلَّا بَغْتَةً ۗ يَسْـَٔلُونَكَ كَأَنَّكَ حَفِىٌّ عَنْهَا ۖ قُلْ إِنَّمَا عِلْمُهَا عِندَ ٱللَّهِ وَلَـٰكِنَّ أَكْثَرَ ٱلنَّاسِ لَا يَعْلَمُونَ ۝

Al-Anfāl (VIII)

In the Name of God, the Infinitely Good, the Ever-Merciful

1. They will question thee concerning the spoils of war. Say: The spoils of war are for God and the messenger... [M]
2. Only those are believers whose hearts thrill with awe at the remembrance of God... [SS]
9. ...I will help you with a thousand of the angels, troop on troop. [M]
12. When thy Lord revealed unto the angels: Lo, I am with you, so make firm the believers. I shall cast terror into the hearts of the disbelievers. It is for you to strike off their heads, and to smite their every finger. [M]
17. ...thou threwest not when thou threwest, but it was God that threw... [SS] [M]
24. ...God cometh in between a man and his own heart... [SS] [S] [IS]

(٨) سُورَةُ الْأَنْفَالِ

بِسْمِ اللَّهِ الرَّحْمَٰنِ الرَّحِيمِ

يَسْـَٔلُونَكَ عَنِ ٱلْأَنفَالِ ۖ قُلِ ٱلْأَنفَالُ لِلَّهِ وَٱلرَّسُولِ ۖ فَٱتَّقُوا۟ ٱللَّهَ وَأَصْلِحُوا۟ ذَاتَ بَيْنِكُمْ ۖ وَأَطِيعُوا۟ ٱللَّهَ وَرَسُولَهُۥٓ إِن كُنتُم مُّؤْمِنِينَ ۝

إِنَّمَا ٱلْمُؤْمِنُونَ ٱلَّذِينَ إِذَا ذُكِرَ ٱللَّهُ وَجِلَتْ قُلُوبُهُمْ وَإِذَا تُلِيَتْ عَلَيْهِمْ ءَايَٰتُهُۥ زَادَتْهُمْ إِيمَٰنًا وَعَلَىٰ رَبِّهِمْ يَتَوَكَّلُونَ ۝

إِذْ تَسْتَغِيثُونَ رَبَّكُمْ فَٱسْتَجَابَ لَكُمْ أَنِّى مُمِدُّكُم بِأَلْفٍ مِّنَ ٱلْمَلَٰٓئِكَةِ مُرْدِفِينَ ۝

إِذْ يُوحِى رَبُّكَ إِلَى ٱلْمَلَٰٓئِكَةِ أَنِّى مَعَكُمْ فَثَبِّتُوا۟ ٱلَّذِينَ ءَامَنُوا۟ ۚ سَأُلْقِى فِى قُلُوبِ ٱلَّذِينَ كَفَرُوا۟ ٱلرُّعْبَ فَٱضْرِبُوا۟ فَوْقَ ٱلْأَعْنَاقِ وَٱضْرِبُوا۟ مِنْهُمْ كُلَّ بَنَانٍ ۝

فَلَمْ تَقْتُلُوهُمْ وَلَٰكِنَّ ٱللَّهَ قَتَلَهُمْ ۚ وَمَا رَمَيْتَ إِذْ رَمَيْتَ وَلَٰكِنَّ ٱللَّهَ رَمَىٰ ۚ وَلِيُبْلِىَ ٱلْمُؤْمِنِينَ مِنْهُ بَلَآءً حَسَنًا ۚ إِنَّ ٱللَّهَ سَمِيعٌ عَلِيمٌ ۝

يَٰٓأَيُّهَا ٱلَّذِينَ ءَامَنُوا۟ ٱسْتَجِيبُوا۟ لِلَّهِ وَلِلرَّسُولِ إِذَا دَعَاكُمْ لِمَا يُحْيِيكُمْ ۖ وَٱعْلَمُوٓا۟ أَنَّ ٱللَّهَ يَحُولُ بَيْنَ ٱلْمَرْءِ وَقَلْبِهِۦ وَأَنَّهُۥٓ إِلَيْهِ تُحْشَرُونَ ۝

39. Fight them until there is no longer any sedition, and religion is all for God... [WS]

57. If thou overcomest them in war, then make of them an example, to strike fear into those that are behind them, that they may take heed. [M]

58. If thou fearest treachery from any folk, then throw back unto them their covenant. Verily God loveth not the treacherous. [M]

61. If they incline unto peace, incline thou also unto it, and trust in God... [M]

62. ...He it is who hath supported thee with His help and with the believers. [ICCT]

63. Whose hearts He has attuned. Hadst thou spent all that is in the earth, thou couldst not have attuned their hearts, but God hath attuned them... [ICCT]

63. ...if thou hadst spent all that is in the earth, thou couldst not have united their hearts. But God hath united their hearts... [M]

67. It is not for a prophet to hold captives until he hath made great slaughter in the land. You would have for yourselves the gains of this world and God would have for you the Hereafter, and God is Mighty, Wise. [M]

69. ...verily God is the All-Forgiving, the All-Merciful. [WS]

70. O Prophet, say unto those captives who are in your hands: If God knoweth any good in your hearts, He will give you better than that which hath been taken from you, and He will forgive you. Verily God is Forgiving, Merciful. [M]

70. ...if God knoweth good in your hearts, He will requite you with good... [SS]

وَقَـٰتِلُوهُمْ حَتَّىٰ لَا تَكُونَ فِتْنَةٌ وَيَكُونَ ٱلدِّينُ كُلُّهُۥ لِلَّهِ ۚ فَإِنِ ٱنتَهَوْا۟ فَإِنَّ ٱللَّهَ بِمَا يَعْمَلُونَ بَصِيرٌ ۝

فَإِمَّا تَثْقَفَنَّهُمْ فِى ٱلْحَرْبِ فَشَرِّدْ بِهِم مَّنْ خَلْفَهُمْ لَعَلَّهُمْ يَذَّكَّرُونَ ۝

وَإِمَّا تَخَافَنَّ مِن قَوْمٍ خِيَانَةً فَٱنبِذْ إِلَيْهِمْ عَلَىٰ سَوَآءٍ ۚ إِنَّ ٱللَّهَ لَا يُحِبُّ ٱلْخَآئِنِينَ ۝

وَإِن جَنَحُوا۟ لِلسَّلْمِ فَٱجْنَحْ لَهَا وَتَوَكَّلْ عَلَى ٱللَّهِ ۚ إِنَّهُۥ هُوَ ٱلسَّمِيعُ ٱلْعَلِيمُ ۝

وَإِن يُرِيدُوٓا۟ أَن يَخْدَعُوكَ فَإِنَّ حَسْبَكَ ٱللَّهُ ۚ هُوَ ٱلَّذِىٓ أَيَّدَكَ بِنَصْرِهِۦ وَبِٱلْمُؤْمِنِينَ ۝

وَأَلَّفَ بَيْنَ قُلُوبِهِمْ ۚ لَوْ أَنفَقْتَ مَا فِى ٱلْأَرْضِ جَمِيعًا مَّآ أَلَّفْتَ بَيْنَ قُلُوبِهِمْ وَلَـٰكِنَّ ٱللَّهَ أَلَّفَ بَيْنَهُمْ ۚ إِنَّهُۥ عَزِيزٌ حَكِيمٌ ۝

مَا كَانَ لِنَبِىٍّ أَن يَكُونَ لَهُۥٓ أَسْرَىٰ حَتَّىٰ يُثْخِنَ فِى ٱلْأَرْضِ ۚ تُرِيدُونَ عَرَضَ ٱلدُّنْيَا وَٱللَّهُ يُرِيدُ ٱلْـَٔاخِرَةَ ۗ وَٱللَّهُ عَزِيزٌ حَكِيمٌ ۝

فَكُلُوا۟ مِمَّا غَنِمْتُمْ حَلَـٰلًا طَيِّبًا ۚ وَٱتَّقُوا۟ ٱللَّهَ ۚ إِنَّ ٱللَّهَ غَفُورٌ رَّحِيمٌ ۝

يَـٰٓأَيُّهَا ٱلنَّبِىُّ قُل لِّمَن فِىٓ أَيْدِيكُم مِّنَ ٱلْأَسْرَىٰٓ إِن يَعْلَمِ ٱللَّهُ فِى قُلُوبِكُمْ خَيْرًا يُؤْتِكُمْ خَيْرًا مِّمَّآ أُخِذَ مِنكُمْ وَيَغْفِرْ لَكُمْ ۗ وَٱللَّهُ غَفُورٌ رَّحِيمٌ ۝

At-Tawbah (IX)

In the Name of God, the Infinitely Good, the Ever-Merciful[1]

25. God hath helped you on many fields, and on the day of Ḥunayn, when ye exulted in your numbers and they availed you naught, and the earth for all its breadth was straitened for you, and ye turned back in flight. [M]
26. Then God sent down His spirit of Peace upon His Messenger and upon the faithful, and sent down hosts that ye saw not, and punished those who disbelieved. Such is the wage of the disbelievers. [M]
27. And afterwards God relenteth unto whom He will, for God is Forgiving, Merciful. [M]
28. O ye who believe, the idolaters are unclean. Therefore let them not come nigh unto the inviolable mosque after this their year. And if ye fear poverty, God will enrich you of His bounty. Verily God is All-Knowing, Infinitely Wise. [M]
33. He it is who hath sent His Messenger with guidance and the religion of Truth, that He may make it prevail over all religion, though the idolaters be averse. [RS][PT]
36. ... wage war on the idolaters totally... [WS]

---

[1] Sūrat at-Tawbah is the only *sūra* in the Qur'ān at the beginning of which the *Basmalah* is not recited. However, as the translation here starts at verse 25, we have retained the *Basmalah*.

(٩) سورة التوبة

بسم الله الرحمن الرحيم

لَقَدْ نَصَرَكُمُ اللَّهُ فِى مَوَاطِنَ كَثِيرَةٍ وَيَوْمَ حُنَيْنٍ إِذْ أَعْجَبَتْكُمْ كَثْرَتُكُمْ فَلَمْ تُغْنِ عَنكُمْ شَيْئًا وَضَاقَتْ عَلَيْكُمُ ٱلْأَرْضُ بِمَا رَحُبَتْ ثُمَّ وَلَّيْتُم مُّدْبِرِينَ ۝

ثُمَّ أَنزَلَ ٱللَّهُ سَكِينَتَهُ عَلَىٰ رَسُولِهِ وَعَلَى ٱلْمُؤْمِنِينَ وَأَنزَلَ جُنُودًا لَّمْ تَرَوْهَا وَعَذَّبَ ٱلَّذِينَ كَفَرُوا۟ وَذَٰلِكَ جَزَآءُ ٱلْكَٰفِرِينَ ۝

ثُمَّ يَتُوبُ ٱللَّهُ مِنۢ بَعْدِ ذَٰلِكَ عَلَىٰ مَن يَشَآءُ وَٱللَّهُ غَفُورٌ رَّحِيمٌ ۝

يَٰٓأَيُّهَا ٱلَّذِينَ ءَامَنُوٓا۟ إِنَّمَا ٱلْمُشْرِكُونَ نَجَسٌ فَلَا يَقْرَبُوا۟ ٱلْمَسْجِدَ ٱلْحَرَامَ بَعْدَ عَامِهِمْ هَٰذَا وَإِنْ خِفْتُمْ عَيْلَةً فَسَوْفَ يُغْنِيكُمُ ٱللَّهُ مِن فَضْلِهِ إِن شَآءَ إِنَّ ٱللَّهَ عَلِيمٌ حَكِيمٌ ۝

هُوَ ٱلَّذِىٓ أَرْسَلَ رَسُولَهُ بِٱلْهُدَىٰ وَدِينِ ٱلْحَقِّ لِيُظْهِرَهُ عَلَى ٱلدِّينِ كُلِّهِ وَلَوْ كَرِهَ ٱلْمُشْرِكُونَ ۝

إِنَّ عِدَّةَ ٱلشُّهُورِ عِندَ ٱللَّهِ ٱثْنَا عَشَرَ شَهْرًا فِى كِتَٰبِ ٱللَّهِ يَوْمَ خَلَقَ ٱلسَّمَٰوَٰتِ وَٱلْأَرْضَ مِنْهَآ أَرْبَعَةٌ حُرُمٌ ذَٰلِكَ ٱلدِّينُ ٱلْقَيِّمُ فَلَا تَظْلِمُوا۟ فِيهِنَّ أَنفُسَكُمْ وَقَٰتِلُوا۟ ٱلْمُشْرِكِينَ كَآفَّةً كَمَا يُقَٰتِلُونَكُمْ كَآفَّةً وَٱعْلَمُوٓا۟ أَنَّ ٱللَّهَ مَعَ ٱلْمُتَّقِينَ ۝

40. ...the second of two when they were both in the cave...
Grieve not, for verily God is with us... [M]

60. The alms are for the poor and needy, and for those who collect them, and those whose hearts are to be reconciled, and to set free slaves and captives, and for the relief of debtors, and for the cause of God, and for the wayfarer—an obligation enjoined by God. And God is Knowing, Wise. [M]

72. God hath promised the believers, the men and the women, gardens that are watered by flowing rivers wherein they shall dwell immortal, abodes of excellence in the Paradises of Eden. And *Riḍwān* from God is greater. That is the Infinite [highest] Beatitude. [M]

72. God hath promised the believers, the men and the women, gardens that are watered by flowing rivers wherein they shall dwell immortal, abodes of excellence in the Paradises of Eden. And *Riḍwān* from God is greater. That is the immense attainment. [NOS]

72. God hath promised the believers, the men and the women, gardens that are watered by flowing rivers wherein they shall dwell immortal... And *Riḍwān* from God is greater. That is the Highest Beatitude. [RS]

72. God hath promised the believers, the men and the women, gardens that are watered by flowing rivers, wherein they shall dwell immortal... And *Riḍwān* from God is greater. That is the Infinite Beatitude. [L-QD]

72. ...God's Beatitude is greater [than Paradise]... [S]

80. Ask forgiveness for them, or ask it not, though thou ask forgiveness for them seventy times, yet will not God forgive them... [M]

84. And never pray the funeral prayer over one of them who dieth, nor stand beside his grave, for verily they disbelieved in God and His Messenger and died in their iniquity. [M]

إِلَّا تَنصُرُوهُ فَقَدْ نَصَرَهُ ٱللَّهُ إِذْ أَخْرَجَهُ ٱلَّذِينَ كَفَرُوا۟ ثَانِىَ ٱثْنَيْنِ إِذْ هُمَا فِى ٱلْغَارِ إِذْ يَقُولُ لِصَٰحِبِهِۦ لَا تَحْزَنْ إِنَّ ٱللَّهَ مَعَنَا ۖ فَأَنزَلَ ٱللَّهُ سَكِينَتَهُۥ عَلَيْهِ وَأَيَّدَهُۥ بِجُنُودٍ لَّمْ تَرَوْهَا وَجَعَلَ كَلِمَةَ ٱلَّذِينَ كَفَرُوا۟ ٱلسُّفْلَىٰ ۗ وَكَلِمَةُ ٱللَّهِ هِىَ ٱلْعُلْيَا ۗ وَٱللَّهُ عَزِيزٌ حَكِيمٌ ۝

إِنَّمَا ٱلصَّدَقَٰتُ لِلْفُقَرَآءِ وَٱلْمَسَٰكِينِ وَٱلْعَٰمِلِينَ عَلَيْهَا وَٱلْمُؤَلَّفَةِ قُلُوبُهُمْ وَفِى ٱلرِّقَابِ وَٱلْغَٰرِمِينَ وَفِى سَبِيلِ ٱللَّهِ وَٱبْنِ ٱلسَّبِيلِ ۖ فَرِيضَةً مِّنَ ٱللَّهِ ۗ وَٱللَّهُ عَلِيمٌ حَكِيمٌ ۝

وَعَدَ ٱللَّهُ ٱلْمُؤْمِنِينَ وَٱلْمُؤْمِنَٰتِ جَنَّٰتٍ تَجْرِى مِن تَحْتِهَا ٱلْأَنْهَٰرُ خَٰلِدِينَ فِيهَا وَمَسَٰكِنَ طَيِّبَةً فِى جَنَّٰتِ عَدْنٍ ۚ وَرِضْوَٰنٌ مِّنَ ٱللَّهِ أَكْبَرُ ۚ ذَٰلِكَ هُوَ ٱلْفَوْزُ ٱلْعَظِيمُ ۝

ٱسْتَغْفِرْ لَهُمْ أَوْ لَا تَسْتَغْفِرْ لَهُمْ إِن تَسْتَغْفِرْ لَهُمْ سَبْعِينَ مَرَّةً فَلَن يَغْفِرَ ٱللَّهُ لَهُمْ ۚ ذَٰلِكَ بِأَنَّهُمْ كَفَرُوا۟ بِٱللَّهِ وَرَسُولِهِۦ ۗ وَٱللَّهُ لَا يَهْدِى ٱلْقَوْمَ ٱلْفَٰسِقِينَ ۝

وَلَا تُصَلِّ عَلَىٰٓ أَحَدٍ مِّنْهُم مَّاتَ أَبَدًا وَلَا تَقُمْ عَلَىٰ قَبْرِهِۦٓ ۖ إِنَّهُمْ كَفَرُوا۟ بِٱللَّهِ وَرَسُولِهِۦ وَمَاتُوا۟ وَهُمْ فَٰسِقُونَ ۝

103. Take alms of their wealth to purify them... [M]

115. It is not God's wont that He should send a folk astray after He hath guided them until He hath made clear unto them that against which they should be upon their guard... [OS]

118. ... when the earth for all its vastness was straitened for them and when their souls were straitened, and they had come to think there is no refuge from God except in Him, then turned He unto them that they might turn in repentance unto Him. Verily God, He is the Ever-Relenting, the Merciful. [M]

118. ... there is no refuge from God except in Him... [WS] [SA]

خُذْ مِنْ أَمْوَالِهِمْ صَدَقَةً تُطَهِّرُهُمْ وَتُزَكِّيهِم بِهَا وَصَلِّ عَلَيْهِمْ ۖ إِنَّ صَلَوٰتَكَ سَكَنٌ لَّهُمْ ۗ وَٱللَّهُ سَمِيعٌ عَلِيمٌ ۝

وَمَا كَانَ ٱللَّهُ لِيُضِلَّ قَوْمًا بَعْدَ إِذْ هَدَىٰهُمْ حَتَّىٰ يُبَيِّنَ لَهُم مَّا يَتَّقُونَ ۚ إِنَّ ٱللَّهَ بِكُلِّ شَيْءٍ عَلِيمٌ ۝

وَعَلَى ٱلثَّلَٰثَةِ ٱلَّذِينَ خُلِّفُوا۟ حَتَّىٰ إِذَا ضَاقَتْ عَلَيْهِمُ ٱلْأَرْضُ بِمَا رَحُبَتْ وَضَاقَتْ عَلَيْهِمْ أَنفُسُهُمْ وَظَنُّوٓا۟ أَن لَّا مَلْجَأَ مِنَ ٱللَّهِ إِلَّآ إِلَيْهِ ثُمَّ تَابَ عَلَيْهِمْ لِيَتُوبُوٓا۟ ۚ إِنَّ ٱللَّهَ هُوَ ٱلتَّوَّابُ ٱلرَّحِيمُ ۝

Yūnus (X)

In the Name of God, the Infinitely Good, the Ever-Merciful

5. He it is Who hath made the sun a splendour and the moon a light... [BC]

7. They who set not their hopes on meeting Us, and who are satisfied with this lower life and find their deepest peace therein, and fail to treat Our signs as signs. [M]

24. Verily this lower life is but as water which we have sent down from the sky... [SA]

25. And Allah calls to the House of Peace, and guides whom He will towards the ascending Way. [UM]

47. For every community there is a Messenger... [SS] [L-II]

47. For every nation there is a Messenger... [NOS]

(١٠) سُورَةُ يُونُسَ

بِسْمِ اللَّهِ الرَّحْمَٰنِ الرَّحِيمِ

هُوَ الَّذِى جَعَلَ الشَّمْسَ ضِيَآءً وَالْقَمَرَ نُورًا وَقَدَّرَهُ مَنَازِلَ لِتَعْلَمُوا۟ عَدَدَ السِّنِينَ وَالْحِسَابَ مَا خَلَقَ اللَّهُ ذَٰلِكَ إِلَّا بِالْحَقِّ يُفَصِّلُ الْآيَٰتِ لِقَوْمٍ يَعْلَمُونَ ۝

إِنَّ الَّذِينَ لَا يَرْجُونَ لِقَآءَنَا وَرَضُوا۟ بِالْحَيَوٰةِ الدُّنْيَا وَاطْمَأَنُّوا۟ بِهَا وَالَّذِينَ هُمْ عَنْ ءَايَٰتِنَا غَٰفِلُونَ ۝

إِنَّمَا مَثَلُ الْحَيَوٰةِ الدُّنْيَا كَمَآءٍ أَنزَلْنَٰهُ مِنَ السَّمَآءِ فَاخْتَلَطَ بِهِ نَبَاتُ الْأَرْضِ مِمَّا يَأْكُلُ النَّاسُ وَالْأَنْعَٰمُ حَتَّىٰ إِذَآ أَخَذَتِ الْأَرْضُ زُخْرُفَهَا وَازَّيَّنَتْ وَظَنَّ أَهْلُهَآ أَنَّهُمْ قَٰدِرُونَ عَلَيْهَآ أَتَىٰهَآ أَمْرُنَا لَيْلًا أَوْ نَهَارًا فَجَعَلْنَٰهَا حَصِيدًا كَأَن لَّمْ تَغْنَ بِالْأَمْسِ كَذَٰلِكَ نُفَصِّلُ الْآيَٰتِ لِقَوْمٍ يَتَفَكَّرُونَ ۝

وَاللَّهُ يَدْعُوٓا۟ إِلَىٰ دَارِ السَّلَٰمِ وَيَهْدِى مَن يَشَآءُ إِلَىٰ صِرَٰطٍ مُّسْتَقِيمٍ ۝

وَلِكُلِّ أُمَّةٍ رَّسُولٌ فَإِذَا جَآءَ رَسُولُهُمْ قُضِىَ بَيْنَهُم بِالْقِسْطِ وَهُمْ لَا يُظْلَمُونَ ۝

Hūd (XI)

In the Name of God, the Infinitely Good, the Ever-Merciful

7. And He it is Who created the Heavens and the earth in six days, and His throne was upon the water... [BC]

7. ...His throne was upon the water... [SA]

17. ...one whom his Lord hath made certain, and whose certainty He hath then followed up with direct evidence... [SS]

37. ...beneath Our eyes... [OS]

56. ...there is no living creature but He graspeth it by its forelock... [OS]

105. On the day when it cometh no soul shall speak but by His leave, wretched some, and others blissful. [M]

106. As for the wretched, in the Fire shall they be, to sigh and to wail is their portion. [M]

(١١) سُورَةُ هُودٍ

بِسْمِ اللَّهِ الرَّحْمَٰنِ الرَّحِيمِ

وَهُوَ الَّذِى خَلَقَ السَّمَٰوَٰتِ وَالْأَرْضَ فِى سِتَّةِ أَيَّامٍ وَكَانَ عَرْشُهُ عَلَى الْمَاءِ لِيَبْلُوَكُمْ أَيُّكُمْ أَحْسَنُ عَمَلًا وَلَئِن قُلْتَ إِنَّكُم مَّبْعُوثُونَ مِنۢ بَعْدِ الْمَوْتِ لَيَقُولَنَّ الَّذِينَ كَفَرُوٓا۟ إِنْ هَٰذَآ إِلَّا سِحْرٌ مُّبِينٌ ۝

أَفَمَن كَانَ عَلَىٰ بَيِّنَةٍ مِّن رَّبِّهِ وَيَتْلُوهُ شَاهِدٌ مِّنْهُ وَمِن قَبْلِهِ كِتَٰبُ مُوسَىٰٓ إِمَامًا وَرَحْمَةً أُو۟لَٰٓئِكَ يُؤْمِنُونَ بِهِ وَمَن يَكْفُرْ بِهِ مِنَ الْأَحْزَابِ فَالنَّارُ مَوْعِدُهُ فَلَا تَكُ فِى مِرْيَةٍ مِّنْهُ إِنَّهُ الْحَقُّ مِن رَّبِّكَ وَلَٰكِنَّ أَكْثَرَ النَّاسِ لَا يُؤْمِنُونَ ۝

وَاصْنَعِ الْفُلْكَ بِأَعْيُنِنَا وَوَحْيِنَا وَلَا تُخَٰطِبْنِى فِى الَّذِينَ ظَلَمُوٓا۟ إِنَّهُم مُّغْرَقُونَ ۝

إِنِّى تَوَكَّلْتُ عَلَى اللَّهِ رَبِّى وَرَبِّكُم مَّا مِن دَآبَّةٍ إِلَّا هُوَ ءَاخِذٌۢ بِنَاصِيَتِهَآ إِنَّ رَبِّى عَلَىٰ صِرَٰطٍ مُّسْتَقِيمٍ ۝

يَوْمَ يَأْتِ لَا تَكَلَّمُ نَفْسٌ إِلَّا بِإِذْنِهِ فَمِنْهُمْ شَقِىٌّ وَسَعِيدٌ ۝

فَأَمَّا الَّذِينَ شَقُوا۟ فَفِى النَّارِ لَهُمْ فِيهَا زَفِيرٌ وَشَهِيقٌ ۝

107. Abiding therein as long as heaven and earth endure, except as God will. Verily thy Lord is ever the doer of what He will. [M]

107. Abiding therein so long as the heavens and the earth endure except as God wisheth. Verily God is ever the doer of what He will. [RS][L-QD]

108. And as for the blissful, in the Garden shall they be, abiding therein as long as heaven and earth endure, except as God will—a gift that shall not be taken away. [M]

108. ... abiding therein so long as the heavens and the earth endure, except as God wisheth. A gift that shall not be taken away. [L-QD]

خَٰلِدِينَ فِيهَا مَا دَامَتِ ٱلسَّمَٰوَٰتُ وَٱلْأَرْضُ إِلَّا مَا شَآءَ رَبُّكَ ۚ إِنَّ رَبَّكَ فَعَّالٌ لِّمَا يُرِيدُ ۝

وَأَمَّا ٱلَّذِينَ سُعِدُوا۟ فَفِى ٱلْجَنَّةِ خَٰلِدِينَ فِيهَا مَا دَامَتِ ٱلسَّمَٰوَٰتُ وَٱلْأَرْضُ إِلَّا مَا شَآءَ رَبُّكَ ۖ عَطَآءً غَيْرَ مَجْذُوذٍ ۝

Yūsuf (XII)

In the Name of God, the Infinitely Good, the Ever-Merciful

18. ...beautiful patience must be mine; and God is He of whom help is to be asked against what they say. [M]

31. ...they said: Peerless is God's Glory! This is not of humankind... [SS] [M]

31. ...glory be to God! This is not a man; this is none other than a noble angel. [QACI] [SQCI]

31. ...this is none other than a noble Angel. [SS]

53. ...verily the soul commandeth unto evil... [M]

76. ...We exalt in degree whom We will; and above each one that hath knowledge is one that knoweth more. [OS] [SS]

84. ...his eyes grew white with blindness for the grief that he was suppressing. [SS]

92. ...this day there shall be no upbraiding of you nor reproach. God forgiveth you, and He is the most of the merciful. [M]

92. ...this day there shall be no upbraiding of you nor reproach. God forgiveth you, and He is the Mercifullest of the merciful. [Mec.]

(١٢) سُورَةُ يُوسُفَ

بِسْمِ اللَّهِ الرَّحْمَٰنِ الرَّحِيمِ

وَجَآءُو عَلَىٰ قَمِيصِهِۦ بِدَمٍ كَذِبٍ قَالَ بَلْ سَوَّلَتْ لَكُمْ أَنفُسُكُمْ أَمْرًا فَصَبْرٌ جَمِيلٌ وَاللَّهُ الْمُسْتَعَانُ عَلَىٰ مَا تَصِفُونَ ۝

فَلَمَّا سَمِعَتْ بِمَكْرِهِنَّ أَرْسَلَتْ إِلَيْهِنَّ وَأَعْتَدَتْ لَهُنَّ مُتَّكَـًٔا وَءَاتَتْ كُلَّ وَٰحِدَةٍ مِّنْهُنَّ سِكِّينًا وَقَالَتِ اخْرُجْ عَلَيْهِنَّ فَلَمَّا رَأَيْنَهُۥ أَكْبَرْنَهُۥ وَقَطَّعْنَ أَيْدِيَهُنَّ وَقُلْنَ حَٰشَ لِلَّهِ مَا هَٰذَا بَشَرًا إِنْ هَٰذَآ إِلَّا مَلَكٌ كَرِيمٌ ۝

وَمَآ أُبَرِّئُ نَفْسِىٓ إِنَّ النَّفْسَ لَأَمَّارَةٌۢ بِالسُّوٓءِ إِلَّا مَا رَحِمَ رَبِّىٓ إِنَّ رَبِّى غَفُورٌ رَّحِيمٌ ۝

فَبَدَأَ بِأَوْعِيَتِهِمْ قَبْلَ وِعَآءِ أَخِيهِ ثُمَّ اسْتَخْرَجَهَا مِن وِعَآءِ أَخِيهِ كَذَٰلِكَ كِدْنَا لِيُوسُفَ مَا كَانَ لِيَأْخُذَ أَخَاهُ فِى دِينِ الْمَلِكِ إِلَّآ أَن يَشَآءَ اللَّهُ نَرْفَعُ دَرَجَٰتٍ مَّن نَّشَآءُ وَفَوْقَ كُلِّ ذِى عِلْمٍ عَلِيمٌ ۝

وَتَوَلَّىٰ عَنْهُمْ وَقَالَ يَٰٓأَسَفَىٰ عَلَىٰ يُوسُفَ وَابْيَضَّتْ عَيْنَاهُ مِنَ الْحُزْنِ فَهُوَ كَظِيمٌ ۝

قَالَ لَا تَثْرِيبَ عَلَيْكُمُ الْيَوْمَ يَغْفِرُ اللَّهُ لَكُمْ وَهُوَ أَرْحَمُ الرَّٰحِمِينَ ۝

Ar-Raʿd (XIII)
In the Name of God, the Infinitely Good, the Ever-Merciful

12. He it is who showeth you the lightning, a fear and a longing, and raiseth the heavy clouds. [SA]

13. And the thunder extolleth and praiseth Him, as do the angels for awe of Him... [SA]

17. He sendeth down water from heaven, so that valleys are in flood with it, each according to its capacity, and the flood beareth swelling foam... thus God coineth the symbols of reality and illusion. Then as for the foam, it goeth as scum upon the banks, and as for what profiteth men, it remaineth in the earth... [SA]

17. He sendeth down water from heaven, so that valleys are in flood with it, each according to its capacity... [SS]

28. Those who believe and whose hearts rest in security in the remembrance of Allah... [UM]

28. Those who believe and whose hearts repose in security through the invocation of God... [UM]

28. ...are not hearts at peace in the remembrance of God? [WS]

28. ...is it not in the remembrance of God that hearts find rest? [UM]

28. ...is it not in the remembrance of God that hearts find repose? [UM]

39. God effaceth and confirmeth what He will, and with Him is the Mother of the Book. [SS]

39. ...the Mother of the Book. [QACI]

(١٣) سُورَةُ ٱلرَّعْدِ

بِسْمِ ٱللَّهِ ٱلرَّحْمَٰنِ ٱلرَّحِيمِ

هُوَ ٱلَّذِي يُرِيكُمُ ٱلْبَرْقَ خَوْفًا وَطَمَعًا وَيُنْشِئُ ٱلسَّحَابَ ٱلثِّقَالَ ۝

وَيُسَبِّحُ ٱلرَّعْدُ بِحَمْدِهِ وَٱلْمَلَٰئِكَةُ مِنْ خِيفَتِهِ وَيُرْسِلُ ٱلصَّوَاعِقَ فَيُصِيبُ بِهَا مَن يَشَاءُ وَهُمْ يُجَٰدِلُونَ فِي ٱللَّهِ وَهُوَ شَدِيدُ ٱلْمِحَالِ ۝

أَنزَلَ مِنَ ٱلسَّمَاءِ مَاءً فَسَالَتْ أَوْدِيَةٌ بِقَدَرِهَا فَٱحْتَمَلَ ٱلسَّيْلُ زَبَدًا رَّابِيًا ۚ وَمِمَّا يُوقِدُونَ عَلَيْهِ فِي ٱلنَّارِ ٱبْتِغَاءَ حِلْيَةٍ أَوْ مَتَٰعٍ زَبَدٌ مِّثْلُهُ ۚ كَذَٰلِكَ يَضْرِبُ ٱللَّهُ ٱلْحَقَّ وَٱلْبَٰطِلَ ۚ فَأَمَّا ٱلزَّبَدُ فَيَذْهَبُ جُفَاءً ۖ وَأَمَّا مَا يَنفَعُ ٱلنَّاسَ فَيَمْكُثُ فِي ٱلْأَرْضِ ۚ كَذَٰلِكَ يَضْرِبُ ٱللَّهُ ٱلْأَمْثَالَ ۝

ٱلَّذِينَ ءَامَنُوا۟ وَتَطْمَئِنُّ قُلُوبُهُم بِذِكْرِ ٱللَّهِ ۗ أَلَا بِذِكْرِ ٱللَّهِ تَطْمَئِنُّ ٱلْقُلُوبُ ۝

يَمْحُوا۟ ٱللَّهُ مَا يَشَاءُ وَيُثْبِتُ ۖ وَعِندَهُۥ أُمُّ ٱلْكِتَٰبِ ۝

Ibrāhīm (XIV)

In the Name of God, the Infinitely Good, the Ever-Merciful

24. Seest thou not how God citeth a symbol. 'A good word is as good as a good tree, its root set (is) firm (and) its branches in heaven.' [BC]

24. Hast thou not seen how God coineth a similitude? A good word is as a good tree, its root firm, its branches in heaven. [QACI] [SQCI]

24. ...a good word is as good as a good tree, its root is firm, its branches are in heaven. [WS]

25. Giving its fruit at every season by the leave of its Lord. God citeth symbols for men that they may remember. [BC]

25. Giving its fruits at every due season by the leave of its Lord. And God coineth similtudes for men that they may remember. [QACI] [SQCI]

26. A bad word is as a bad tree which lies uprooted on the surface of the earth... [BC]

26. ...a bad tree sprawling uprooted across the ground for lack of firm foundation. [WS]

37. Verily I have settled a line of mine offspring in a tilthless valley at Thy Holy House... Therefore incline unto them men's hearts, and sustain them with fruits that they may be thankful. [M]

(١٤) سُورَةُ إِبْرَاهِيمَ

بِسْمِ ٱللَّهِ ٱلرَّحْمَٰنِ ٱلرَّحِيمِ

أَلَمْ تَرَ كَيْفَ ضَرَبَ ٱللَّهُ مَثَلًا كَلِمَةً طَيِّبَةً كَشَجَرَةٍ طَيِّبَةٍ أَصْلُهَا ثَابِتٌ وَفَرْعُهَا فِى ٱلسَّمَآءِ ۝

تُؤْتِىٓ أُكُلَهَا كُلَّ حِينٍ بِإِذْنِ رَبِّهَا ۗ وَيَضْرِبُ ٱللَّهُ ٱلْأَمْثَالَ لِلنَّاسِ لَعَلَّهُمْ يَتَذَكَّرُونَ ۝

وَمَثَلُ كَلِمَةٍ خَبِيثَةٍ كَشَجَرَةٍ خَبِيثَةٍ ٱجْتُثَّتْ مِن فَوْقِ ٱلْأَرْضِ مَا لَهَا مِن قَرَارٍ ۝

رَّبَّنَآ إِنِّىٓ أَسْكَنتُ مِن ذُرِّيَّتِى بِوَادٍ غَيْرِ ذِى زَرْعٍ عِندَ بَيْتِكَ ٱلْمُحَرَّمِ رَبَّنَا لِيُقِيمُوا۟ ٱلصَّلَوٰةَ فَٱجْعَلْ أَفْـِٔدَةً مِّنَ ٱلنَّاسِ تَهْوِىٓ إِلَيْهِمْ وَٱرْزُقْهُم مِّنَ ٱلثَّمَرَٰتِ لَعَلَّهُمْ يَشْكُرُونَ ۝

Al-Ḥijr (XV)
In the Name of God, the Infinitely Good, the Ever-Merciful

21. Nor is there anything but with Us are the treasuries thereof, and We send it not down save in known measure. [SA]

23. And verily it is We who give life and make to die, and We are the Inheritor. [SA]

29. ...I breathed into him of My Spirit... [SS]

42. Over my slaves thou hast no power... [L-QOS]

47. And we remove whatever there may be of rancour in their breasts... [M]

An-Naḥl (XVI)
In the Name of God, the Infinitely Good, the Ever-Merciful

13. And whatsoever He hath created for you on earth of diverse hues, verily therein is a sign for people bent on remembrance. [SA]

42. Those who have patience and trust in their Lord. [UM]

78. ...He hath given you hearing and sight and heart knowledge that ye may be thankful. [M]

126. If ye inflict punishment, then inflict only so much as ye have suffered; but if ye endure patiently, that is better for the patient. [M]

(١٥) سُورَةُ الْحِجْرِ

بِسْمِ اللَّهِ الرَّحْمَٰنِ الرَّحِيمِ

وَإِن مِّن شَيْءٍ إِلَّا عِندَنَا خَزَائِنُهُ وَمَا نُنَزِّلُهُ إِلَّا بِقَدَرٍ مَّعْلُومٍ ۝

وَإِنَّا لَنَحْنُ نُحْيِـۦ وَنُمِيتُ وَنَحْنُ الْوَارِثُونَ ۝

فَإِذَا سَوَّيْتُهُ وَنَفَخْتُ فِيهِ مِن رُّوحِي فَقَعُوا لَهُ سَاجِدِينَ ۝

إِنَّ عِبَادِي لَيْسَ لَكَ عَلَيْهِمْ سُلْطَانٌ إِلَّا مَنِ اتَّبَعَكَ مِنَ الْغَاوِينَ ۝

وَنَزَعْنَا مَا فِي صُدُورِهِم مِّنْ غِلٍّ إِخْوَانًا عَلَىٰ سُرُرٍ مُّتَقَابِلِينَ ۝

(١٦) سُورَةُ النَّحْلِ

بِسْمِ اللَّهِ الرَّحْمَٰنِ الرَّحِيمِ

وَمَا ذَرَأَ لَكُمْ فِي الْأَرْضِ مُخْتَلِفًا أَلْوَانُهُ ۗ إِنَّ فِي ذَٰلِكَ لَآيَةً لِّقَوْمٍ يَذَّكَّرُونَ ۝

الَّذِينَ صَبَرُوا وَعَلَىٰ رَبِّهِمْ يَتَوَكَّلُونَ ۝

وَاللَّهُ أَخْرَجَكُم مِّن بُطُونِ أُمَّهَاتِكُمْ لَا تَعْلَمُونَ شَيْئًا وَجَعَلَ لَكُمُ السَّمْعَ وَالْأَبْصَارَ وَالْأَفْئِدَةَ لَعَلَّكُمْ تَشْكُرُونَ ۝

وَإِنْ عَاقَبْتُمْ فَعَاقِبُوا بِمِثْلِ مَا عُوقِبْتُم بِهِ ۖ وَلَئِن صَبَرْتُمْ لَهُوَ خَيْرٌ لِّلصَّابِرِينَ ۝

Al-Isrā' (XVII)

In the Name of God, the Infinitely Good, the Ever-Merciful

1. Glory be to Him who took His slave by night from the inviolable Mosque unto that furthest Mosque whose precincts We have made blessed... [Mec.]

21. Behold how We have given precedence of favour unto some over others; and verily the Beyond is greater in degrees, and greater in hierarchic precedences. [SCR-SA]

21. Behold how We have favoured some of them above others; and verily the Hereafter is greater in degrees and greater in hierarchic precedences. [M] [L-QD] [PT]

21. Behold how We have favoured some of them above others; and verily the Hereafter is greater in degrees and greater in precedences of favouring. [SA]

21. Behold how We have favoured some of them above others; and verily the Hereafter is greater in degrees and greater in precedences. [RS]

41. Verily We have given them in this Koran ample reason to take heed, yet it doth but increase them in aversion. [M]

44. The seven Heavens and the earth extol Him, and all that is therein, and there is naught that hymneth not His praise, yet ye understand not their praising... [BC]

44. The seven heavens and the earth and all that is therein extol Him, nor is there anything which doth not glorify Him with praise; yet ye understand not their glorification... [WS]

44. The seven heavens and the earth and all therein glorify Him. Nothing is, but glorifieth Him with Praise... [NOS]

44. The seven Heavens and the earth and all that is therein glorify Him, nor is there anything but glorifieth Him with praise; yet ye understand not their glorification... [SA]

44. ...there is nothing that doth not praise Him... [SA]

(١٧) سُورَةُ الْإِسْرَاء

بِسْمِ اللَّهِ الرَّحْمَٰنِ الرَّحِيمِ

سُبْحَانَ الَّذِي أَسْرَىٰ بِعَبْدِهِ لَيْلًا مِنَ الْمَسْجِدِ الْحَرَامِ إِلَى الْمَسْجِدِ الْأَقْصَى الَّذِي بَارَكْنَا حَوْلَهُ لِنُرِيَهُ مِنْ آيَاتِنَا ۚ إِنَّهُ هُوَ السَّمِيعُ الْبَصِيرُ ۝

انْظُرْ كَيْفَ فَضَّلْنَا بَعْضَهُمْ عَلَىٰ بَعْضٍ ۚ وَلَلْآخِرَةُ أَكْبَرُ دَرَجَاتٍ وَأَكْبَرُ تَفْضِيلًا ۝

وَلَقَدْ صَرَّفْنَا فِي هَٰذَا الْقُرْآنِ لِيَذَّكَّرُوا وَمَا يَزِيدُهُمْ إِلَّا نُفُورًا ۝

تُسَبِّحُ لَهُ السَّمَاوَاتُ السَّبْعُ وَالْأَرْضُ وَمَنْ فِيهِنَّ ۚ وَإِنْ مِنْ شَيْءٍ إِلَّا يُسَبِّحُ بِحَمْدِهِ وَلَٰكِنْ لَا تَفْقَهُونَ تَسْبِيحَهُمْ ۗ إِنَّهُ كَانَ حَلِيمًا غَفُورًا ۝

44. ...and there is nothing that does not sing His praises... [UM]

44. ...there is nothing which does not praise Him... [PT]

55. ...and We have favoured some of the Prophets above others, and unto David we gave the Psalms. [BC] [SCR-SA]

55. ...some of the Prophets We have favoured above others, and unto David We gave the Psalms. [Mec.]

60. ...We give them cause to fear, yet it doth but increase them in monstrous outrage. [M]

65. Verily over my slaves thou [Satan] hast no power... [BC]

65. As to My slaves, over them thou hast no power... [M]

79. And part of the night, keep vigil as a free devotion from thee; perchance thy Lord shall resurrect thee in a glorious station. [UM]

81. ...the Truth hath come and the false hath vanished. Verily the false is ever a vanisher. [M]

81. ...Reality hath come and vanity hath disappeared; indeed vanity is ephemeral. [UM]

85. They will question thee concerning the Spirit. Say: the Spirit proceedeth from the command of my Lord; and ye have not been given knowledge, save only a little. [M]

95. ...if the angels walked at their ease upon earth, verily We had sent down upon them an angel messenger. [M]

95. ...if there were on earth angels walking at their ease, We had sent down upon them an angel as messenger. [SA]

110. ...invoke God (*Allāh*) or invoke the Infinitely-Good (*Ar-Raḥmān*), whichever ye invoke, His are the names most Beautiful... [M]

110. ...call upon *Allāh* or call upon *Ar-Raḥmān*... [UM]

تُسَبِّحُ لَهُ ٱلسَّمَـٰوَٰتُ ٱلسَّبْعُ وَٱلْأَرْضُ وَمَن فِيهِنَّ وَإِن مِّن شَىْءٍ إِلَّا يُسَبِّحُ بِحَمْدِهِۦ وَلَـٰكِن لَّا تَفْقَهُونَ تَسْبِيحَهُمْ إِنَّهُۥ كَانَ حَلِيمًا غَفُورًا ۝

وَرَبُّكَ أَعْلَمُ بِمَن فِى ٱلسَّمَـٰوَٰتِ وَٱلْأَرْضِ وَلَقَدْ فَضَّلْنَا بَعْضَ ٱلنَّبِيِّـۧنَ عَلَىٰ بَعْضٍ وَءَاتَيْنَا دَاوُۥدَ زَبُورًا ۝

وَإِذْ قُلْنَا لَكَ إِنَّ رَبَّكَ أَحَاطَ بِٱلنَّاسِ وَمَا جَعَلْنَا ٱلرُّءْيَا ٱلَّتِىٓ أَرَيْنَـٰكَ إِلَّا فِتْنَةً لِّلنَّاسِ وَٱلشَّجَرَةَ ٱلْمَلْعُونَةَ فِى ٱلْقُرْءَانِ وَنُخَوِّفُهُمْ فَمَا يَزِيدُهُمْ إِلَّا طُغْيَـٰنًا كَبِيرًا ۝

إِنَّ عِبَادِى لَيْسَ لَكَ عَلَيْهِمْ سُلْطَـٰنٌ وَكَفَىٰ بِرَبِّكَ وَكِيلًا ۝

وَمِنَ ٱلَّيْلِ فَتَهَجَّدْ بِهِۦ نَافِلَةً لَّكَ عَسَىٰٓ أَن يَبْعَثَكَ رَبُّكَ مَقَامًا مَّحْمُودًا ۝

وَقُلْ جَآءَ ٱلْحَقُّ وَزَهَقَ ٱلْبَـٰطِلُ إِنَّ ٱلْبَـٰطِلَ كَانَ زَهُوقًا ۝

وَيَسْـَٔلُونَكَ عَنِ ٱلرُّوحِ قُلِ ٱلرُّوحُ مِنْ أَمْرِ رَبِّى وَمَآ أُوتِيتُم مِّنَ ٱلْعِلْمِ إِلَّا قَلِيلًا ۝

قُل لَّوْ كَانَ فِى ٱلْأَرْضِ مَلَـٰٓئِكَةٌ يَمْشُونَ مُطْمَئِنِّينَ لَنَزَّلْنَا عَلَيْهِم مِّنَ ٱلسَّمَآءِ مَلَكًا رَّسُولًا ۝

قُلِ ٱدْعُوا۟ ٱللَّهَ أَوِ ٱدْعُوا۟ ٱلرَّحْمَـٰنَ أَيًّا مَّا تَدْعُوا۟ فَلَهُ ٱلْأَسْمَآءُ ٱلْحُسْنَىٰ وَلَا تَجْهَرْ بِصَلَاتِكَ وَلَا تُخَافِتْ بِهَا وَٱبْتَغِ بَيْنَ ذَٰلِكَ سَبِيلًا ۝

Al-Kahf (XVIII)

In the Name of God, the Infinitely Good, the Ever-Merciful

23. And say not of anything: verily I shall do that tomorrow. [M]

24. Except thou sayest: if God will... [M]

28. ...they seek His Face... [OS]

60. ...I will not give up until I reach the meeting-place of the two Seas... [BC]

60. ...I will not cease until I reach the meeting-place of the two seas... [WS] [SA]

65. ...one of Our slaves unto whom We had given mercy from Our Mercy and knowledge from Our Knowledge. [SA]

66. Moses said unto him: May I follow thee that from what thou hast been taught thou mayst teach me with right guidance. [SA]

67. He said: Verily thou canst not be patient with me. [SA]

68. For how shouldst thou be patient in respect of that which is beyond the compass of thine experience? [SA]

69. He said: God willing, thou shalt find me patient, nor will I gainsay thee in aught. [SA]

70. He said: Then if thou go with me, question me of naught until of myself I mention it to thee. [SA]

109. ...if the sea were ink for the Words of thy Lord, the sea would be used up before the Words of the Lord were used up... [SA]

(١٨) سُورَةُ الْكَهْفِ
بِسْمِ اللَّهِ الرَّحْمَٰنِ الرَّحِيمِ

وَلَا تَقُولَنَّ لِشَاْىْءٍ إِنِّى فَاعِلٌ ذَٰلِكَ غَدًا ۝

إِلَّا أَن يَشَاءَ ٱللَّهُ ۚ وَٱذْكُر رَّبَّكَ إِذَا نَسِيتَ وَقُلْ عَسَىٰ أَن يَهْدِيَنِ رَبِّى لِأَقْرَبَ مِنْ هَٰذَا رَشَدًا ۝

وَٱصْبِرْ نَفْسَكَ مَعَ ٱلَّذِينَ يَدْعُونَ رَبَّهُم بِٱلْغَدَوٰةِ وَٱلْعَشِىِّ يُرِيدُونَ وَجْهَهُۥ ۖ وَلَا تَعْدُ عَيْنَاكَ عَنْهُمْ تُرِيدُ زِينَةَ ٱلْحَيَوٰةِ ٱلدُّنْيَا ۖ وَلَا تُطِعْ مَنْ أَغْفَلْنَا قَلْبَهُۥ عَن ذِكْرِنَا وَٱتَّبَعَ هَوَىٰهُ وَكَانَ أَمْرُهُۥ فُرُطًا ۝

وَإِذْ قَالَ مُوسَىٰ لِفَتَىٰهُ لَآ أَبْرَحُ حَتَّىٰٓ أَبْلُغَ مَجْمَعَ ٱلْبَحْرَيْنِ أَوْ أَمْضِىَ حُقُبًا ۝ فَوَجَدَا عَبْدًا مِّنْ عِبَادِنَآ ءَاتَيْنَٰهُ رَحْمَةً مِّنْ عِندِنَا وَعَلَّمْنَٰهُ مِن لَّدُنَّا عِلْمًا ۝ قَالَ لَهُۥ مُوسَىٰ هَلْ أَتَّبِعُكَ عَلَىٰٓ أَن تُعَلِّمَنِ مِمَّا عُلِّمْتَ رُشْدًا ۝ قَالَ إِنَّكَ لَن تَسْتَطِيعَ مَعِىَ صَبْرًا ۝ وَكَيْفَ تَصْبِرُ عَلَىٰ مَا لَمْ تُحِطْ بِهِۦ خُبْرًا ۝ قَالَ سَتَجِدُنِىٓ إِن شَآءَ ٱللَّهُ صَابِرًا وَلَآ أَعْصِى لَكَ أَمْرًا ۝ قَالَ فَإِنِ ٱتَّبَعْتَنِى فَلَا تَسْـَٔلْنِى عَن شَىْءٍ حَتَّىٰٓ أُحْدِثَ لَكَ مِنْهُ ذِكْرًا ۝

قُل لَّوْ كَانَ ٱلْبَحْرُ مِدَادًا لِّكَلِمَٰتِ رَبِّى لَنَفِدَ ٱلْبَحْرُ قَبْلَ أَن تَنفَدَ كَلِمَٰتُ رَبِّى وَلَوْ جِئْنَا بِمِثْلِهِۦ مَدَدًا ۝

Maryam (XIX)

In the Name of God, the Infinitely Good, the Ever-Merciful

16. And make mention of Mary in the Book, when she withdrew from her people unto a place towards the east. [M]
17. And secluded herself from them. And We sent unto her Our Spirit and it appeared unto her in the likeness of a perfect man. [M]
18. She said: I take refuge from thee in the Infinitely Good, if any piety thou hast. [M]
19. He said: I am none other than a messenger from thy Lord, that I may bestow on thee a son most pure. [M]
20. She said: How can there be for me a son, when no man hath touched me, nor am I unchaste? [M]
21. He said: Even so shall it be; thy Lord saith: It is easy for Me. That We may make him a sign for mankind and a mercy from Us; and it is a thing ordained. [M]
40. .... [We will] inherit the earth and all who are on it... [SS]

(١٩) سُورَةُ مَرْيَمَ

بِسْمِ اللَّهِ الرَّحْمَٰنِ الرَّحِيمِ

وَاذْكُرْ فِي الْكِتَابِ مَرْيَمَ إِذِ انتَبَذَتْ مِنْ أَهْلِهَا مَكَانًا شَرْقِيًّا ۝

فَاتَّخَذَتْ مِن دُونِهِمْ حِجَابًا فَأَرْسَلْنَا إِلَيْهَا رُوحَنَا فَتَمَثَّلَ لَهَا بَشَرًا سَوِيًّا ۝

قَالَتْ إِنِّي أَعُوذُ بِالرَّحْمَٰنِ مِنكَ إِن كُنتَ تَقِيًّا ۝

قَالَ إِنَّمَا أَنَا رَسُولُ رَبِّكِ لِأَهَبَ لَكِ غُلَامًا زَكِيًّا ۝

قَالَتْ أَنَّىٰ يَكُونُ لِي غُلَامٌ وَلَمْ يَمْسَسْنِي بَشَرٌ وَلَمْ أَكُ بَغِيًّا ۝

قَالَ كَذَٰلِكِ قَالَ رَبُّكِ هُوَ عَلَيَّ هَيِّنٌ ۖ وَلِنَجْعَلَهُ آيَةً لِّلنَّاسِ وَرَحْمَةً مِّنَّا ۚ وَكَانَ أَمْرًا مَّقْضِيًّا ۝

إِنَّا نَحْنُ نَرِثُ الْأَرْضَ وَمَنْ عَلَيْهَا وَإِلَيْنَا يُرْجَعُونَ ۝

Ṭā Hā (XX)

In the Name of God, the Infinitely Good, the Ever-Merciful

11. And when he reached it, he was called. O Moses! [BC]
12. Verily I am thy Lord. So take off thy two sandals. Verily thou art in the holy Valley of Tuwa. [BC]
14. ... perform the prayer in remembrance of Me. [SS]
26. Make easy my task. [SS]
27. Untie my tongue. [SS]
32. Let one share my burden. [SS]
41. I have fashioned thee as a work of art for Myself. [QACI] [RS] [SQCI]
109. On that day no intercession availeth save his whom the All-Merciful permitteth to speak, with whose words He is well pleased. [SS]
111. The day when faces are all humbled before the eternal Living... [SS]
114. ... and hasten not with the Qoran until its revelation hath been perfected unto thee and say: Lord, increase me in knowledge. [SS]
120. Then Satan whispered unto him and said: 'O Adam shall I show thee the Tree of Immortality and a kingdom that fadeth not away?' [BC] [SA]

(٢٠) سُورَةُ طه

بِسْمِ ٱللَّهِ ٱلرَّحْمَٰنِ ٱلرَّحِيمِ

فَلَمَّآ أَتَىٰهَا نُودِيَ يَٰمُوسَىٰٓ ۝

إِنِّىٓ أَنَا۠ رَبُّكَ فَٱخْلَعْ نَعْلَيْكَ إِنَّكَ بِٱلْوَادِ ٱلْمُقَدَّسِ طُوًى ۝

إِنَّنِىٓ أَنَا ٱللَّهُ لَآ إِلَٰهَ إِلَّآ أَنَا۠ فَٱعْبُدْنِى وَأَقِمِ ٱلصَّلَوٰةَ لِذِكْرِىٓ ۝

وَيَسِّرْ لِىٓ أَمْرِى ۝

وَٱحْلُلْ عُقْدَةً مِّن لِّسَانِى ۝

وَأَشْرِكْهُ فِىٓ أَمْرِى ۝

وَٱصْطَنَعْتُكَ لِنَفْسِى ۝

يَوْمَئِذٍ لَّا تَنفَعُ ٱلشَّفَٰعَةُ إِلَّا مَنْ أَذِنَ لَهُ ٱلرَّحْمَٰنُ وَرَضِىَ لَهُۥ قَوْلًا ۝

وَعَنَتِ ٱلْوُجُوهُ لِلْحَىِّ ٱلْقَيُّومِ وَقَدْ خَابَ مَنْ حَمَلَ ظُلْمًا ۝

فَتَعَٰلَى ٱللَّهُ ٱلْمَلِكُ ٱلْحَقُّ وَلَا تَعْجَلْ بِٱلْقُرْءَانِ مِن قَبْلِ أَن يُقْضَىٰٓ إِلَيْكَ وَحْيُهُۥ وَقُل رَّبِّ زِدْنِى عِلْمًا ۝

فَوَسْوَسَ إِلَيْهِ ٱلشَّيْطَٰنُ قَالَ يَٰٓـَٔادَمُ هَلْ أَدُلُّكَ عَلَىٰ شَجَرَةِ ٱلْخُلْدِ وَمُلْكٍ لَّا يَبْلَىٰ ۝

Al-Anbiyā' (XXI)
In the Name of God, the Infinitely Good, the Ever-Merciful

16. Not in play did We create the heaven and the earth and all that is between them. [M]

23. He is not questioned as to what He doth, but they are questioned. [SS]

30. Have not the infidels seen that the Heavens and the earth were of one piece? Then We rifted them asunder, and from the water We made every living thing... [BC]

35. ...We try you both with evil and with good... [SS]

78. And [remember] David and Solomon when they gave judgement concerning the field wherein the people's sheep had grazed by night, and We were witness unto their judgement. [UM]

79. And We gave Solomon understanding of the case, and unto each gave We judgement authoritative and lore... [UM]

91. ...a sign for the worlds. [SA]

104. The day when we shall roll up the heavens as at the rolling up of a written scroll... [BC] [RS]

104. On the day when We shall roll up the heavens as the rolling up of a written scroll... [L-QD]

104. ...like the folding of a written scroll... [SS]

107. We sent thee not save as a mercy for the worlds. [M]

(٢١) سُورَةُ الْأَنْبِيَاءِ
بِسْمِ اللَّهِ الرَّحْمَٰنِ الرَّحِيمِ

وَمَا خَلَقْنَا السَّمَاءَ وَالْأَرْضَ وَمَا بَيْنَهُمَا لَاعِبِينَ ۝

لَا يُسْأَلُ عَمَّا يَفْعَلُ وَهُمْ يُسْأَلُونَ ۝

أَوَلَمْ يَرَ الَّذِينَ كَفَرُوا أَنَّ السَّمَاوَاتِ وَالْأَرْضَ كَانَتَا رَتْقًا فَفَتَقْنَاهُمَا وَجَعَلْنَا مِنَ الْمَاءِ كُلَّ شَيْءٍ حَيٍّ ۖ أَفَلَا يُؤْمِنُونَ ۝

كُلُّ نَفْسٍ ذَائِقَةُ الْمَوْتِ ۗ وَنَبْلُوكُم بِالشَّرِّ وَالْخَيْرِ فِتْنَةً ۖ وَإِلَيْنَا تُرْجَعُونَ ۝

وَدَاوُودَ وَسُلَيْمَانَ إِذْ يَحْكُمَانِ فِي الْحَرْثِ إِذْ نَفَشَتْ فِيهِ غَنَمُ الْقَوْمِ وَكُنَّا لِحُكْمِهِمْ شَاهِدِينَ ۝

فَفَهَّمْنَاهَا سُلَيْمَانَ ۚ وَكُلًّا آتَيْنَا حُكْمًا وَعِلْمًا ۚ وَسَخَّرْنَا مَعَ دَاوُودَ الْجِبَالَ يُسَبِّحْنَ وَالطَّيْرَ ۚ وَكُنَّا فَاعِلِينَ ۝

وَالَّتِي أَحْصَنَتْ فَرْجَهَا فَنَفَخْنَا فِيهَا مِن رُّوحِنَا وَجَعَلْنَاهَا وَابْنَهَا آيَةً لِّلْعَالَمِينَ ۝

يَوْمَ نَطْوِي السَّمَاءَ كَطَيِّ السِّجِلِّ لِلْكُتُبِ ۚ كَمَا بَدَأْنَا أَوَّلَ خَلْقٍ نُّعِيدُهُ ۚ وَعْدًا عَلَيْنَا ۚ إِنَّا كُنَّا فَاعِلِينَ ۝

وَمَا أَرْسَلْنَاكَ إِلَّا رَحْمَةً لِّلْعَالَمِينَ ۝

Al-Ḥajj (XXII)
In the Name of God, the Infinitely Good, the Ever-Merciful

26. ... purify My House for those who go the rounds of it and who stand beside it and bow and make prostration. [M]
27. And proclaim unto men the pilgrimage, that they may come unto thee on foot and on every lean camel out of every deep ravine. [M] [Mec.]
39. Permission to fight is given unto those who fight because they have been wronged; and God is Able to give them victory. [M]
40. Those who have been driven from their homes unjustly, for no cause other than for their saying: Our Lord is God... [M]
46. ... not blind are the eyes, but blind are the hearts within the breasts. [M]
46. ... it is not the eyes that are blind but the hearts. [WS]
46. ... for verily it is not the sight that is blind, but the hearts... that are blind. [SA]
46. ... it is not the eyes that are blind, but blind are the hearts that are in the breasts. [L-QOS]
46. ... it is not the eye-sights which are blind, it is the hearts in the breasts which are blind. [L-MPP]

(۲۲) سُورَةُ الحَجّ

بِسْمِ اللَّهِ الرَّحْمَٰنِ الرَّحِيمِ

وَإِذْ بَوَّأْنَا لِإِبْرَٰهِيمَ مَكَانَ ٱلْبَيْتِ أَن لَّا تُشْرِكْ بِى شَيْـًٔا وَطَهِّرْ بَيْتِىَ لِلطَّآئِفِينَ وَٱلْقَآئِمِينَ وَٱلرُّكَّعِ ٱلسُّجُودِ ۝

وَأَذِّن فِى ٱلنَّاسِ بِٱلْحَجِّ يَأْتُوكَ رِجَالًا وَعَلَىٰ كُلِّ ضَامِرٍ يَأْتِينَ مِن كُلِّ فَجٍّ عَمِيقٍ ۝

أُذِنَ لِلَّذِينَ يُقَٰتَلُونَ بِأَنَّهُمْ ظُلِمُوا۟ ۚ وَإِنَّ ٱللَّهَ عَلَىٰ نَصْرِهِمْ لَقَدِيرٌ ۝

ٱلَّذِينَ أُخْرِجُوا۟ مِن دِيَٰرِهِم بِغَيْرِ حَقٍّ إِلَّآ أَن يَقُولُوا۟ رَبُّنَا ٱللَّهُ ۗ وَلَوْلَا دَفْعُ ٱللَّهِ ٱلنَّاسَ بَعْضَهُم بِبَعْضٍ لَّهُدِّمَتْ صَوَٰمِعُ وَبِيَعٌ وَصَلَوَٰتٌ وَمَسَٰجِدُ يُذْكَرُ فِيهَا ٱسْمُ ٱللَّهِ كَثِيرًا ۗ وَلَيَنصُرَنَّ ٱللَّهُ مَن يَنصُرُهُۥٓ ۗ إِنَّ ٱللَّهَ لَقَوِىٌّ عَزِيزٌ ۝

أَفَلَمْ يَسِيرُوا۟ فِى ٱلْأَرْضِ فَتَكُونَ لَهُمْ قُلُوبٌ يَعْقِلُونَ بِهَآ أَوْ ءَاذَانٌ يَسْمَعُونَ بِهَا ۖ فَإِنَّهَا لَا تَعْمَى ٱلْأَبْصَٰرُ وَلَٰكِن تَعْمَى ٱلْقُلُوبُ ٱلَّتِى فِى ٱلصُّدُورِ ۝

47. ...verily a day in the sight of thy Lord is as a thousand years of what ye count. [M]

74. They esteem not God as He hath the right to be esteemed... [NOS]

74. They have not rated God at His true worth... [PT]

Al-Mu'minūn (XXIII)

In the Name of God, the Infinitely Good, the Ever-Merciful

115. Deem ye that We did but create you in vain and that ye shall not be brought back unto Us. [M]

وَيَسْتَعْجِلُونَكَ بِالْعَذَابِ وَلَن يُخْلِفَ اللَّهُ وَعْدَهُ وَإِنَّ يَوْمًا عِندَ رَبِّكَ كَأَلْفِ سَنَةٍ مِّمَّا تَعُدُّونَ ۝

مَا قَدَرُوا اللَّهَ حَقَّ قَدْرِهِ إِنَّ اللَّهَ لَقَوِيٌّ عَزِيزٌ ۝

(٢٣) سُورَةُ الْمُؤْمِنُونَ

بِسْمِ اللَّهِ الرَّحْمَٰنِ الرَّحِيمِ

أَفَحَسِبْتُمْ أَنَّمَا خَلَقْنَاكُمْ عَبَثًا وَأَنَّكُمْ إِلَيْنَا لَا تُرْجَعُونَ ۝

An-Nūr (XXIV)
In the Name of God, the Infinitely Good, the Ever-Merciful

11. Verily they who brought forth the lie are a party amongst you... [M]
15. When ye took it upon your tongues, uttering with your mouths that whereof ye had no knowledge, ye counted it but a trifle. Yet in the sight of God it is enormous. [M]
16. Why said ye not when ye heard it: To speak of this is not for us. Glory be to Thee! This is a monstrous calumny. [M]
17. God biddeth you beware of ever repeating the like thereof, if ye are believers. [M]
22. Let not the men of dignity and wealth amongst you swear that they will not give unto kinsmen and unto the needy and unto those who have migrated for the sake of God. Let them forgive and let them be indulgent. Do you not long that God should forgive you? And God is Forgiving, Merciful. [M]

(٢٤) سُورَةُ النُّورِ

بِسْمِ اللَّهِ الرَّحْمَنِ الرَّحِيمِ

إِنَّ الَّذِينَ جَاءُو بِالْإِفْكِ عُصْبَةٌ مِنكُمْ لَا تَحْسَبُوهُ شَرًّا لَكُم بَلْ هُوَ خَيْرٌ لَكُمْ لِكُلِّ امْرِئٍ مِنْهُم مَّا اكْتَسَبَ مِنَ الْإِثْمِ وَالَّذِي تَوَلَّىٰ كِبْرَهُ مِنْهُمْ لَهُ عَذَابٌ عَظِيمٌ ۝

إِذْ تَلَقَّوْنَهُ بِأَلْسِنَتِكُمْ وَتَقُولُونَ بِأَفْوَاهِكُم مَّا لَيْسَ لَكُم بِهِ عِلْمٌ وَتَحْسَبُونَهُ هَيِّنًا وَهُوَ عِندَ اللَّهِ عَظِيمٌ ۝

وَلَوْلَا إِذْ سَمِعْتُمُوهُ قُلْتُم مَّا يَكُونُ لَنَا أَن نَّتَكَلَّمَ بِهَٰذَا سُبْحَانَكَ هَٰذَا بُهْتَانٌ عَظِيمٌ ۝

يَعِظُكُمُ اللَّهُ أَن تَعُودُوا لِمِثْلِهِ أَبَدًا إِن كُنتُم مُّؤْمِنِينَ ۝

وَلَا يَأْتَلِ أُولُو الْفَضْلِ مِنكُمْ وَالسَّعَةِ أَن يُؤْتُوا أُولِي الْقُرْبَىٰ وَالْمَسَاكِينَ وَالْمُهَاجِرِينَ فِي سَبِيلِ اللَّهِ وَلْيَعْفُوا وَلْيَصْفَحُوا أَلَا تُحِبُّونَ أَن يَغْفِرَ اللَّهُ لَكُمْ وَاللَّهُ غَفُورٌ رَّحِيمٌ ۝

THE HOLY QUR'ĀN: SELECTED VERSES

35. God is the Light of the Heavens and the earth. The symbol of His light is as a tabernacle wherein is a lamp. The lamp is in glass. The glass is as it were a gleaming planet. The lamp is kindled from a blessed tree, an olive that is neither of the East nor of the West, whose oil well nigh blazeth in splendour even though the fire hath not yet touched it. Light upon light! God leadeth to His light whom he will, and God citeth symbols for men, and God of all things hath Knowledge. [BC]

35. ... God leadeth to His light whom He will... [OS]

35. God is the Light of the Heavens and the earth. His light [on earth] is like a niche wherein is a lamp. The lamp is of glass; the glass is like a shining planet. It is lit from a sacred olive tree that is neither of the East nor of the West, the oil whereof well nigh blazeth though the fire have not touched it—Light upon Light! God leadeth to His light whom he will, and God citeth symbols for men, and God is the Knower of all things. [SS]

35. ... a sacred olive tree that is neither of the East nor of the West; its oil well-nigh blazeth in splendour though the fire hath not touched it... [QACI] [SQCI]

35. God is the Light of the Heavens and the earth. His light is as a niche wherein is a lamp. The lamp is in a glass; the glass is as it were a shining planet. It is kindled from a blessed tree, an olive neither of the east nor of the west. The oil thereof well nigh blazeth in splendour even though the fire have not touched it. Light upon light. God guideth to His light whom he will, and God citeth symbols for men, and God is of all things the Knower. [M] [SA]

ٱللَّهُ نُورُ ٱلسَّمَٰوَٰتِ وَٱلۡأَرۡضِۚ مَثَلُ نُورِهِۦ كَمِشۡكَوٰةٖ فِيهَا مِصۡبَاحٌۖ ٱلۡمِصۡبَاحُ فِي زُجَاجَةٍۖ ٱلزُّجَاجَةُ كَأَنَّهَا كَوۡكَبٞ دُرِّيّٞ يُوقَدُ مِن شَجَرَةٖ مُّبَٰرَكَةٖ زَيۡتُونَةٖ لَّا شَرۡقِيَّةٖ وَلَا غَرۡبِيَّةٖ يَكَادُ زَيۡتُهَا يُضِيٓءُ وَلَوۡ لَمۡ تَمۡسَسۡهُ نَارٞۚ نُّورٌ عَلَىٰ نُورٖۚ يَهۡدِي ٱللَّهُ لِنُورِهِۦ مَن يَشَآءُۚ وَيَضۡرِبُ ٱللَّهُ ٱلۡأَمۡثَٰلَ لِلنَّاسِۗ وَٱللَّهُ بِكُلِّ شَيۡءٍ عَلِيمٞ ۝

37. Men whom neither bartering nor selling diverteth from the remembrance of God... [ss]

39. ...as a mirage in the desert that the thirsty man taketh to be water until he cometh unto it and findeth it to be nothing, and where he thought it to be, there findeth he God... [ss]

39. ...a mirage in the desert which the thirsty man reckoneth to be water... [sa]

42. Of God is the Sovereignty over the heavens and the earth; and unto God is the ultimate becoming. [rs]

رِجَالٌ لَّا تُلْهِيهِمْ تِجَٰرَةٌ وَلَا بَيْعٌ عَن ذِكْرِ ٱللَّهِ وَإِقَامِ ٱلصَّلَوٰةِ وَإِيتَآءِ ٱلزَّكَوٰةِ ۙ يَخَافُونَ يَوْمًا تَتَقَلَّبُ فِيهِ ٱلْقُلُوبُ وَٱلْأَبْصَٰرُ ۝

وَٱلَّذِينَ كَفَرُوٓا۟ أَعْمَٰلُهُمْ كَسَرَابٍۭ بِقِيعَةٍ يَحْسَبُهُ ٱلظَّمْـَٔانُ مَآءً حَتَّىٰٓ إِذَا جَآءَهُۥ لَمْ يَجِدْهُ شَيْـًٔا وَوَجَدَ ٱللَّهَ عِندَهُۥ فَوَفَّىٰهُ حِسَابَهُۥ ۗ وَٱللَّهُ سَرِيعُ ٱلْحِسَابِ ۝

وَلِلَّهِ مُلْكُ ٱلسَّمَٰوَٰتِ وَٱلْأَرْضِ ۖ وَإِلَى ٱللَّهِ ٱلْمَصِيرُ ۝

Al-Furqān (XXV)

In the Name of God, the Infinitely Good, the Ever-Merciful

1. Blessed be He Who hath made the distinct revelation unto His servant, that he might be for all the worlds a warner. [BC]

15. ...the Garden of Immortality which is promised to the pious... [M]

16. For them therein is that which they desire, for ever and Ever—a promise that thy Lord hath bound Himself to fulfil. [M]

21. They who place not their hopes in meeting Us say: Why are the angels not sent down unto us? Or why see we not our Lord? Verily they are proud with pride in themselves, and arrogant with a great arrogance. [M]

22. The day they behold the angels, on that day there will be no good tidings for the evil-doers, and they will say: A barrier that bars! [M]

48. ...and We have sent down from Heaven pure water. [BC]

49. That thereof We may quicken a dead land, and that thereof We may give drink to Our creatures to cattle and men in plenty. [BC]

50. And verily We have given of it freely unto them that they might remember... [BC]

53. And He it is Who hath let loose the two seas, one sweet and fresh, the other salt and bitter, and hath set between them an isthmus, an impassable barrier. [BC]

53. ...the sweet fresh water sea...the brackish salt sea... [WS]

53. ...one sweet and fresh, the other salt and bitter... [SA]

53. ...one sweet and fresh, the other salted and bitter... [L-HOD]

54. And He it is Who from water hath created man... [BC]

(٢٥) سُورَةُ الْفُرْقَانِ

بِسْمِ اللَّهِ الرَّحْمَٰنِ الرَّحِيمِ

تَبَارَكَ الَّذِي نَزَّلَ الْفُرْقَانَ عَلَىٰ عَبْدِهِ لِيَكُونَ لِلْعَالَمِينَ نَذِيرًا ۝

قُلْ أَذَٰلِكَ خَيْرٌ أَمْ جَنَّةُ الْخُلْدِ الَّتِي وُعِدَ الْمُتَّقُونَ ۚ كَانَتْ لَهُمْ جَزَاءً وَمَصِيرًا ۝

لَهُمْ فِيهَا مَا يَشَاءُونَ خَالِدِينَ ۚ كَانَ عَلَىٰ رَبِّكَ وَعْدًا مَسْئُولًا ۝

وَقَالَ الَّذِينَ لَا يَرْجُونَ لِقَاءَنَا لَوْلَا أُنزِلَ عَلَيْنَا الْمَلَائِكَةُ أَوْ نَرَىٰ رَبَّنَا ۗ لَقَدِ اسْتَكْبَرُوا فِي أَنفُسِهِمْ وَعَتَوْا عُتُوًّا كَبِيرًا ۝ يَوْمَ يَرَوْنَ الْمَلَائِكَةَ لَا بُشْرَىٰ يَوْمَئِذٍ لِّلْمُجْرِمِينَ وَيَقُولُونَ حِجْرًا مَّحْجُورًا ۝

وَهُوَ الَّذِي أَرْسَلَ الرِّيَاحَ بُشْرًا بَيْنَ يَدَيْ رَحْمَتِهِ ۚ وَأَنزَلْنَا مِنَ السَّمَاءِ مَاءً طَهُورًا ۝

لِّنُحْيِيَ بِهِ بَلْدَةً مَّيْتًا وَنُسْقِيَهُ مِمَّا خَلَقْنَا أَنْعَامًا وَأَنَاسِيَّ كَثِيرًا ۝

وَلَقَدْ صَرَّفْنَاهُ بَيْنَهُمْ لِيَذَّكَّرُوا فَأَبَىٰ أَكْثَرُ النَّاسِ إِلَّا كُفُورًا ۝

وَهُوَ الَّذِي مَرَجَ الْبَحْرَيْنِ هَٰذَا عَذْبٌ فُرَاتٌ وَهَٰذَا مِلْحٌ أُجَاجٌ وَجَعَلَ بَيْنَهُمَا بَرْزَخًا وَحِجْرًا مَّحْجُورًا ۝

وَهُوَ الَّذِي خَلَقَ مِنَ الْمَاءِ بَشَرًا فَجَعَلَهُ نَسَبًا وَصِهْرًا ۚ وَكَانَ رَبُّكَ قَدِيرًا ۝

61. Blessed is He who hath placed in the heavens the constellations of the zodiac, and hath placed therein a lamp and a light-giving moon. [M]
62. And He it is who hath made the night and the day to succeed one the other, as a sign for him who would reflect or give thanks. [M]
70. ...God will change their evils into goods, and God is All-Forgiving, All-Merciful. [SA]

Ash-Shu'arā' (XXVI)

In the Name of God, the Infinitely Good, the Ever-Merciful

192. Verily it is a revelation from the Lord of the Worlds. [SQCI]
193. Which the faithful Spirit hath brought down. [SQCI]
194. Upon thy heart for thee to be a warner. [SQCI]
214. Warn thy family who are thy nearest of kin. [M]
215. Lower thy wing unto those that follow thee... [WS]

تَبَارَكَ ٱلَّذِى جَعَلَ فِى ٱلسَّمَآءِ بُرُوجًا وَجَعَلَ فِيهَا سِرَاجًا وَقَمَرًا مُّنِيرًا ۝

وَهُوَ ٱلَّذِى جَعَلَ ٱلَّيْلَ وَٱلنَّهَارَ خِلْفَةً لِّمَنْ أَرَادَ أَن يَذَّكَّرَ أَوْ أَرَادَ شُكُورًا ۝

إِلَّا مَن تَابَ وَءَامَنَ وَعَمِلَ عَمَلًا صَٰلِحًا فَأُوْلَٰٓئِكَ يُبَدِّلُ ٱللَّهُ سَيِّـَٔاتِهِمْ حَسَنَٰتٍ ۗ وَكَانَ ٱللَّهُ غَفُورًا رَّحِيمًا ۝

(٢٦) سُورَةُ ٱلشُّعَرَاءِ
بِسْمِ ٱللَّهِ ٱلرَّحْمَٰنِ ٱلرَّحِيمِ

وَإِنَّهُۥ لَتَنزِيلُ رَبِّ ٱلْعَٰلَمِينَ ۝

نَزَلَ بِهِ ٱلرُّوحُ ٱلْأَمِينُ ۝

عَلَىٰ قَلْبِكَ لِتَكُونَ مِنَ ٱلْمُنذِرِينَ ۝

وَأَنذِرْ عَشِيرَتَكَ ٱلْأَقْرَبِينَ ۝

وَٱخْفِضْ جَنَاحَكَ لِمَنِ ٱتَّبَعَكَ مِنَ ٱلْمُؤْمِنِينَ ۝

An-Naml (XXVII)

In the Name of God, the Infinitely Good, the Ever-Merciful

7. Moses said to his household: Verily beyond all doubt I have seen a fire. I will bring you tidings of it or I will bring you a flaming brand that ye may warm yourselves. [BC]

8. Then when he reached it he was called: Blessed is He who is in the fire and He who is about it, and Glory be to God the Lord of the worlds. [BC]

29. She said: Ye lords, there hath been cast down before me a noble letter. [UM]

30. It is from Solomon, and it is in the Name of God, the All-Merciful the Meed-Giver of Mercy. [UM]

38. He [Solomon] said: Ye Lords, which of you will bring me her throne ere they come unto me in surrender. [UM]

38. ...which of you will bring me her throne before they come unto me in surrender. [SA]

39. Said a demon from among the jinn: I will bring it thee ere thou canst rise from thy seat, for verily even such is my strength, such my trustiness. [UM]

40. Said he that had lore from the scriptures: I will bring it thee ere thy glance can return unto thee. And [Solomon] seeing it firm-set in his presence said: this is of the Favour of my Lord... [UM]

41. He [Solomon] said: Disguise for her her throne, that we may see if she will be guided or if she be of those that receive not guidance. [UM]

41. ...disguise her throne for her; we shall see if she is on the right path, or if she is of those who are not rightly guided. [SA]

(۲۷) سُورَةُ النَّمْل
بِسْمِ اللَّهِ الرَّحْمَٰنِ الرَّحِيمِ

إِذْ قَالَ مُوسَىٰ لِأَهْلِهِ إِنِّي آنَسْتُ نَارًا سَآتِيكُم مِّنْهَا بِخَبَرٍ أَوْ آتِيكُم بِشِهَابٍ قَبَسٍ لَّعَلَّكُمْ تَصْطَلُونَ ۝

فَلَمَّا جَاءَهَا نُودِيَ أَن بُورِكَ مَن فِي النَّارِ وَمَنْ حَوْلَهَا وَسُبْحَانَ اللَّهِ رَبِّ الْعَالَمِينَ ۝

قَالَتْ يَا أَيُّهَا الْمَلَأُ إِنِّي أُلْقِيَ إِلَيَّ كِتَابٌ كَرِيمٌ ۝

إِنَّهُ مِن سُلَيْمَانَ وَإِنَّهُ بِسْمِ اللَّهِ الرَّحْمَٰنِ الرَّحِيمِ ۝

قَالَ يَا أَيُّهَا الْمَلَأُ أَيُّكُمْ يَأْتِينِي بِعَرْشِهَا قَبْلَ أَن يَأْتُونِي مُسْلِمِينَ ۝

قَالَ عِفْرِيتٌ مِّنَ الْجِنِّ أَنَا آتِيكَ بِهِ قَبْلَ أَن تَقُومَ مِن مَّقَامِكَ وَإِنِّي عَلَيْهِ لَقَوِيٌّ أَمِينٌ ۝

قَالَ الَّذِي عِندَهُ عِلْمٌ مِّنَ الْكِتَابِ أَنَا آتِيكَ بِهِ قَبْلَ أَن يَرْتَدَّ إِلَيْكَ طَرْفُكَ ۚ فَلَمَّا رَآهُ مُسْتَقِرًّا عِندَهُ قَالَ هَٰذَا مِن فَضْلِ رَبِّي لِيَبْلُوَنِي أَأَشْكُرُ أَمْ أَكْفُرُ ۖ وَمَن شَكَرَ فَإِنَّمَا يَشْكُرُ لِنَفْسِهِ ۖ وَمَن كَفَرَ فَإِنَّ رَبِّي غَنِيٌّ كَرِيمٌ ۝

قَالَ نَكِّرُوا لَهَا عَرْشَهَا نَنظُرْ أَتَهْتَدِي أَمْ تَكُونُ مِنَ الَّذِينَ لَا يَهْتَدُونَ ۝

42. Then when she came was it said unto her: Is thy throne such as this? She said: It is as if it were indeed my throne. And [Solomon pondered in his heart]: The lore unto us was given ere it was given unto her, and before God our surrender had we made. [UM]

42. And when she came it was said unto her: Is thy throne like unto this? She said: It is as if it were it. And [Solomon reflected] we had been given the knowledge before her and had surrendered unto God. [SA]

43. And that which she had been wont to worship in the place of God was as a stumbling block before her. Verily she came of an infidel folk. [UM]

43. And she was barred from it by what she was wont to worship apart from God. Verily she was from a disbelieving people. [SA]

44. It was said unto her: Enter the palace. And when she saw it she thought it a deep of water, and she bared her legs. He said: A palace is it indeed, made smooth, of glass. She said: My Lord, verily I have wronged myself, and with Solomon do I surrender unto God, the Lord of the worlds. [UM]

44. She was told: Enter the courtyard; and when she saw it she reckoned it to be a pool of water and bared her legs. He said: It is a courtyard made smooth with glass. She said: O my Lord, verily I have done wrong unto my soul, and I surrender with Solomon unto God, the Lord of the Worlds. [SA]

فَلَمَّا جَآءَتْ قِيلَ أَهَٰكَذَا عَرْشُكِ ۖ قَالَتْ كَأَنَّهُۥ هُوَ ۚ وَأُوتِينَا ٱلْعِلْمَ مِن قَبْلِهَا وَكُنَّا مُسْلِمِينَ ۝

وَصَدَّهَا مَا كَانَت تَّعْبُدُ مِن دُونِ ٱللَّهِ ۖ إِنَّهَا كَانَتْ مِن قَوْمٍ كَٰفِرِينَ ۝

قِيلَ لَهَا ٱدْخُلِى ٱلصَّرْحَ ۖ فَلَمَّا رَأَتْهُ حَسِبَتْهُ لُجَّةً وَكَشَفَتْ عَن سَاقَيْهَا ۚ قَالَ إِنَّهُۥ صَرْحٌ مُّمَرَّدٌ مِّن قَوَارِيرَ ۗ قَالَتْ رَبِّ إِنِّى ظَلَمْتُ نَفْسِى وَأَسْلَمْتُ مَعَ سُلَيْمَٰنَ لِلَّهِ رَبِّ ٱلْعَٰلَمِينَ ۝

Al-Qaṣaṣ (XXVIII)
In the Name of God, the Infinitely Good, the Ever-Merciful

56. Verily thou guidest not whom thou lovest, but God guideth whom He will... [M]

68. God createth what He will, according to His Choice... [SS]

71. Say: Have ye thought if God made night everlasting upon you till the Day of the Resurrection, who is a god beside God to bring you light? Will ye then not hear? [M]

72. Say: Have ye thought, if God made day everlasting upon you till the Day of the Resurrection, who is a god beside God to bring you a night wherein to rest? Will ye not then see? [M]

73. And of his mercy hath he made for you night and day, that therein ye may rest and that ye may go seek His favours, and that ye may be thankful. [M]

85. Verily He who hath made binding upon thee the Koran will bring thee home once more... [M]

88. ... there is no god save Him. Everything will perish save His Face. His is the command, and unto Him ye will be brought back. [NOS]

88. ... everything perisheth but His Face... [SS] [WS]

88. ... all things perish but His Face... [S]

88. ... there is no God but He: all things are perishable but His Face... [OS]

(۲۸) سُورَةُ الْقَصَصِ

بِسْمِ اللَّهِ الرَّحْمَنِ الرَّحِيمِ

إِنَّكَ لَا تَهْدِي مَنْ أَحْبَبْتَ وَلَكِنَّ اللَّهَ يَهْدِي مَن يَشَاءُ وَهُوَ أَعْلَمُ بِالْمُهْتَدِينَ ۝

وَرَبُّكَ يَخْلُقُ مَا يَشَاءُ وَيَخْتَارُ مَا كَانَ لَهُمُ الْخِيَرَةُ سُبْحَانَ اللَّهِ وَتَعَالَى عَمَّا يُشْرِكُونَ ۝

قُلْ أَرَأَيْتُمْ إِن جَعَلَ اللَّهُ عَلَيْكُمُ اللَّيْلَ سَرْمَدًا إِلَى يَوْمِ الْقِيَامَةِ مَنْ إِلَهٌ غَيْرُ اللَّهِ يَأْتِيكُم بِضِيَاءٍ أَفَلَا تَسْمَعُونَ ۝

قُلْ أَرَأَيْتُمْ إِن جَعَلَ اللَّهُ عَلَيْكُمُ النَّهَارَ سَرْمَدًا إِلَى يَوْمِ الْقِيَامَةِ مَنْ إِلَهٌ غَيْرُ اللَّهِ يَأْتِيكُم بِلَيْلٍ تَسْكُنُونَ فِيهِ أَفَلَا تُبْصِرُونَ ۝

وَمِن رَّحْمَتِهِ جَعَلَ لَكُمُ اللَّيْلَ وَالنَّهَارَ لِتَسْكُنُوا فِيهِ وَلِتَبْتَغُوا مِن فَضْلِهِ وَلَعَلَّكُمْ تَشْكُرُونَ ۝

إِنَّ الَّذِي فَرَضَ عَلَيْكَ الْقُرْآنَ لَرَادُّكَ إِلَى مَعَادٍ قُل رَّبِّي أَعْلَمُ مَن جَاءَ بِالْهُدَى وَمَنْ هُوَ فِي ضَلَالٍ مُّبِينٍ ۝

وَلَا تَدْعُ مَعَ اللَّهِ إِلَهًا آخَرَ لَا إِلَهَ إِلَّا هُوَ كُلُّ شَيْءٍ هَالِكٌ إِلَّا وَجْهَهُ لَهُ الْحُكْمُ وَإِلَيْهِ تُرْجَعُونَ ۝

Al-ʿAnkabūt (XXIX)

In the Name of God, the Infinitely Good, the Ever-Merciful

43. ...none understandeth it save the wise. [SS]
45. ...verily the ritual prayer preserveth from iniquity and abomination; but the remembrance of God is greater... [M]
45. ...and verily the remembrance is of all things the most great... [UM]
45. ...and certainly the invocation of God is the greatest thing... [UM]
45. ...and verily the remembrance of Allah is greater [or infinitely great]... [UM]
45. ...the remembrance of God is greater... [WS]
45. ...the invocation of Allah is greater... [L-QOS]
64. This lower life is but a diversion and a game; and verily the abode of the Hereafter, that, that is Life, did they but know. [M]
64. This lower life is naught but a pastime and a game; and verily the abode of the Hereafter, that, that is Life, did they but know. [RS] [L-QD]
64. ...verily the abode of the Hereafter, that, that is Life, did they but know. [SA]
64. ...surely, the Last Abode is Life, did they but know. [PT]
69. Whoso striveth after Us, verily We shall lead them upon Our paths... [SS]

(٢٩) سُورَةُ العَنكَبُوتِ

بِسْمِ اللَّهِ الرَّحْمَٰنِ الرَّحِيمِ

وَتِلْكَ الْأَمْثَٰلُ نَضْرِبُهَا لِلنَّاسِ ۖ وَمَا يَعْقِلُهَا إِلَّا الْعَٰلِمُونَ ۝

اتْلُ مَا أُوحِىَ إِلَيْكَ مِنَ الْكِتَٰبِ وَأَقِمِ الصَّلَوٰةَ ۖ إِنَّ الصَّلَوٰةَ تَنْهَىٰ عَنِ الْفَحْشَآءِ وَالْمُنكَرِ ۗ وَلَذِكْرُ اللَّهِ أَكْبَرُ ۗ وَاللَّهُ يَعْلَمُ مَا تَصْنَعُونَ ۝

وَمَا هَٰذِهِ الْحَيَوٰةُ الدُّنْيَآ إِلَّا لَهْوٌ وَلَعِبٌ ۚ وَإِنَّ الدَّارَ الْءَاخِرَةَ لَهِىَ الْحَيَوَانُ ۚ لَوْ كَانُوا۟ يَعْلَمُونَ ۝

وَالَّذِينَ جَٰهَدُوا۟ فِينَا لَنَهْدِيَنَّهُمْ سُبُلَنَا ۚ وَإِنَّ اللَّهَ لَمَعَ الْمُحْسِنِينَ ۝

Ar-Rūm (XXX)

In the Name of God, the Infinitely Good, the Ever-Merciful

4. ...that day the believers will rejoice. [M]
7. They know only an outward appearance of this lower life... [SA]
8. ...God created not the heavens and the earth and what lieth between them save from Truth and an appointed term... [SA]
21. And of His signs is His creation for you of consorts from amongst yourselves, that ye may find rest in them, and His ordaining of love between you and mercy. Verily therein are signs for people who reflect. [M]
30. And turn thy face towards the religion in a pure fashion, in conformity with the primordial Nature, in which God hath created men; one must not exchange this creation (this Nature) for another. This is the immutable Religion, but most men know it not. [UM]
30. ...God's original upon which he originated mankind... [NOS]

(٣٠) سُورَةُ الرُّومِ
بِسْمِ اللَّهِ الرَّحْمَٰنِ الرَّحِيمِ

فِي بِضْعِ سِنِينَ ۗ لِلَّهِ الْأَمْرُ مِن قَبْلُ وَمِن بَعْدُ ۚ وَيَوْمَئِذٍ يَفْرَحُ الْمُؤْمِنُونَ ۝ يَعْلَمُونَ ظَاهِرًا مِّنَ الْحَيَاةِ الدُّنْيَا وَهُمْ عَنِ الْآخِرَةِ هُمْ غَافِلُونَ ۝ أَوَلَمْ يَتَفَكَّرُوا فِي أَنفُسِهِم ۗ مَّا خَلَقَ اللَّهُ السَّمَاوَاتِ وَالْأَرْضَ وَمَا بَيْنَهُمَا إِلَّا بِالْحَقِّ وَأَجَلٍ مُّسَمًّى ۗ وَإِنَّ كَثِيرًا مِّنَ النَّاسِ بِلِقَاءِ رَبِّهِمْ لَكَافِرُونَ ۝ وَمِنْ آيَاتِهِ أَنْ خَلَقَ لَكُم مِّنْ أَنفُسِكُمْ أَزْوَاجًا لِّتَسْكُنُوا إِلَيْهَا وَجَعَلَ بَيْنَكُم مَّوَدَّةً وَرَحْمَةً ۚ إِنَّ فِي ذَٰلِكَ لَآيَاتٍ لِّقَوْمٍ يَتَفَكَّرُونَ ۝ فَأَقِمْ وَجْهَكَ لِلدِّينِ حَنِيفًا ۚ فِطْرَتَ اللَّهِ الَّتِي فَطَرَ النَّاسَ عَلَيْهَا ۚ لَا تَبْدِيلَ لِخَلْقِ اللَّهِ ۚ ذَٰلِكَ الدِّينُ الْقَيِّمُ وَلَٰكِنَّ أَكْثَرَ النَّاسِ لَا يَعْلَمُونَ ۝

Luqmān (XXXI)

In the Name of God, the Infinitely Good, the Ever-Merciful

15. ... unto Me is your return... [SS]
27. If all the trees in the earth were pens, and if the sea eked out by the seven seas more were ink, the Words of God could not be written out unto their end... [QACI] [M] [SQCI]

As-Sajdah (XXXII)

In the Name of God, the Infinitely Good, the Ever-Merciful

16. They turn aside from their beds to invoke their Lord in fear and longing, and of what We have given them they give. [M]
16. Their sides shrink away from their beds, and they call upon their Lord in fear and in longing... [OS]
16. ... whose sides shrink away from beds... [SS]
17. And no soul knoweth the hidden bliss that lieth in store for them as meed for that which they were wont to do. [M]
17. No soul knoweth what is secretly stored up for them of coolness of the eyes in reward for what they were wont to do. [RS][L-QD]

(٣١) سُورَةُ لُقْمَان

بِسْمِ ٱللَّهِ ٱلرَّحْمَٰنِ ٱلرَّحِيمِ

وَإِن جَٰهَدَاكَ عَلَىٰٓ أَن تُشْرِكَ بِى مَا لَيْسَ لَكَ بِهِۦ عِلْمٌ فَلَا تُطِعْهُمَا ۖ وَصَاحِبْهُمَا فِى ٱلدُّنْيَا مَعْرُوفًا ۖ وَٱتَّبِعْ سَبِيلَ مَنْ أَنَابَ إِلَىَّ ۚ ثُمَّ إِلَىَّ مَرْجِعُكُمْ فَأُنَبِّئُكُم بِمَا كُنتُمْ تَعْمَلُونَ ﴿١٥﴾

وَلَوْ أَنَّمَا فِى ٱلْأَرْضِ مِن شَجَرَةٍ أَقْلَٰمٌ وَٱلْبَحْرُ يَمُدُّهُۥ مِنۢ بَعْدِهِۦ سَبْعَةُ أَبْحُرٍ مَّا نَفِدَتْ كَلِمَٰتُ ٱللَّهِ ۗ إِنَّ ٱللَّهَ عَزِيزٌ حَكِيمٌ ﴿٢٧﴾

(٣٢) سُورَةُ ٱلسَّجْدَة

بِسْمِ ٱللَّهِ ٱلرَّحْمَٰنِ ٱلرَّحِيمِ

تَتَجَافَىٰ جُنُوبُهُمْ عَنِ ٱلْمَضَاجِعِ يَدْعُونَ رَبَّهُمْ خَوْفًا وَطَمَعًا وَمِمَّا رَزَقْنَٰهُمْ يُنفِقُونَ ﴿١٦﴾

فَلَا تَعْلَمُ نَفْسٌ مَّآ أُخْفِىَ لَهُم مِّن قُرَّةِ أَعْيُنٍ جَزَآءًۢ بِمَا كَانُوا۟ يَعْمَلُونَ ﴿١٧﴾

Al-Aḥzāb (XXXIII)

In the Name of God, the Infinitely Good, the Ever-Merciful

9. O ye who believe, remember God's favour unto you when hosts came at you and We sent against them a wind and hosts ye saw not... [M]

10. ...when eyes could no longer look with steadiness, and when men's hearts rose up into their throats, and ye were thinking strange thoughts about God. [M]

11. There the believers were tested and tried, and their souls were quaked with a mighty quaking. [M]

21. Verily in the Messenger of God is a fair example for those of you that set their hopes on God and the Last Day, and remember God much. [WS]

21. Ye have in God's Messenger a fair example for whoso setteth his hopes on God and the Last Day and invoketh God much. [UM]

21. Verily ye have in God's Apostle a pattern most fair... [UM]

21. Indeed, in the Messenger of Allah ye have a fair example for whosoever hopes in Allah and in the Last Day and who invokes Allah much. [UM]

21. Verily ye have a fair pattern in God's Apostle... [OS]

21. Verily ye have a fair pattern in the Messenger of God... [SS]

22. ...this is that which God and His Messenger did promise us. That which God and His Messenger foretold hath truly come to pass. And it did but increase them in faith and in submission. [M]

23. Of the believers are men who are true to their covenant with God. Some of them have made good their vow by death, and some are waiting, and they waver not nor change. [M]

(٣٣) سُورَةُ الْأَحْزَابِ

بِسْمِ اللَّهِ الرَّحْمَٰنِ الرَّحِيمِ

يَٰٓأَيُّهَا ٱلَّذِينَ ءَامَنُواْ ٱذْكُرُواْ نِعْمَةَ ٱللَّهِ عَلَيْكُمْ إِذْ جَآءَتْكُمْ جُنُودٌ فَأَرْسَلْنَا عَلَيْهِمْ رِيحًا وَجُنُودًا لَّمْ تَرَوْهَا وَكَانَ ٱللَّهُ بِمَا تَعْمَلُونَ بَصِيرًا ۝

إِذْ جَآءُوكُم مِّن فَوْقِكُمْ وَمِنْ أَسْفَلَ مِنكُمْ وَإِذْ زَاغَتِ ٱلْأَبْصَٰرُ وَبَلَغَتِ ٱلْقُلُوبُ ٱلْحَنَاجِرَ وَتَظُنُّونَ بِٱللَّهِ ٱلظُّنُونَا۠ ۝

هُنَالِكَ ٱبْتُلِيَ ٱلْمُؤْمِنُونَ وَزُلْزِلُواْ زِلْزَالًا شَدِيدًا ۝

لَّقَدْ كَانَ لَكُمْ فِي رَسُولِ ٱللَّهِ أُسْوَةٌ حَسَنَةٌ لِّمَن كَانَ يَرْجُواْ ٱللَّهَ وَٱلْيَوْمَ ٱلْآخِرَ وَذَكَرَ ٱللَّهَ كَثِيرًا ۝

وَلَمَّا رَءَا ٱلْمُؤْمِنُونَ ٱلْأَحْزَابَ قَالُواْ هَٰذَا مَا وَعَدَنَا ٱللَّهُ وَرَسُولُهُۥ وَصَدَقَ ٱللَّهُ وَرَسُولُهُۥ وَمَا زَادَهُمْ إِلَّآ إِيمَٰنًا وَتَسْلِيمًا ۝

مِّنَ ٱلْمُؤْمِنِينَ رِجَالٌ صَدَقُواْ مَا عَٰهَدُواْ ٱللَّهَ عَلَيْهِ فَمِنْهُم مَّن قَضَىٰ نَحْبَهُۥ وَمِنْهُم مَّن يَنتَظِرُ وَمَا بَدَّلُواْ تَبْدِيلًا ۝

28. O Prophet, say unto thy wives: If ye desire this lower life and its adornments, then come and I will bestow its goods upon you, and I will release you with a fair release. [M]

29. But if ye desire God and His messenger and the abode of the Hereafter, then verily God hath laid in store for you a meed immense, for such of you as do good. [M]

35. ...those who remember God much... [SS]

37. ...We have married her to thee... [M]

40. Muḥammad is not the father of any man amongst you, but he is the Messenger of God and the Seal of the Prophets... [M]

يَـٰٓأَيُّهَا ٱلنَّبِىُّ قُل لِّأَزْوَٰجِكَ إِن كُنتُنَّ تُرِدْنَ ٱلْحَيَوٰةَ ٱلدُّنْيَا وَزِينَتَهَا فَتَعَالَيْنَ أُمَتِّعْكُنَّ وَأُسَرِّحْكُنَّ سَرَاحًا جَمِيلًا ۝

وَإِن كُنتُنَّ تُرِدْنَ ٱللَّهَ وَرَسُولَهُۥ وَٱلدَّارَ ٱلْـَٔاخِرَةَ فَإِنَّ ٱللَّهَ أَعَدَّ لِلْمُحْسِنَـٰتِ مِنكُنَّ أَجْرًا عَظِيمًا ۝

إِنَّ ٱلْمُسْلِمِينَ وَٱلْمُسْلِمَـٰتِ وَٱلْمُؤْمِنِينَ وَٱلْمُؤْمِنَـٰتِ وَٱلْقَـٰنِتِينَ وَٱلْقَـٰنِتَـٰتِ وَٱلصَّـٰدِقِينَ وَٱلصَّـٰدِقَـٰتِ وَٱلصَّـٰبِرِينَ وَٱلصَّـٰبِرَٰتِ وَٱلْخَـٰشِعِينَ وَٱلْخَـٰشِعَـٰتِ وَٱلْمُتَصَدِّقِينَ وَٱلْمُتَصَدِّقَـٰتِ وَٱلصَّـٰٓئِمِينَ وَٱلصَّـٰٓئِمَـٰتِ وَٱلْحَـٰفِظِينَ فُرُوجَهُمْ وَٱلْحَـٰفِظَـٰتِ وَٱلذَّٰكِرِينَ ٱللَّهَ كَثِيرًا وَٱلذَّٰكِرَٰتِ أَعَدَّ ٱللَّهُ لَهُم مَّغْفِرَةً وَأَجْرًا عَظِيمًا ۝

وَإِذْ تَقُولُ لِلَّذِىٓ أَنْعَمَ ٱللَّهُ عَلَيْهِ وَأَنْعَمْتَ عَلَيْهِ أَمْسِكْ عَلَيْكَ زَوْجَكَ وَٱتَّقِ ٱللَّهَ وَتُخْفِى فِى نَفْسِكَ مَا ٱللَّهُ مُبْدِيهِ وَتَخْشَى ٱلنَّاسَ وَٱللَّهُ أَحَقُّ أَن تَخْشَىٰهُ ۖ فَلَمَّا قَضَىٰ زَيْدٌ مِّنْهَا وَطَرًا زَوَّجْنَـٰكَهَا لِكَىْ لَا يَكُونَ عَلَى ٱلْمُؤْمِنِينَ حَرَجٌ فِىٓ أَزْوَٰجِ أَدْعِيَآئِهِمْ إِذَا قَضَوْا۟ مِنْهُنَّ وَطَرًا ۚ وَكَانَ أَمْرُ ٱللَّهِ مَفْعُولًا ۝

مَّا كَانَ مُحَمَّدٌ أَبَآ أَحَدٍ مِّن رِّجَالِكُمْ وَلَـٰكِن رَّسُولَ ٱللَّهِ وَخَاتَمَ ٱلنَّبِيِّـۧنَ ۗ وَكَانَ ٱللَّهُ بِكُلِّ شَىْءٍ عَلِيمًا ۝

53. O ye who have faith, enter not the dwellings of the Prophet unto a meal without waiting for its time to come, except if leave be given you. But if ye are invited then enter, and when you have fed then disperse. Linger not in the hope of discourse. Verily that would be irksome unto the Prophet, and he would shrink from telling you, but God shrinketh not from the truth... [M]

56. Verily God and His angels invoke blessings upon the Prophet. O ye who believe, invoke blessings upon him and greetings of peace. [SCR-SA]

56. Verily God and His angels whelm in blessings the prophet. O ye who believe invoke blessings upon him and give him greetings of Peace. [M]

72. We offered the trust [of being Our representative] unto the heavens and the earth and the mountains, but they shrank from bearing it, and were afraid of it. And man took it upon himself. Verily he hath proved an ignorant tyrant. [SS]

يَٰٓأَيُّهَا ٱلَّذِينَ ءَامَنُوا۟ لَا تَدْخُلُوا۟ بُيُوتَ ٱلنَّبِيِّ إِلَّآ أَن يُؤْذَنَ لَكُمْ إِلَىٰ طَعَامٍ غَيْرَ نَٰظِرِينَ إِنَىٰهُ وَلَٰكِنْ إِذَا دُعِيتُمْ فَٱدْخُلُوا۟ فَإِذَا طَعِمْتُمْ فَٱنتَشِرُوا۟ وَلَا مُسْتَـْٔنِسِينَ لِحَدِيثٍ إِنَّ ذَٰلِكُمْ كَانَ يُؤْذِى ٱلنَّبِىَّ فَيَسْتَحْىِۦ مِنكُمْ وَٱللَّهُ لَا يَسْتَحْىِۦ مِنَ ٱلْحَقِّ وَإِذَا سَأَلْتُمُوهُنَّ مَتَٰعًا فَسْـَٔلُوهُنَّ مِن وَرَآءِ حِجَابٍ ذَٰلِكُمْ أَطْهَرُ لِقُلُوبِكُمْ وَقُلُوبِهِنَّ وَمَا كَانَ لَكُمْ أَن تُؤْذُوا۟ رَسُولَ ٱللَّهِ وَلَآ أَن تَنكِحُوٓا۟ أَزْوَٰجَهُۥ مِنۢ بَعْدِهِۦٓ أَبَدًا إِنَّ ذَٰلِكُمْ كَانَ عِندَ ٱللَّهِ عَظِيمًا ۝

إِنَّ ٱللَّهَ وَمَلَٰٓئِكَتَهُۥ يُصَلُّونَ عَلَى ٱلنَّبِىِّ يَٰٓأَيُّهَا ٱلَّذِينَ ءَامَنُوا۟ صَلُّوا۟ عَلَيْهِ وَسَلِّمُوا۟ تَسْلِيمًا ۝

إِنَّا عَرَضْنَا ٱلْأَمَانَةَ عَلَى ٱلسَّمَٰوَٰتِ وَٱلْأَرْضِ وَٱلْجِبَالِ فَأَبَيْنَ أَن يَحْمِلْنَهَا وَأَشْفَقْنَ مِنْهَا وَحَمَلَهَا ٱلْإِنسَٰنُ إِنَّهُۥ كَانَ ظَلُومًا جَهُولًا ۝

Sabā' (XXXIV)

In the Name of God, the Infinitely Good, the Ever-Merciful

9. ...if We will, We shall make the earth gape and swallow them, or make fall the firmament in pieces upon them... [M]

Fāṭir (XXXV)

In the Name of God, the Infinitely Good, the Ever-Merciful

15. O men, ye are the poor in relation to God, and He is the Rich, the Praiseworthy. [UM]

15. O men, ye are the poor unto God, and God—He is the Rich, the Object of all Praise. [WS]

15. O men, ye are the poor, and God is the Rich, the Owner of Praise. [L-QOS]

(٣٤) سُورَةُ سَبَإٍ

بِسْمِ ٱللَّهِ ٱلرَّحْمَٰنِ ٱلرَّحِيمِ

أَفَلَمْ يَرَوْا۟ إِلَىٰ مَا بَيْنَ أَيْدِيهِمْ وَمَا خَلْفَهُم مِّنَ ٱلسَّمَآءِ وَٱلْأَرْضِ إِن نَّشَأْ نَخْسِفْ بِهِمُ ٱلْأَرْضَ أَوْ نُسْقِطْ عَلَيْهِمْ كِسَفًا مِّنَ ٱلسَّمَآءِ إِنَّ فِى ذَٰلِكَ لَآيَةً لِّكُلِّ عَبْدٍ مُّنِيبٍ ۝

(٣٥) سُورَةُ فَاطِرٍ

بِسْمِ ٱللَّهِ ٱلرَّحْمَٰنِ ٱلرَّحِيمِ

يَـٰٓأَيُّهَا ٱلنَّاسُ أَنتُمُ ٱلْفُقَرَآءُ إِلَى ٱللَّهِ وَٱللَّهُ هُوَ ٱلْغَنِىُّ ٱلْحَمِيدُ ۝

THE HOLY QUR'ĀN: SELECTED VERSES

Yā Sīn (XXXVI)

In the Name of God, the Infinitely Good, the Ever-Merciful

1. Yā Sīn. [UM]
2. And by the Wise Qur'ān. [UM]
3. Verily thou art one of those sent by God. [UM]
4. Upon the straight path. [UM]
5. This is a revelation of the Mighty, the Merciful. [UM]
6. That thou mightest warn a people whose fathers were not warned and the people were heedless. [UM]
7. Already hath sentence been passed on most of them, so that they will not believe. [UM]
8. Verily We have put shackles upon their necks even up to their chins, so that they are stiff-necked. [UM]
8. Verily we have put chains upon their necks, and they reach up to their neck and their heads are forced up. [BC]
9. And we have placed in front of them a barrier and behind them a barrier and We have veiled them so that they shall not see. [UM]
9. And before them We have placed a barrier and behind them a barrier, and We have blindfolded them so that they see not. [BC]
9. ...and We have enshrouded them, so that they see not. [M]
10. Alike is it to them whether thou warnest them or not, for they will not believe. [BC]
11. Thou shalt only warn him who hearkeneth to the reminder... and give him good tidings of forgiveness and of a noble reward. [UM]

(٣٦) سُورَةُ يسٓ

بِسْمِ اللَّهِ الرَّحْمَٰنِ الرَّحِيمِ

يسٓ ۝

وَالْقُرْءَانِ الْحَكِيمِ ۝

إِنَّكَ لَمِنَ الْمُرْسَلِينَ ۝

عَلَىٰ صِرَاطٍ مُّسْتَقِيمٍ ۝

تَنزِيلَ الْعَزِيزِ الرَّحِيمِ ۝

لِتُنذِرَ قَوْمًا مَّا أُنذِرَ ءَابَاؤُهُمْ فَهُمْ غَافِلُونَ ۝

لَقَدْ حَقَّ الْقَوْلُ عَلَىٰ أَكْثَرِهِمْ فَهُمْ لَا يُؤْمِنُونَ ۝

إِنَّا جَعَلْنَا فِي أَعْنَاقِهِمْ أَغْلَالًا فَهِيَ إِلَى الْأَذْقَانِ فَهُم مُّقْمَحُونَ ۝

وَجَعَلْنَا مِنْ بَيْنِ أَيْدِيهِمْ سَدًّا وَمِنْ خَلْفِهِمْ سَدًّا فَأَغْشَيْنَاهُمْ فَهُمْ لَا يُبْصِرُونَ ۝

وَسَوَاءٌ عَلَيْهِمْ ءَأَنذَرْتَهُمْ أَمْ لَمْ تُنذِرْهُمْ لَا يُؤْمِنُونَ ۝

إِنَّمَا تُنذِرُ مَنِ اتَّبَعَ الذِّكْرَ وَخَشِيَ الرَّحْمَٰنَ بِالْغَيْبِ فَبَشِّرْهُ بِمَغْفِرَةٍ وَأَجْرٍ كَرِيمٍ ۝

THE HOLY QUR'ĀN: SELECTED VERSES

13. And give them the parable of the townsfolk... [UM]
22. Why should I not worship Him who created me, Him to whom ye shall return? [UM]
26. It was said to him: Enter Paradise. He said: O that my people knew. [M]
26. ...Oh that my people knew. [UM]
27. How my Lord hath forgiven me and ennobled me. [M]
27. How God hath forgiven my sins and lavished upon me His bounty! [M]
36. Glory be to Him Who hath created all the pairs, of what growth from the earth, and of themselves and of what they know not. [BC]
36. Glory be to Him who hath created all the pairs, of that which the earth growth, and of themselves, and of that whereof they know not. [SA]
37. And a sign to them is the night. We take from it the day and lo they are in darkness. [UM]
38. And the sun runneth to its resting place. Such is the decree of the Mighty, the Knower. [UM]
38. And the sun runneth on unto its resting place. Such is the Decree of the Almighty, the All-Knowing. [BC]
39. And for the moon we have appointed phases until it becometh like unto an old palm branch. [UM]
40. It is not for the sun to overtake the moon and the night outstrippeth not the day. And each in a sphere glideth onwards. [UM]
41. And a sign to them is Our carrying their offspring in the full-laden ark. [UM]
42. And We have created for them others in its likeness upon which they ride. [UM]
55. Verily the people of Paradise on that day shall be joyful at their work. [UM]
56. ...in shades upon couches reclining. [UM]

وَٱضْرِبْ لَهُم مَّثَلًا أَصْحَٰبَ ٱلْقَرْيَةِ إِذْ جَآءَهَا ٱلْمُرْسَلُونَ ۞

وَمَا لِيَ لَآ أَعْبُدُ ٱلَّذِى فَطَرَنِى وَإِلَيْهِ تُرْجَعُونَ ۞

قِيلَ ٱدْخُلِ ٱلْجَنَّةَ ۖ قَالَ يَٰلَيْتَ قَوْمِى يَعْلَمُونَ ۞

بِمَا غَفَرَ لِى رَبِّى وَجَعَلَنِى مِنَ ٱلْمُكْرَمِينَ ۞

سُبْحَٰنَ ٱلَّذِى خَلَقَ ٱلْأَزْوَٰجَ كُلَّهَا مِمَّا تُنۢبِتُ ٱلْأَرْضُ وَمِنْ أَنفُسِهِمْ وَمِمَّا لَا يَعْلَمُونَ ۞

وَءَايَةٌ لَّهُمُ ٱلَّيْلُ نَسْلَخُ مِنْهُ ٱلنَّهَارَ فَإِذَا هُم مُّظْلِمُونَ ۞

وَٱلشَّمْسُ تَجْرِى لِمُسْتَقَرٍّ لَّهَا ۚ ذَٰلِكَ تَقْدِيرُ ٱلْعَزِيزِ ٱلْعَلِيمِ ۞

وَٱلْقَمَرَ قَدَّرْنَٰهُ مَنَازِلَ حَتَّىٰ عَادَ كَٱلْعُرْجُونِ ٱلْقَدِيمِ ۞

لَا ٱلشَّمْسُ يَنۢبَغِى لَهَآ أَن تُدْرِكَ ٱلْقَمَرَ وَلَا ٱلَّيْلُ سَابِقُ ٱلنَّهَارِ ۚ وَكُلٌّ فِى فَلَكٍ يَسْبَحُونَ ۞

وَءَايَةٌ لَّهُمْ أَنَّا حَمَلْنَا ذُرِّيَّتَهُمْ فِى ٱلْفُلْكِ ٱلْمَشْحُونِ ۞

وَخَلَقْنَا لَهُم مِّن مِّثْلِهِۦ مَا يَرْكَبُونَ ۞

إِنَّ أَصْحَٰبَ ٱلْجَنَّةِ ٱلْيَوْمَ فِى شُغُلٍ فَٰكِهُونَ ۞

هُمْ وَأَزْوَٰجُهُمْ فِى ظِلَٰلٍ عَلَى ٱلْأَرَآئِكِ مُتَّكِـُٔونَ ۞

57. Therein shall they have fruits and they shall have what they ask. [UM]

58. Peace. A word from the Merciful Lord. [UM]

78. ... he forgot his own createdness and said: Who will give life to bones when they are rotten? [M]

79. Say: He who gave them being the first time will give them life again... [M]

82. It needeth but his command if He wisheth aught... [UM]

83. Glory be to Him who hath the Sovranty over all things and to Whom ye shall return. [UM]

لَهُمْ فِيهَا فَٰكِهَةٌ وَلَهُم مَّا يَدَّعُونَ ۝

سَلَٰمٌ قَوْلًا مِّن رَّبٍّ رَّحِيمٍ ۝

وَضَرَبَ لَنَا مَثَلًا وَنَسِيَ خَلْقَهُۥ ۖ قَالَ مَن يُحْىِ ٱلْعِظَٰمَ وَهِىَ رَمِيمٌ ۝

قُلْ يُحْيِيهَا ٱلَّذِىٓ أَنشَأَهَآ أَوَّلَ مَرَّةٍ ۖ وَهُوَ بِكُلِّ خَلْقٍ عَلِيمٌ ۝

إِنَّمَآ أَمْرُهُۥٓ إِذَآ أَرَادَ شَيْـًٔا أَن يَقُولَ لَهُۥ كُن فَيَكُونُ ۝

فَسُبْحَٰنَ ٱلَّذِى بِيَدِهِۦ مَلَكُوتُ كُلِّ شَىْءٍ وَإِلَيْهِ تُرْجَعُونَ ۝

THE HOLY QUR'ĀN: SELECTED VERSES

Aṣ-Ṣāffāt (XXXVII)
In the Name of God, the Infinitely Good, the Ever-Merciful

28. ... verily ye had come unto us from the right hand. [UM]
177. When it alighteth in front of their dwellings, bad morning then to those who have been warned. [UM]

Ṣād (XXXVIII)
In the Name of God, the Infinitely Good, the Ever-Merciful

35. ... my Lord, grant me Thy Pardon, and give me a sovereignty that shall not belong unto any after me. Verily it is Thou Who art the Giver. [UM]
67. ... great tidings. [SS]
75. ... what hath prevented thee from bowing down before him whom My Hands have created... [UM]

(٣٧) سُورَةُ الصَّافَّاتِ

بِسْمِ اللَّهِ الرَّحْمَنِ الرَّحِيمِ

قَالُوا إِنَّكُمْ كُنتُمْ تَأْتُونَنَا عَنِ الْيَمِينِ ۝

فَإِذَا نَزَلَ بِسَاحَتِهِمْ فَسَاءَ صَبَاحُ الْمُنذَرِينَ ۝

(٣٨) سُورَةُ ص

بِسْمِ اللَّهِ الرَّحْمَنِ الرَّحِيمِ

قَالَ رَبِّ اغْفِرْ لِي وَهَبْ لِي مُلْكًا لَّا يَنبَغِي لِأَحَدٍ مِّن بَعْدِي ۖ إِنَّكَ أَنتَ الْوَهَّابُ ۝

قُلْ هُوَ نَبَأٌ عَظِيمٌ ۝

قَالَ يَا إِبْلِيسُ مَا مَنَعَكَ أَن تَسْجُدَ لِمَا خَلَقْتُ بِيَدَيَّ ۖ أَسْتَكْبَرْتَ أَمْ كُنتَ مِنَ الْعَالِينَ ۝

Az-Zumar (XXXIX)

In the Name of God, the Infinitely Good, the Ever-Merciful

23. ...it causeth the skins of those that fear their Lord to thrill. Then their skins and their hearts grow pliant (or supple) unto the remembrance of God... [WS]

53. ...O My slaves who have acted unwisely against yourselves, despair not of God's Mercy. Verily God forgiveth sins in their entirety. He is the All-Forgiving, the All-Merciful. [M]

54. And turn unto your Lord in repentance and surrender unto Him before there come unto you the punishment, when ye shall not be helped. [M]

67. They esteem not God as He hath the right to be esteemed... [NOS]

67. They have not rated God at His true worth... [PT]

(٣٩) سورة الزمر

بسم الله الرحمن الرحيم

الله نزل أحسن الحديث كتابا متشابها مثاني تقشعر منه جلود الذين يخشون ربهم ثم تلين جلودهم وقلوبهم إلى ذكر الله ذلك هدى الله يهدي به من يشاء ومن يضلل الله فما له من هاد ۝

قل يا عبادي الذين أسرفوا على أنفسهم لا تقنطوا من رحمة الله إن الله يغفر الذنوب جميعا إنه هو الغفور الرحيم ۝

وأنيبوا إلى ربكم وأسلموا له من قبل أن يأتيكم العذاب ثم لا تنصرون ۝

وما قدروا الله حق قدره والأرض جميعا قبضته يوم القيامة والسماوات مطويات بيمينه سبحانه وتعالى عما يشركون ۝

Ghāfir (XL)

In the Name of God, the Infinitely Good, the Ever-Merciful

16. ...unto whom on that day belongeth the Kingdom? Unto God the One, the Irresistible. [BC]

16. ...unto whom this day is the Kingdom? Unto God, the One, the Irrestistible. [SS]

44. ...I submit my case unto God. Verily God is the Seer of His slaves. [SS]

60. Your Lord hath said: Call upon Me and I will answer you... [WS]

78. Verily We have sent messengers before thee. About some of them have We told thee, and about some have We not told thee... [SS] [NOS] [RS]

78. We have sent messengers before thee. About some of them We have told thee, and about some We have not told thee... [L-II]

78. ...some of them We have mentioned. Others We have not mentioned... [L-UQ]

(٤٠) سُورَةُ غَافِرٍ

بِسْمِ اللَّهِ الرَّحْمَنِ الرَّحِيمِ

يَوْمَ هُم بَارِزُونَ لَا يَخْفَىٰ عَلَى اللَّهِ مِنْهُمْ شَيْءٌ لِّمَنِ الْمُلْكُ الْيَوْمَ لِلَّهِ الْوَاحِدِ الْقَهَّارِ ۝

فَسَتَذْكُرُونَ مَا أَقُولُ لَكُمْ وَأُفَوِّضُ أَمْرِي إِلَى اللَّهِ إِنَّ اللَّهَ بَصِيرٌ بِالْعِبَادِ ۝

وَقَالَ رَبُّكُمُ ادْعُونِي أَسْتَجِبْ لَكُمْ إِنَّ الَّذِينَ يَسْتَكْبِرُونَ عَنْ عِبَادَتِي سَيَدْخُلُونَ جَهَنَّمَ دَاخِرِينَ ۝

وَلَقَدْ أَرْسَلْنَا رُسُلًا مِّن قَبْلِكَ مِنْهُم مَّن قَصَصْنَا عَلَيْكَ وَمِنْهُم مَّن لَّمْ نَقْصُصْ عَلَيْكَ وَمَا كَانَ لِرَسُولٍ أَن يَأْتِيَ بِآيَةٍ إِلَّا بِإِذْنِ اللَّهِ فَإِذَا جَاءَ أَمْرُ اللَّهِ قُضِيَ بِالْحَقِّ وَخَسِرَ هُنَالِكَ الْمُبْطِلُونَ ۝

Fuṣṣilat (XLI)

In the Name of God, the Infinitely Good, the Ever-Merciful

30. Verily those who say: 'Our Lord is God,' and who then follow straight His path, on them descend the Angels saying: 'Fear not nor grieve, but hearken to good tidings of the Paradise which ye are promised.' [M]

31. 'We are your protecting friends in this lower life, and in the Hereafter wherein ye shall be given that which your souls long for, that which ye pray for.' [M]

32. 'In bounty from Him who is All-Forgiving, All-Merciful.' [M]

35. ... none meeteth it face to face save him whose destined portion is immeasurably blessed. [SS]

37. And of His signs are the night and the day and the sun and the moon. Bow not down in adoration unto the sun nor unto the moon, but bow down in adoration unto God their Creator, if Him indeed ye worship. [M]

53. We shall show them Our signs upon the horizons and within themselves, until it be clear to them that He is the truth... [BC]

53. We shall show them Our signs on the horizons and in themselves... [WS] [SA]

(٤١) سُورَةُ فُصِّلَتْ

بِسْمِ اللَّهِ الرَّحْمَٰنِ الرَّحِيمِ

إِنَّ الَّذِينَ قَالُوا رَبُّنَا اللَّهُ ثُمَّ اسْتَقَامُوا تَتَنَزَّلُ عَلَيْهِمُ الْمَلَائِكَةُ أَلَّا تَخَافُوا وَلَا تَحْزَنُوا وَأَبْشِرُوا بِالْجَنَّةِ الَّتِي كُنتُمْ تُوعَدُونَ ۞

نَحْنُ أَوْلِيَاؤُكُمْ فِي الْحَيَاةِ الدُّنْيَا وَفِي الْآخِرَةِ ۖ وَلَكُمْ فِيهَا مَا تَشْتَهِي أَنفُسُكُمْ وَلَكُمْ فِيهَا مَا تَدَّعُونَ ۞

نُزُلًا مِّنْ غَفُورٍ رَّحِيمٍ ۞

وَمَا يُلَقَّاهَا إِلَّا الَّذِينَ صَبَرُوا وَمَا يُلَقَّاهَا إِلَّا ذُو حَظٍّ عَظِيمٍ ۞

وَمِنْ آيَاتِهِ اللَّيْلُ وَالنَّهَارُ وَالشَّمْسُ وَالْقَمَرُ ۚ لَا تَسْجُدُوا لِلشَّمْسِ وَلَا لِلْقَمَرِ وَاسْجُدُوا لِلَّهِ الَّذِي خَلَقَهُنَّ إِن كُنتُمْ إِيَّاهُ تَعْبُدُونَ ۞

سَنُرِيهِمْ آيَاتِنَا فِي الْآفَاقِ وَفِي أَنفُسِهِمْ حَتَّىٰ يَتَبَيَّنَ لَهُمْ أَنَّهُ الْحَقُّ ۗ أَوَلَمْ يَكْفِ بِرَبِّكَ أَنَّهُ عَلَىٰ كُلِّ شَيْءٍ شَهِيدٌ ۞

Ash-Shūrā (XLII)

In the Name of God, the Infinitely Good, the Ever-Merciful

11. ...naught is like unto Him, and He is the Hearer, the Seer. [SS]
11. ...nothing is like unto Him... [UM]
11. ...there is naught like unto Him, and He is the Hearer, the Seer. [SS]
52. ...We have made it a light whereby We guide whom We will... [QACI] [SQCI]
53. ...do not all things return to God? [WS] [RS]
53. ...all things come unto God. [SS]

Az-Zukhruf (XLIII)

In the Name of God, the Infinitely Good, the Ever-Merciful

84. He it is who is God in Heaven and God on earth... [SS]

(٤٢) سُورَةُ الشُّورَىٰ

بِسْمِ اللَّهِ الرَّحْمَٰنِ الرَّحِيمِ

فَاطِرُ ٱلسَّمَٰوَٰتِ وَٱلْأَرْضِ جَعَلَ لَكُم مِّنْ أَنفُسِكُمْ أَزْوَٰجًا وَمِنَ ٱلْأَنْعَٰمِ أَزْوَٰجًا يَذْرَؤُكُمْ فِيهِ لَيْسَ كَمِثْلِهِۦ شَىْءٌ وَهُوَ ٱلسَّمِيعُ ٱلْبَصِيرُ ۝

وَكَذَٰلِكَ أَوْحَيْنَآ إِلَيْكَ رُوحًا مِّنْ أَمْرِنَا مَا كُنتَ تَدْرِى مَا ٱلْكِتَٰبُ وَلَا ٱلْإِيمَٰنُ وَلَٰكِن جَعَلْنَٰهُ نُورًا نَّهْدِى بِهِۦ مَن نَّشَآءُ مِنْ عِبَادِنَا وَإِنَّكَ لَتَهْدِىٓ إِلَىٰ صِرَٰطٍ مُّسْتَقِيمٍ ۝

صِرَٰطِ ٱللَّهِ ٱلَّذِى لَهُۥ مَا فِى ٱلسَّمَٰوَٰتِ وَمَا فِى ٱلْأَرْضِ أَلَآ إِلَى ٱللَّهِ تَصِيرُ ٱلْأُمُورُ ۝

(٤٣) سُورَةُ الزُّخْرُفِ

بِسْمِ اللَّهِ الرَّحْمَٰنِ الرَّحِيمِ

وَهُوَ ٱلَّذِى فِى ٱلسَّمَآءِ إِلَٰهٌ وَفِى ٱلْأَرْضِ إِلَٰهٌ وَهُوَ ٱلْحَكِيمُ ٱلْعَلِيمُ ۝

Ad-Dukhān (XLIV)

In the Name of God, the Infinitely Good, the Ever-Merciful

38. Not in play did We create the heavens and the earth and all that is between them. [M]

Al-Aḥqāf (XLVI)

In the Name of God, the Infinitely Good, the Ever-Merciful

3. We created the heavens and the earth and all that is between them with naught but Truth... [SS]

Muḥammad (XLVII)

In the Name of God, the Infinitely Good, the Ever-Merciful

38. ...God is the Rich, and ye are the poor... [BC] [WS]

(٤٤) سُورَةُ الدُّخَانِ

بِسْمِ اللَّهِ الرَّحْمَٰنِ الرَّحِيمِ

وَمَا خَلَقْنَا السَّمَاوَاتِ وَالْأَرْضَ وَمَا بَيْنَهُمَا لَاعِبِينَ ۞

(٤٦) سُورَةُ الْأَحْقَافِ

بِسْمِ اللَّهِ الرَّحْمَٰنِ الرَّحِيمِ

مَا خَلَقْنَا السَّمَاوَاتِ وَالْأَرْضَ وَمَا بَيْنَهُمَا إِلَّا بِالْحَقِّ وَأَجَلٍ مُّسَمًّى وَالَّذِينَ كَفَرُوا عَمَّا أُنذِرُوا مُعْرِضُونَ ۞

(٤٧) سُورَةُ مُحَمَّدٍ

بِسْمِ اللَّهِ الرَّحْمَٰنِ الرَّحِيمِ

هَا أَنتُمْ هَٰؤُلَاءِ تُدْعَوْنَ لِتُنفِقُوا فِي سَبِيلِ اللَّهِ فَمِنكُم مَّن يَبْخَلُ وَمَن يَبْخَلْ فَإِنَّمَا يَبْخَلُ عَن نَّفْسِهِ وَاللَّهُ الْغَنِيُّ وَأَنتُمُ الْفُقَرَاءُ وَإِن تَتَوَلَّوْا يَسْتَبْدِلْ قَوْمًا غَيْرَكُمْ ثُمَّ لَا يَكُونُوا أَمْثَالَكُم ۞

Al-Fatḥ (XLVIII)

In the Name of God, the Infinitely Good, the Ever-Merciful

1. Verily We have made thee victorious by a manifest victory. [BC]
1. Verily We have given thee a clear victory. [M]
2. That God may forgive thee thy trespasses past and those which are to come... [BC]
4. He it is who causes the spirit of Peace to descend into the hearts of the believers, that they might add [new] faith to their [former] faith... [UM]
4. He it is Who hath sent down the Spirit of Peace into the hearts of the faithful that they may increase in faith upon faith... [OS] [SS]
4. He it is who sent down the Spirit of Peace into the hearts of the believers that they may increase in faith upon their faith... [M]
5. That He may bring the believing men and the believing women into gardens that are watered by flowing rivers, gardens wherein they shall dwell immortal, and that He may take from them all guilt of evil. Triumph immense for them is that in the sight of God. [M]
10. Verily those who swear allegiance unto Thee, swear allegiance only unto Allah. The Hand of Allah is above their hands. And whosoever breaketh his oath, breaketh it only with himself. And whosoever keepeth his covenant with Allah, on him will He bestow immense reward. [UM]
10. Verily they that swear allegiance unto thee swear it unto none but God. The Hand of God is over their hands. Therefore whomsoever breaketh his oath breaketh it only unto his soul's hurt, and whomsoever keepeth his covenant with God, verily unto him will He give Immense Reward. [BC]

(٤٨) سُورَةُ الفَتْح

بِسْمِ اللَّهِ الرَّحْمَنِ الرَّحِيمِ

إِنَّا فَتَحْنَا لَكَ فَتْحًا مُبِينًا ۝

لِيَغْفِرَ لَكَ اللَّهُ مَا تَقَدَّمَ مِن ذَنبِكَ وَمَا تَأَخَّرَ وَيُتِمَّ نِعْمَتَهُ عَلَيْكَ وَيَهْدِيَكَ صِرَاطًا مُسْتَقِيمًا ۝

هُوَ الَّذِي أَنزَلَ السَّكِينَةَ فِي قُلُوبِ الْمُؤْمِنِينَ لِيَزْدَادُوا إِيمَانًا مَّعَ إِيمَانِهِمْ وَلِلَّهِ جُنُودُ السَّمَاوَاتِ وَالْأَرْضِ وَكَانَ اللَّهُ عَلِيمًا حَكِيمًا ۝

لِيُدْخِلَ الْمُؤْمِنِينَ وَالْمُؤْمِنَاتِ جَنَّاتٍ تَجْرِي مِن تَحْتِهَا الْأَنْهَارُ خَالِدِينَ فِيهَا وَيُكَفِّرَ عَنْهُمْ سَيِّئَاتِهِمْ وَكَانَ ذَلِكَ عِندَ اللَّهِ فَوْزًا عَظِيمًا ۝

إِنَّ الَّذِينَ يُبَايِعُونَكَ إِنَّمَا يُبَايِعُونَ اللَّهَ يَدُ اللَّهِ فَوْقَ أَيْدِيهِمْ فَمَن نَّكَثَ فَإِنَّمَا يَنكُثُ عَلَى نَفْسِهِ وَمَنْ أَوْفَى بِمَا عَاهَدَ عَلَيْهُ اللَّهَ فَسَيُؤْتِيهِ أَجْرًا عَظِيمًا ۝

10. Verily they who pledge unto thee their allegiance pledge it unto none but God. The Hand of God is above their hands... [WS]

18. God was well pleased with the believers when they swore allegiance unto thee beneath the tree. He knew what was in their hearts and sent down the Spirit of Peace upon them and hath rewarded them with a near victory. [BC]

18. God was well pleased with the believers when they pledged allegiance unto thee beneath the tree. He knew what was in their hearts and sent down the Spirit of Peace upon them and hath rewarded them with a near victory. [WS]

18. God was well pleased with the believers when they pledged allegiance unto thee beneath the tree. He knew what was in their hearts and sent down the Spirit of Peace upon them and hath given them the meed of a near victory. [M]

21. Other [spoils] which ye have not yet been able to achieve but which God encompasseth... [WS]

27. God hath fulfilled for His Messenger the vision: God willing ye shall enter the inviolable mosque in safety, not fearing, with the hair of your heads shaven or cut. But He knoweth what ye know not, and before that hath He given you a near victory. [M]

إِنَّ ٱلَّذِينَ يُبَايِعُونَكَ إِنَّمَا يُبَايِعُونَ ٱللَّهَ يَدُ ٱللَّهِ فَوْقَ أَيْدِيهِمْ فَمَن نَّكَثَ فَإِنَّمَا يَنكُثُ عَلَىٰ نَفْسِهِۦ ۖ وَمَنْ أَوْفَىٰ بِمَا عَٰهَدَ عَلَيْهُ ٱللَّهَ فَسَيُؤْتِيهِ أَجْرًا عَظِيمًا ۝

لَّقَدْ رَضِيَ ٱللَّهُ عَنِ ٱلْمُؤْمِنِينَ إِذْ يُبَايِعُونَكَ تَحْتَ ٱلشَّجَرَةِ فَعَلِمَ مَا فِى قُلُوبِهِمْ فَأَنزَلَ ٱلسَّكِينَةَ عَلَيْهِمْ وَأَثَٰبَهُمْ فَتْحًا قَرِيبًا ۝

وَأُخْرَىٰ لَمْ تَقْدِرُوا۟ عَلَيْهَا قَدْ أَحَاطَ ٱللَّهُ بِهَا ۚ وَكَانَ ٱللَّهُ عَلَىٰ كُلِّ شَىْءٍ قَدِيرًا ۝

لَّقَدْ صَدَقَ ٱللَّهُ رَسُولَهُ ٱلرُّءْيَا بِٱلْحَقِّ ۖ لَتَدْخُلُنَّ ٱلْمَسْجِدَ ٱلْحَرَامَ إِن شَآءَ ٱللَّهُ ءَامِنِينَ مُحَلِّقِينَ رُءُوسَكُمْ وَمُقَصِّرِينَ لَا تَخَافُونَ ۖ فَعَلِمَ مَا لَمْ تَعْلَمُوا۟ فَجَعَلَ مِن دُونِ ذَٰلِكَ فَتْحًا قَرِيبًا ۝

Al-Ḥujurāt (XLIX)

In the Name of God, the Infinitely Good, the Ever-Merciful

14. The Arabs of the desert say: 'We believe.' Say thou [Muhammad]: 'Ye believe not, but say rather "we submit", for faith hath not yet entered your hearts. Yet if ye obey God and His Messenger, He will not withhold from you any reward that your deeds deserve. Verily God is Forgiving, Merciful.' [SS]

14. The Arabs say: We believe. Say thou: Ye believe not. Say rather: 'We have submitted', for faith hath not entered your hearts... [BC]

14. The Arabs of the desert say: We have faith. Say thou: Faith ye have not, but say 'we submit', for faith hath not yet entered your hearts. And if ye obey God and His Messenger, He will in no wise withhold from you your meed for what ye do... [M]

Qāf (L)

In the Name of God, the Infinitely Good, the Ever-Merciful

16. ... We are nearer to him (man) than his jugular vein. [OS] [BC] [NOS] [SP] [L-QD] [L-QOS]

16. ... We (God) are nearer to him (man) than his jugular vein. [SS] [S] [WS] [SA]

37. ... who giveth ear with full intelligence. [SS]

(٤٩) سورة الحجرات

بسم الله الرحمن الرحيم

قَالَتِ ٱلْأَعْرَابُ ءَامَنَّا ۖ قُل لَّمْ تُؤْمِنُوا۟ وَلَٰكِن قُولُوٓا۟ أَسْلَمْنَا وَلَمَّا يَدْخُلِ ٱلْإِيمَٰنُ فِى قُلُوبِكُمْ ۖ وَإِن تُطِيعُوا۟ ٱللَّهَ وَرَسُولَهُۥ لَا يَلِتْكُم مِّنْ أَعْمَٰلِكُمْ شَيْـًٔا ۚ إِنَّ ٱللَّهَ غَفُورٌ رَّحِيمٌ ۝١٤

(٥٠) سورة ق

بسم الله الرحمن الرحيم

وَلَقَدْ خَلَقْنَا ٱلْإِنسَٰنَ وَنَعْلَمُ مَا تُوَسْوِسُ بِهِۦ نَفْسُهُۥ ۖ وَنَحْنُ أَقْرَبُ إِلَيْهِ مِنْ حَبْلِ ٱلْوَرِيدِ ۝١٦

إِنَّ فِى ذَٰلِكَ لَذِكْرَىٰ لِمَن كَانَ لَهُۥ قَلْبٌ أَوْ أَلْقَى ٱلسَّمْعَ وَهُوَ شَهِيدٌ ۝٣٧

Adh-Dhāriyāt (LI)
In the Name of God, the Infinitely Good, the Ever-Merciful

50. Flee unto God... [S] [WS]
55. Be a remembrancer, for verily remembrancing profiteth the believers. [SS]
56. I did not create jinn and men except that they should worship Me. [RS] [L-QD]

At-Ṭūr (LII)
In the Name of God, the Infinitely Good, the Ever-Merciful

48. Wait patiently for the fulfillment of they Lord's decree, for verily thou art in Our sight; and glorify thy Lord with praise when thou uprisest. [M]
48. ... verily thou art beneath Our Eyes... [OS]
49. And glorify Him in the night, and at the dimming of the stars. [M]

(٥١) سُورَةُ الذَّارِيَاتِ

بِسْمِ اللَّهِ الرَّحْمَٰنِ الرَّحِيمِ

فَفِرُّوا إِلَى اللَّهِ ۖ إِنِّي لَكُم مِّنْهُ نَذِيرٌ مُّبِينٌ ۝

وَذَكِّرْ فَإِنَّ الذِّكْرَىٰ تَنفَعُ الْمُؤْمِنِينَ ۝

وَمَا خَلَقْتُ الْجِنَّ وَالْإِنسَ إِلَّا لِيَعْبُدُونِ ۝

(٥٢) سُورَةُ الطُّورِ

بِسْمِ اللَّهِ الرَّحْمَٰنِ الرَّحِيمِ

وَاصْبِرْ لِحُكْمِ رَبِّكَ فَإِنَّكَ بِأَعْيُنِنَا ۖ وَسَبِّحْ بِحَمْدِ رَبِّكَ حِينَ تَقُومُ ۝

وَمِنَ اللَّيْلِ فَسَبِّحْهُ وَإِدْبَارَ النُّجُومِ ۝

An-Najm (LIII)

In the Name of God, the Infinitely Good, the Ever-Merciful

13. And verily he saw him at another revelation. [BC] [SS]
14. Beside the lote-tree of the uttermost boundary. [BC]
14. By the Lote Tree of the Uttermost End. [SS]
15. Whereby is the Garden of Refuge. [BC]
15. Even here is the Garden of Ultimate Refuge. [SS]
16. When there enshrouded the lote-tree That Which enshroudeth. [BC] [SS] [M]
17. The sight wavered not, nor did it transgress. [BC]
17. The eye wavered not nor did it transgress. [SS] [M]
18. Verily he saw, of the Signs of his Lord, the Greatest. [BC]
18. Verily he beheld, of all the signs of his Lord, the Greatest. [SS] [M]
42. Thy Lord is the Uttermost end. [SS]

Al-Qamar (LIV)

In the Name of God, the Infinitely Good, the Ever-Merciful

55. In the abode of truthfulness at the court of an Almighty King. [SS]

(٥٣) سُورَةُ النَّجْمِ

بِسْمِ اللَّهِ الرَّحْمَٰنِ الرَّحِيمِ

وَلَقَدْ رَءَاهُ نَزْلَةً أُخْرَىٰ ۝

عِندَ سِدْرَةِ الْمُنتَهَىٰ ۝

عِندَهَا جَنَّةُ الْمَأْوَىٰ ۝

إِذْ يَغْشَى السِّدْرَةَ مَا يَغْشَىٰ ۝

مَا زَاغَ الْبَصَرُ وَمَا طَغَىٰ ۝

لَقَدْ رَأَىٰ مِنْ ءَايَٰتِ رَبِّهِ الْكُبْرَىٰ ۝

وَأَنَّ إِلَىٰ رَبِّكَ الْمُنتَهَىٰ ۝

(٥٤) سُورَةُ الْقَمَرِ

بِسْمِ اللَّهِ الرَّحْمَٰنِ الرَّحِيمِ

فِى مَقْعَدِ صِدْقٍ عِندَ مَلِيكٍ مُّقْتَدِرٍ ۝

Ar-Raḥmān (LV)

In the Name of God, the Infinitely Good, the Ever-Merciful

1. The God of Mercy All-Transcendent. [UM]
1. The Infinitely-Good. [QACI] [M] [SA] [SQCI]
2. Hath taught the Qur'an. [UM]
2. Taught the Koran. [QACI] [M] [SA] [SQCI]
3. He hath created man. [UM]
4. He hath taught him speech. [UM]
5. The sun and the moon have their span. [UM]
6. And the star and the tree do obeisance. [UM]
7. The heaven hath He raised aloft; and He hath let down the scales. [UM]
8. That ye transgress not in the measure. [UM]
9. Set ye the weight right; nor come ye short of the measure. [UM]
10. And the earth hath He laid down for mankind. [UM]
11. Therein is fruit and the date palm bearing sheaths. [UM]
12. And grains decked in greenery and odorous herbs. [UM]
13. Which of your Lord's boons will ye twain belie? [UM]

(٥٥) سُورَةُ الرَّحْمَٰنِ
بِسْمِ اللَّهِ الرَّحْمَٰنِ الرَّحِيمِ

الرَّحْمَٰنُ ۝

عَلَّمَ الْقُرْآنَ ۝

خَلَقَ الْإِنسَانَ ۝

عَلَّمَهُ الْبَيَانَ ۝

الشَّمْسُ وَالْقَمَرُ بِحُسْبَانٍ ۝

وَالنَّجْمُ وَالشَّجَرُ يَسْجُدَانِ ۝

وَالسَّمَاءَ رَفَعَهَا وَوَضَعَ الْمِيزَانَ ۝

أَلَّا تَطْغَوْا فِي الْمِيزَانِ ۝

وَأَقِيمُوا الْوَزْنَ بِالْقِسْطِ وَلَا تُخْسِرُوا الْمِيزَانَ ۝

وَالْأَرْضَ وَضَعَهَا لِلْأَنَامِ ۝

فِيهَا فَاكِهَةٌ وَالنَّخْلُ ذَاتُ الْأَكْمَامِ ۝

وَالْحَبُّ ذُو الْعَصْفِ وَالرَّيْحَانُ ۝

فَبِأَيِّ آلَاءِ رَبِّكُمَا تُكَذِّبَانِ ۝

14. He hath created man from clay even as earthenware. [UM]
15. And He created the jinn from clear flame of fire. [UM]
16. Which of your Lord's boons will ye twain belie? [UM]
17. He is Lord of the two Easts, and Lord of the two Wests. [UM]
18. Which of your Lord's boons will ye twain belie? [UM]
19. He hath let loose the two seas, and they meet each other. [UM]
19. He hath let loose the two seas; they come together. [SS]
20. Between them is an isthmus: beyond it they trespass not. [UM]
20. But an isthmus is between them, and they encroach not beyond it. [SS]
21. Which of your Lord's boons will ye twain belie? [UM]
22. Forth from them come pearls great and small. [UM]
23. Which of your Lord's boons will ye twain belie? [UM]
24. He hath ships towering aloft upon the sea like standards. [UM]
25. Which of your Lord's boons will ye twain belie? [UM]
26. All that is thereon passeth away. [UM]
26. Everyone therein (in the worlds of creation) passeth away. [WS]
26. All that is therein suffereth extinction. [SS]
26. All that is therein (in creation) passeth away. [S]
26. All that is thereon suffereth extinction. [NOS]
27. And the Face of thy Lord endureth forever in its Majesty and Bounty. [UM]
27. And there remaineth the Face of thy Lord in Its Majesty and Bounty. [SS] [S] [WS] [NOS]
27. Eternal is the face of thy Lord in its Majesty and Bounty. [M]
28. Which of your Lord's boons will ye twain belie? [UM]

خَلَقَ ٱلْإِنسَٰنَ مِن صَلْصَٰلٍ كَٱلْفَخَّارِ ۝

وَخَلَقَ ٱلْجَانَّ مِن مَّارِجٍ مِّن نَّارٍ ۝

فَبِأَيِّ ءَالَآءِ رَبِّكُمَا تُكَذِّبَانِ ۝

رَبُّ ٱلْمَشْرِقَيْنِ وَرَبُّ ٱلْمَغْرِبَيْنِ ۝

فَبِأَيِّ ءَالَآءِ رَبِّكُمَا تُكَذِّبَانِ ۝

مَرَجَ ٱلْبَحْرَيْنِ يَلْتَقِيَانِ ۝

بَيْنَهُمَا بَرْزَخٌ لَّا يَبْغِيَانِ ۝

فَبِأَيِّ ءَالَآءِ رَبِّكُمَا تُكَذِّبَانِ ۝

يَخْرُجُ مِنْهُمَا ٱللُّؤْلُؤُ وَٱلْمَرْجَانُ ۝

فَبِأَيِّ ءَالَآءِ رَبِّكُمَا تُكَذِّبَانِ ۝

وَلَهُ ٱلْجَوَارِ ٱلْمُنشَـَٔاتُ فِي ٱلْبَحْرِ كَٱلْأَعْلَٰمِ ۝

فَبِأَيِّ ءَالَآءِ رَبِّكُمَا تُكَذِّبَانِ ۝

كُلُّ مَنْ عَلَيْهَا فَانٍ ۝

وَيَبْقَىٰ وَجْهُ رَبِّكَ ذُو ٱلْجَلَٰلِ وَٱلْإِكْرَامِ ۝

فَبِأَيِّ ءَالَآءِ رَبِّكُمَا تُكَذِّبَانِ ۝

29. He is petitioned by those who are in the heavens and on earth: every day bringeth He things to pass. [UM]
30. Which of your Lord's boons will ye twain belie? [UM]
31. We shall have leisure for you both, O ye heavy ones. [UM]
32. Which of your Lord's boons will ye twain belie? [UM]
33. O band of jinn and men, if ye can pass beyond the limits of the Heavens and the earth, then pass! Yet shall ye not pass if ye have not the authority. [UM] [BC]
33. ...if you would pass beyond the boundary of Heaven and earth do so, but you cannot pass without authority. [L-MPP]
34. Which of your Lord's boons will ye twain belie? [UM]
35. There shall be sent against you a flash of fire and brass, and ye shall not prevail. [UM]
36. Which of your Lord's boons will ye twain belie? [UM]
37. When the heaven shall be cleft and when it shall turn ruddy like oils? [UM]
38. Which of your Lord's boons will ye twain belie? [UM]
39. On that day no man shall be questioned as to his sins, neither shall any jinn. [UM]
40. Which of your Lord's boons will ye twain belie? [UM]
41. The guilty shall be known by their marks: seized shall they be by the forelock and the feet. [UM]
42. Which of your Lord's boons will ye twain belie? [UM]

يَسْـَٔلُهُۥ مَن فِى ٱلسَّمَوَٰتِ وَٱلْأَرْضِ ۚ كُلَّ يَوْمٍ هُوَ فِى شَأْنٍ ۝

فَبِأَىِّ ءَالَآءِ رَبِّكُمَا تُكَذِّبَانِ ۝

سَنَفْرُغُ لَكُمْ أَيُّهَ ٱلثَّقَلَانِ ۝

فَبِأَىِّ ءَالَآءِ رَبِّكُمَا تُكَذِّبَانِ ۝

يَٰمَعْشَرَ ٱلْجِنِّ وَٱلْإِنسِ إِنِ ٱسْتَطَعْتُمْ أَن تَنفُذُوا۟ مِنْ أَقْطَارِ ٱلسَّمَوَٰتِ وَٱلْأَرْضِ فَٱنفُذُوا۟ ۚ لَا تَنفُذُونَ إِلَّا بِسُلْطَٰنٍ ۝

فَبِأَىِّ ءَالَآءِ رَبِّكُمَا تُكَذِّبَانِ ۝

يُرْسَلُ عَلَيْكُمَا شُوَاظٌ مِّن نَّارٍ وَنُحَاسٌ فَلَا تَنتَصِرَانِ ۝

فَبِأَىِّ ءَالَآءِ رَبِّكُمَا تُكَذِّبَانِ ۝

فَإِذَا ٱنشَقَّتِ ٱلسَّمَآءُ فَكَانَتْ وَرْدَةً كَٱلدِّهَانِ ۝

فَبِأَىِّ ءَالَآءِ رَبِّكُمَا تُكَذِّبَانِ ۝

فَيَوْمَئِذٍ لَّا يُسْـَٔلُ عَن ذَنۢبِهِۦٓ إِنسٌ وَلَا جَآنٌّ ۝

فَبِأَىِّ ءَالَآءِ رَبِّكُمَا تُكَذِّبَانِ ۝

يُعْرَفُ ٱلْمُجْرِمُونَ بِسِيمَٰهُمْ فَيُؤْخَذُ بِٱلنَّوَٰصِى وَٱلْأَقْدَامِ ۝

فَبِأَىِّ ءَالَآءِ رَبِّكُمَا تُكَذِّبَانِ ۝

43. This is Hell, which the guilty belied. [UM]
44. To and fro shall they pass between it and the scalding waters. [UM]
45. Which of your Lord's boons will ye twain belie? [UM]
46. And for him that feareth the High Degree of his Lord there are two gardens. [UM] [BC]
47. Which of your Lord's boons will ye twain belie? [UM]
48. Each aboundeth in green branches. [UM]
49. Which of your Lord's boons will ye twain belie? [UM]
50. Therein are two fountains flowing. [UM] [BC]
51. Which of your Lord's boons will ye twain belie? [UM]
52. Therein of every fruit there are two kinds. [UM]
52. Therein of every fruit two kinds. [BC]
53. Which of your Lord's boons will ye twain belie? [UM]
54. Therein shall they rest upon beds lined with brocade of silver, and at hand shall be the fruits of the two gardens. [UM]
55. Which of your Lord's boons will ye twain belie? [UM]
56. Thereon are maidens shy of glance. Never until now were they deflowered by man or jinn. [UM]
57. Which of your Lord's boons will ye twain belie? [UM]

هَـٰذِهِۦ جَهَنَّمُ ٱلَّتِى يُكَذِّبُ بِهَا ٱلْمُجْرِمُونَ ۝

يَطُوفُونَ بَيْنَهَا وَبَيْنَ حَمِيمٍ ءَانٍ ۝

فَبِأَىِّ ءَالَآءِ رَبِّكُمَا تُكَذِّبَانِ ۝

وَلِمَنْ خَافَ مَقَامَ رَبِّهِۦ جَنَّتَانِ ۝

فَبِأَىِّ ءَالَآءِ رَبِّكُمَا تُكَذِّبَانِ ۝

ذَوَاتَآ أَفْنَانٍ ۝

فَبِأَىِّ ءَالَآءِ رَبِّكُمَا تُكَذِّبَانِ ۝

فِيهِمَا عَيْنَانِ تَجْرِيَانِ ۝

فَبِأَىِّ ءَالَآءِ رَبِّكُمَا تُكَذِّبَانِ ۝

فِيهِمَا مِن كُلِّ فَـٰكِهَةٍ زَوْجَانِ ۝

فَبِأَىِّ ءَالَآءِ رَبِّكُمَا تُكَذِّبَانِ ۝

مُتَّكِـِٔينَ عَلَىٰ فُرُشٍۭ بَطَآئِنُهَا مِنْ إِسْتَبْرَقٍ وَجَنَى ٱلْجَنَّتَيْنِ دَانٍ ۝

فَبِأَىِّ ءَالَآءِ رَبِّكُمَا تُكَذِّبَانِ ۝

فِيهِنَّ قَـٰصِرَٰتُ ٱلطَّرْفِ لَمْ يَطْمِثْهُنَّ إِنسٌ قَبْلَهُمْ وَلَا جَآنٌّ ۝

فَبِأَىِّ ءَالَآءِ رَبِّكُمَا تُكَذِّبَانِ ۝

58. Even as the ruby are they, even as the finest pearl. [UM]
59. Which of your Lord's boons will ye twain belie? [UM]
60. What is the meed of excellence if it be not excellence? [UM]
61. Which of your Lord's boons will ye twain belie? [UM]
62. And beyond them are two other gardens. [UM]
62. And beyond these are two other gardens. [BC]
63. Which of your Lord's boons will ye twain belie? [UM]
64. Of the deepest green are they. [UM]
65. Which of your Lord's boons will ye twain belie? [UM]
66. Therein are two fountains gushing. [UM] [BC]
67. Which of your Lord's boons will ye twain belie? [UM]
68. Therein is fruit and the date palm, and the pomegranate. [UM] [BC]
69. Which of your Lord's boons will ye twain belie? [UM]
70. Therein are All-excelling lovely ones. [UM]
71. Which of your Lord's boons will ye twain belie? [UM]
72. Huri's secluded in the tents. [UM]

كَأَنَّهُنَّ ٱلْيَاقُوتُ وَٱلْمَرْجَانُ ۝

فَبِأَيِّ ءَالَآءِ رَبِّكُمَا تُكَذِّبَانِ ۝

هَلْ جَزَآءُ ٱلْإِحْسَٰنِ إِلَّا ٱلْإِحْسَٰنُ ۝

فَبِأَيِّ ءَالَآءِ رَبِّكُمَا تُكَذِّبَانِ ۝

وَمِن دُونِهِمَا جَنَّتَانِ ۝

فَبِأَيِّ ءَالَآءِ رَبِّكُمَا تُكَذِّبَانِ ۝

مُدْهَآمَّتَانِ ۝

فَبِأَيِّ ءَالَآءِ رَبِّكُمَا تُكَذِّبَانِ ۝

فِيهِمَا عَيْنَانِ نَضَّاخَتَانِ ۝

فَبِأَيِّ ءَالَآءِ رَبِّكُمَا تُكَذِّبَانِ ۝

فِيهِمَا فَٰكِهَةٌ وَنَخْلٌ وَرُمَّانٌ ۝

فَبِأَيِّ ءَالَآءِ رَبِّكُمَا تُكَذِّبَانِ ۝

فِيهِنَّ خَيْرَٰتٌ حِسَانٌ ۝

فَبِأَيِّ ءَالَآءِ رَبِّكُمَا تُكَذِّبَانِ ۝

حُورٌ مَّقْصُورَٰتٌ فِى ٱلْخِيَامِ ۝

73. Which of your Lord's boons will ye twain belie? [UM]
74. Never until now were they deflowered by man or jinn. [UM]
75. Which of your Lord's boons will ye twain belie? [UM]
76. Therein shall they rest upon tissue of green and upon fabric rarest and loveliest. [UM]
77. Which of your Lord's boons will ye twain belie? [UM]
78. Blessed be the Name of thy Lord in His Majesty and Bounty. [UM]

فَبِأَيِّ آلَاءِ رَبِّكُمَا تُكَذِّبَانِ ۝

لَمْ يَطْمِثْهُنَّ إِنسٌ قَبْلَهُمْ وَلَا جَانٌّ ۝

فَبِأَيِّ آلَاءِ رَبِّكُمَا تُكَذِّبَانِ ۝

مُتَّكِئِينَ عَلَىٰ رَفْرَفٍ خُضْرٍ وَعَبْقَرِيٍّ حِسَانٍ ۝

فَبِأَيِّ آلَاءِ رَبِّكُمَا تُكَذِّبَانِ ۝

تَبَارَكَ اسْمُ رَبِّكَ ذِي الْجَلَالِ وَالْإِكْرَامِ ۝

Al-Wāqiʿah (LVI)

In the Name of God, the Infinitely Good, the Ever-Merciful

10. The foremost in excellence. [ICCT]
10. The Foremost are the Foremost. [SS]
11. It is they who are brought nigh. [SS]
11. Those who are brought near [to God]. [L-QD]
11. They are those who are brought near. [L-QOS]
13. A multitude of those of old. [ICCT]
13. Many among the earlier generations. [SS] [RS]
13. Many amongst the first generations. [WS]
13. Many in former generations. [L-QD]
14. And a few of those of the later time. [ICCT]
14. And few among the later generations. [SS] [RS]
14. And few amongst the later generations. [WS]
14. And few in later generations. [L-QD]
25. Therein (in Paradise) hear they no vain word, nor any incitement to sin. [UM]
25. There (in the Garden of Paradise) they shall hear no idle speaking nor any incitement to evil. [UM]
25. ... they hear no vain talk or incitement to evil. [UM]
26. Only the utterance: Peace, Peace. [UM]
26. But only the word; Peace. Peace. [UM]
26. Only the word: Peace. Peace. [UM]
38. ... those on the right hand. [ICCT]
38. ... the Companions of the Right. [SS]
39. A multitude of those of old. [ICCT]
39. Many among the earlier generations. [SS]
39. Many among the first. [SS]
39. Many in early generations. [L-QD]
40. And a multitude of those of later time. [ICCT]
40. And many among the later generations. [SS]

(٥٦) سُورَةُ الوَاقِعَةِ
بِسْمِ اللَّهِ الرَّحْمَٰنِ الرَّحِيمِ

وَالسَّابِقُونَ السَّابِقُونَ ۝

أُولَٰئِكَ الْمُقَرَّبُونَ ۝

ثُلَّةٌ مِّنَ الْأَوَّلِينَ ۝

وَقَلِيلٌ مِّنَ الْآخِرِينَ ۝

لَا يَسْمَعُونَ فِيهَا لَغْوًا وَلَا تَأْثِيمًا ۝

إِلَّا قِيلًا سَلَامًا سَلَامًا ۝

لِأَصْحَابِ الْيَمِينِ ۝

ثُلَّةٌ مِّنَ الْأَوَّلِينَ ۝

وَثُلَّةٌ مِّنَ الْآخِرِينَ ۝

40. And many among the last. [RS]
40. And many in later generations. [L-QD]
41. The companions of the Left... [SS]
77. Verily this is an All-bountiful recitation. [QACI]
77. Verily it is an All-bountiful utterance. [SQCI]
78. In a hidden book. [QACI] [SQCI]
79. Which none toucheth save the purified. [QACI]
79. Touched by none save the purified. [SQCI]
80. A revelation from the Lord of the worlds. [QACI] [SQCI]
85. We are nearer to him than ye are, although ye see not. [SS]
85. We are nearer to him [the dying man about whom ye are gathered] than ye are but ye see not. [NOS]

وَثُلَّةٌ مِّنَ ٱلْآخِرِينَ ۝

وَأَصْحَٰبُ ٱلشِّمَالِ مَآ أَصْحَٰبُ ٱلشِّمَالِ ۝

إِنَّهُۥ لَقُرْءَانٌ كَرِيمٌ ۝

فِى كِتَٰبٍ مَّكْنُونٍ ۝

لَّا يَمَسُّهُۥٓ إِلَّا ٱلْمُطَهَّرُونَ ۝

تَنزِيلٌ مِّن رَّبِّ ٱلْعَٰلَمِينَ ۝

وَنَحْنُ أَقْرَبُ إِلَيْهِ مِنكُمْ وَلَٰكِن لَّا تُبْصِرُونَ ۝

Al-Ḥadīd (LVII)

In the Name of God, the Infinitely Good, the Ever-Merciful

3. He is the First and the Last and the Outward and the Inward and He has knowledge of all things. [UM]

3. He is the First and the Last and the Outwardly Manifest and the Inwardly Hidden... [SS] [S] [SA]

3. He is the First and the Last and the Outward and the Inward... [WS] [QACI] [RS] [SQCI]

4. ...He is with you wheresoe'er ye be... [SS]

11. Who will lend unto God a goodly loan that He may double it for him and add thereunto a bountiful reward. [WS]

16. ...a long length of time passed over them so that their hearts were hardened... [RS]

16. ...that their hearts were hardened... [L-II]

(٥٧) سُورَةُ الْحَدِيدِ

بِسْمِ اللَّهِ الرَّحْمَنِ الرَّحِيمِ

هُوَ الْأَوَّلُ وَالْآخِرُ وَالظَّاهِرُ وَالْبَاطِنُ وَهُوَ بِكُلِّ شَيْءٍ عَلِيمٌ ۝

هُوَ الَّذِي خَلَقَ السَّمَوَاتِ وَالْأَرْضَ فِي سِتَّةِ أَيَّامٍ ثُمَّ اسْتَوَى عَلَى الْعَرْشِ يَعْلَمُ مَا يَلِجُ فِي الْأَرْضِ وَمَا يَخْرُجُ مِنْهَا وَمَا يَنزِلُ مِنَ السَّمَاءِ وَمَا يَعْرُجُ فِيهَا وَهُوَ مَعَكُمْ أَيْنَ مَا كُنتُمْ وَاللَّهُ بِمَا تَعْمَلُونَ بَصِيرٌ ۝

مَن ذَا الَّذِي يُقْرِضُ اللَّهَ قَرْضًا حَسَنًا فَيُضَاعِفَهُ لَهُ وَلَهُ أَجْرٌ كَرِيمٌ ۝

أَلَمْ يَأْنِ لِلَّذِينَ آمَنُوا أَن تَخْشَعَ قُلُوبُهُمْ لِذِكْرِ اللَّهِ وَمَا نَزَلَ مِنَ الْحَقِّ وَلَا يَكُونُوا كَالَّذِينَ أُوتُوا الْكِتَابَ مِن قَبْلُ فَطَالَ عَلَيْهِمُ الْأَمَدُ فَقَسَتْ قُلُوبُهُمْ وَكَثِيرٌ مِّنْهُمْ فَاسِقُونَ ۝

Al-Ḥashr (LIX)

In the Name of God, the Infinitely Good, the Ever-Merciful

8. The poor emigrants who have been driven from their homes... [M]

14. ...ill feeling is rife amongst them. Thou countest them as one whole, but their hearts are divided... [M]

21. If We had sent down this Qur'ān upon a mountain, thou wouldst have seen it humbled, split asunder through fear of God. We coin such similitudes for men, that they may meditate. [L-QOS]

21. If We caused this Qoran to descend upon a mountain, thou wouldst see the mountain lying prostrate with humility, rent asunder through fear of God... [SS]

21. If We had sent down this Qur'ān upon a mountain, thou wouldst have seen it lying prostrate in humility, rent asunder through fear of God... [QACI] [SQCI]

21. If We sent down this Koran upon a mountain, thou wouldst see it prostrate in humility, rent asunder through fear of God... [M]

21. If We had sent down this Quran upon a mountain, thou wouldst have seen it humbled, split asunder out of the fear of God... [NOS]

21. If We had sent down this Qur'ān upon a mountain, thou wouldst have seen it lying prostrate in humility, rent asunder through fear of God... [SA]

(٥٩) سُورَةُ الحَشْرِ

بِسْمِ ٱللَّهِ ٱلرَّحْمَٰنِ ٱلرَّحِيمِ

لِلْفُقَرَاءِ ٱلْمُهَٰجِرِينَ ٱلَّذِينَ أُخْرِجُوا۟ مِن دِيَٰرِهِمْ وَأَمْوَٰلِهِمْ يَبْتَغُونَ فَضْلًا مِّنَ ٱللَّهِ وَرِضْوَٰنًا وَيَنصُرُونَ ٱللَّهَ وَرَسُولَهُۥٓ أُو۟لَٰٓئِكَ هُمُ ٱلصَّٰدِقُونَ ۝

لَا يُقَٰتِلُونَكُمْ جَمِيعًا إِلَّا فِى قُرًى مُّحَصَّنَةٍ أَوْ مِن وَرَآءِ جُدُرٍۭ بَأْسُهُم بَيْنَهُمْ شَدِيدٌ تَحْسَبُهُمْ جَمِيعًا وَقُلُوبُهُمْ شَتَّىٰ ذَٰلِكَ بِأَنَّهُمْ قَوْمٌ لَّا يَعْقِلُونَ ۝

لَوْ أَنزَلْنَا هَٰذَا ٱلْقُرْءَانَ عَلَىٰ جَبَلٍ لَّرَأَيْتَهُۥ خَٰشِعًا مُّتَصَدِّعًا مِّنْ خَشْيَةِ ٱللَّهِ وَتِلْكَ ٱلْأَمْثَٰلُ نَضْرِبُهَا لِلنَّاسِ لَعَلَّهُمْ يَتَفَكَّرُونَ ۝

Al-Mumtaḥanah (LX)

In the Name of God, the Infinitely Good, the Ever-Merciful

7. It may be that God will establish love between you and those with whom ye are at enmity... [M]

Aṣ-Ṣaff (LXI)

In the Name of God, the Infinitely Good, the Ever-Merciful

4. Verily God loveth those who fight for His cause in ranks as if they were a close-built block. [M]

9. He it is who has sent His Messenger with the guidance and the Religion of Truth, that He may make it prevail over all religion, though the idolaters be averse. [L-UQ]

Al-Munāfiqūn (LXIII)

In the Name of God, the Infinitely Good, the Ever-Merciful

9. ...let neither your possessions nor children divert you from the remembrance of God... [SS]

(٦٠) سُورَةُ الْمُمْتَحَنَةِ

بِسْمِ اللَّهِ الرَّحْمَنِ الرَّحِيمِ

عَسَى اللَّهُ أَن يَجْعَلَ بَيْنَكُمْ وَبَيْنَ الَّذِينَ عَادَيْتُم مِّنْهُم مَّوَدَّةً وَاللَّهُ قَدِيرٌ وَاللَّهُ غَفُورٌ رَّحِيمٌ ۝

(٦١) سُورَةُ الصَّفِّ

بِسْمِ اللَّهِ الرَّحْمَنِ الرَّحِيمِ

إِنَّ اللَّهَ يُحِبُّ الَّذِينَ يُقَاتِلُونَ فِي سَبِيلِهِ صَفًّا كَأَنَّهُم بُنْيَانٌ مَّرْصُوصٌ ۝ هُوَ الَّذِي أَرْسَلَ رَسُولَهُ بِالْهُدَى وَدِينِ الْحَقِّ لِيُظْهِرَهُ عَلَى الدِّينِ كُلِّهِ وَلَوْ كَرِهَ الْمُشْرِكُونَ ۝

(٦٣) سُورَةُ الْمُنَافِقُونَ

بِسْمِ اللَّهِ الرَّحْمَنِ الرَّحِيمِ

يَا أَيُّهَا الَّذِينَ آمَنُوا لَا تُلْهِكُمْ أَمْوَالُكُمْ وَلَا أَوْلَادُكُمْ عَن ذِكْرِ اللَّهِ وَمَن يَفْعَلْ ذَلِكَ فَأُولَئِكَ هُمُ الْخَاسِرُونَ ۝

At-Taḥrīm (LXVI)
In the Name of God, the Infinitely Good, the Ever-Merciful

1. O Prophet why bannest thou, to please thy wives, that which God hath made lawful unto thee?... [M]

4. If ye twain repent unto God ye have cause, for your hearts were set upon the ban; and if ye aid each the other against him, verily God, even He, is his Protecting Friend, and Gabriel, and the elect of the faithful; and beyond these, the angels are massed to help him. [M]

5. It may be, if he divorce you, that his Lord will give him wives in your stead who are better than you, submissive unto God, believing, devout, penitent, inclined unto worship and fasting, widows and virgin maids. [M]

10. God citeth as an example for those who disbelieve, the wife of Noah and the wife of Lot. They were under two righteous men from amongst Our slaves, men whom they betrayed and who thus availed them naught against God; and it was said unto both: Enter ye the fire with them who enter it. [M]

11. And God citeth as example for those who believe the wife of Pharaoh when she said: 'My Lord, build for me a dwelling unto Thee in Paradise, and save me from Pharaoh and his deeds, and save me from the people who transgress.' [M]

12. And Maryam, daughter of ʿImrān, who kept intact her virginity; and We breathed into her of Our Spirit; and she believed in the Words of her Lord and in His Books, and was one of those who are absorbed in Invocation. [UM]

(٦٦) سُورَةُ التَّحْرِيمِ

بِسْمِ اللَّهِ الرَّحْمَنِ الرَّحِيمِ

يَاأَيُّهَا النَّبِيُّ لِمَ تُحَرِّمُ مَا أَحَلَّ اللَّهُ لَكَ تَبْتَغِي مَرْضَاتَ أَزْوَاجِكَ وَاللَّهُ غَفُورٌ رَحِيمٌ ۝

إِنْ تَتُوبَا إِلَى اللَّهِ فَقَدْ صَغَتْ قُلُوبُكُمَا وَإِنْ تَظَاهَرَا عَلَيْهِ فَإِنَّ اللَّهَ هُوَ مَوْلَاهُ وَجِبْرِيلُ وَصَالِحُ الْمُؤْمِنِينَ وَالْمَلَائِكَةُ بَعْدَ ذَلِكَ ظَهِيرٌ ۝

عَسَى رَبُّهُ إِنْ طَلَّقَكُنَّ أَنْ يُبْدِلَهُ أَزْوَاجًا خَيْرًا مِنْكُنَّ مُسْلِمَاتٍ مُؤْمِنَاتٍ قَانِتَاتٍ تَائِبَاتٍ عَابِدَاتٍ سَائِحَاتٍ ثَيِّبَاتٍ وَأَبْكَارًا ۝

ضَرَبَ اللَّهُ مَثَلًا لِلَّذِينَ كَفَرُوا امْرَأَتَ نُوحٍ وَامْرَأَتَ لُوطٍ كَانَتَا تَحْتَ عَبْدَيْنِ مِنْ عِبَادِنَا صَالِحَيْنِ فَخَانَتَاهُمَا فَلَمْ يُغْنِيَا عَنْهُمَا مِنَ اللَّهِ شَيْئًا وَقِيلَ ادْخُلَا النَّارَ مَعَ الدَّاخِلِينَ ۝

وَضَرَبَ اللَّهُ مَثَلًا لِلَّذِينَ آمَنُوا امْرَأَتَ فِرْعَوْنَ إِذْ قَالَتْ رَبِّ ابْنِ لِي عِنْدَكَ بَيْتًا فِي الْجَنَّةِ وَنَجِّنِي مِنْ فِرْعَوْنَ وَعَمَلِهِ وَنَجِّنِي مِنَ الْقَوْمِ الظَّالِمِينَ ۝

وَمَرْيَمَ ابْنَتَ عِمْرَانَ الَّتِي أَحْصَنَتْ فَرْجَهَا فَنَفَخْنَا فِيهِ مِنْ رُوحِنَا وَصَدَّقَتْ بِكَلِمَاتِ رَبِّهَا وَكُتُبِهِ وَكَانَتْ مِنَ الْقَانِتِينَ ۝

12. [God citeth as example] Maryam, daughter of 'Imrān, who kept inviolate her virginity; and We breathed therein of Our Spirit; and she accepted the Words of her Lord and His Books; and she was of those who are absorbed in the orison. [UM]

12. And Mary, the daughter of 'Imrān, who kept chaste her womb and We breathed therein of Our Spirit. And she testified to the truth of the words of her Lord and His scriptures, and was of those who are absorbed in prayer. [M]

وَمَرْيَمَ ٱبْنَتَ عِمْرَٰنَ ٱلَّتِىٓ أَحْصَنَتْ فَرْجَهَا فَنَفَخْنَا فِيهِ مِن رُّوحِنَا وَصَدَّقَتْ بِكَلِمَٰتِ رَبِّهَا وَكُتُبِهِۦ وَكَانَتْ مِنَ ٱلْقَٰنِتِينَ ۝

THE HOLY QUR'ĀN: SELECTED VERSES

Al-Qalam (LXVIII)
In the Name of God, the Infinitely Good, the Ever-Merciful

1. Nūn. By the pen, and by that which they write. [M]
2. No madman art thou, through the grace of thy Lord unto thee. [M]
3. And thine shall be a meed unfailing. [M]
4. And verily thou art [O Prophet] of an immense nature. [UM]
4. Verily thou art of a tremendous nature. [PI] [SS]
4. Verily thou art beyond all doubt of a nature of wondrous magnitude. [QACI]
4. And verily of an immense magnitude is thy nature. [SCR-SA] [M] [SA] [RS] [SQCI] [L-QOS]

Al-Jinn (LXXII)
In the Name of God, the Infinitely Good, the Ever-Merciful

1. Say: it hath been revealed unto me that a company of the jinn gave ear, and then said: Verily we have heard a wondrous recitation. [M]
2. Which guideth unto rightness, and we believe in it... [M]

(٦٨) سُورَةُ القَلَمِ

بِسْمِ اللَّهِ الرَّحْمَٰنِ الرَّحِيمِ

نٓ ۚ وَالْقَلَمِ وَمَا يَسْطُرُونَ ۝

مَا أَنتَ بِنِعْمَةِ رَبِّكَ بِمَجْنُونٍ ۝

وَإِنَّ لَكَ لَأَجْرًا غَيْرَ مَمْنُونٍ ۝

وَإِنَّكَ لَعَلَىٰ خُلُقٍ عَظِيمٍ ۝

(٧٢) سُورَةُ الجِنِّ

بِسْمِ اللَّهِ الرَّحْمَٰنِ الرَّحِيمِ

قُلْ أُوحِيَ إِلَيَّ أَنَّهُ اسْتَمَعَ نَفَرٌ مِّنَ الْجِنِّ فَقَالُوٓا۟ إِنَّا سَمِعْنَا قُرْءَانًا عَجَبًا ۝

يَهْدِىٓ إِلَى الرُّشْدِ فَـَٔامَنَّا بِهِۦ ۖ وَلَن نُّشْرِكَ بِرَبِّنَآ أَحَدًا ۝

THE HOLY QUR'ĀN: SELECTED VERSES

Al-Muzzammil (LXXIII)
In the Name of God, the Infinitely Good, the Ever-Merciful

1. O thou who art wrapped in thy raiment. [M]
1. O thou who art enshrouded in thy raiment. [L-QOS]
2. Keep vigil all the night save a little. [SS] [S] [M] [L-QOS]
2. Keep vigil the night long save a little. [NOS]
3. Half the night or lessen than half a little. [M]
3. A half thereof, or abate a little thereof. [NOS]
3. A half of it, or take from that a little. [L-QOS]
4. Or add to it, and with care and clarity chant the Koran. [M]
4. Or add [a little] thereto and chant the Quran in measure. [NOS]
4. Or add to it, and recite the Qur'ān with exact recital. [L-QOS]
5. Verily We shall load thee with a word of heavy weight. [M]
8. Invoke the Name of thy Lord and consecrate thyself unto Him with a total consecration. [UM]
8. Invoke in remembrance the Name of thy Lord, and devote thyself to Him with an utter devotion. [OS] [SS] [S] [M] [NOS] [L-QOS]
9. Lord of the east and of the west—no god but He. Him therefore take, on Him place thy reliance. [M]
10. Bear with patience what they say, and part from them with a courteous farewell. [M]
17. ...a day that shall turn the hair of children grey. [M]
19. Surely this [the Revelation] is a Reminder; so let him who will, take unto his Lord a way. [NOS]
19. Verily this is a reminder, so let him who will take unto his Lord a way. [L-QOS]

(٧٣) سُورَةُ المُزَّمِّلِ

بِسْمِ اللَّهِ الرَّحْمَنِ الرَّحِيمِ

يَـٰٓأَيُّهَا ٱلْمُزَّمِّلُ ۝

قُمِ ٱلَّيْلَ إِلَّا قَلِيلًا ۝

نِّصْفَهُۥ أَوِ ٱنقُصْ مِنْهُ قَلِيلًا ۝

أَوْ زِدْ عَلَيْهِ وَرَتِّلِ ٱلْقُرْءَانَ تَرْتِيلًا ۝

إِنَّا سَنُلْقِى عَلَيْكَ قَوْلًا ثَقِيلًا ۝

وَٱذْكُرِ ٱسْمَ رَبِّكَ وَتَبَتَّلْ إِلَيْهِ تَبْتِيلًا ۝

رَّبُّ ٱلْمَشْرِقِ وَٱلْمَغْرِبِ لَآ إِلَـٰهَ إِلَّا هُوَ فَٱتَّخِذْهُ وَكِيلًا ۝

وَٱصْبِرْ عَلَىٰ مَا يَقُولُونَ وَٱهْجُرْهُمْ هَجْرًا جَمِيلًا ۝

فَكَيْفَ تَتَّقُونَ إِن كَفَرْتُمْ يَوْمًا يَجْعَلُ ٱلْوِلْدَٰنَ شِيبًا ۝

إِنَّ هَـٰذِهِۦ تَذْكِرَةٌ ۖ فَمَن شَآءَ ٱتَّخَذَ إِلَىٰ رَبِّهِۦ سَبِيلًا ۝

20. Verily thy Lord knoweth that thou keepest vigil well-nigh two thirds of the night, and sometimes half of it or a third of it, thou and a group of those that are with thee. God measureth the night and the day. He knoweth that ye will not be able to come up to the full measure of it, and therefore hath He relented unto you. Recite then even so much of the Koran as is easy for you... [M]

20. Thy Lord knoweth that thou keepest vigil nearly two thirds of the night, or half the night or a third thereof, thou and a group of those that are with thee... [OS]

20. Verily thy Lord knoweth that thou keepest vigil nearly two thirds of the night, or its half, or a third, thou and a group of those who are with thee... [L-QOS]

20. ...a group of those that are with thee... [NOS]

20. ...whatever good ye have accomplished for yourselves in advance, ye will find it with Allah; but it will be better [than your action] and a greater recompense [than that which your action merits]. And ask forgiveness of Allah; verily, Allah is full of forgiveness and mercy. [UM]

إِنَّ رَبَّكَ يَعْلَمُ أَنَّكَ تَقُومُ أَدْنَىٰ مِن ثُلُثَيِ ٱلَّيْلِ وَنِصْفَهُۥ وَثُلُثَهُۥ وَطَآئِفَةٌ مِّنَ ٱلَّذِينَ مَعَكَ ۚ وَٱللَّهُ يُقَدِّرُ ٱلَّيْلَ وَٱلنَّهَارَ ۚ عَلِمَ أَن لَّن تُحْصُوهُ فَتَابَ عَلَيْكُمْ ۖ فَٱقْرَءُوا۟ مَا تَيَسَّرَ مِنَ ٱلْقُرْءَانِ ۚ عَلِمَ أَن سَيَكُونُ مِنكُم مَّرْضَىٰ ۙ وَءَاخَرُونَ يَضْرِبُونَ فِى ٱلْأَرْضِ يَبْتَغُونَ مِن فَضْلِ ٱللَّهِ ۙ وَءَاخَرُونَ يُقَٰتِلُونَ فِى سَبِيلِ ٱللَّهِ ۖ فَٱقْرَءُوا۟ مَا تَيَسَّرَ مِنْهُ ۚ وَأَقِيمُوا۟ ٱلصَّلَوٰةَ وَءَاتُوا۟ ٱلزَّكَوٰةَ وَأَقْرِضُوا۟ ٱللَّهَ قَرْضًا حَسَنًا ۚ وَمَا تُقَدِّمُوا۟ لِأَنفُسِكُم مِّنْ خَيْرٍ تَجِدُوهُ عِندَ ٱللَّهِ هُوَ خَيْرًا وَأَعْظَمَ أَجْرًا ۚ وَٱسْتَغْفِرُوا۟ ٱللَّهَ ۖ إِنَّ ٱللَّهَ غَفُورٌ رَّحِيمٌ ۝

THE HOLY QUR'ĀN: SELECTED VERSES

Al-Muddaththir (LXXIV)

In the Name of God, the Infinitely Good, the Ever-Merciful

1. O thou who art wrapped in thy cloak. [M] [L-QOS]
2. Arise and warn! [M] [L-QOS]
3. Thy Lord magnify! [M]
4. Thy raiment purify! [M]
5. Defilement shun! [M]
8. For when the trumpet shall be blown. [M]
9. That shall be a day of anguish. [M]
10. Not of ease, for disbelievers. [M]

Al-Qiyāmah (LXXV)

In the Name of God, the Infinitely Good, the Ever-Merciful

2. ...the Ever-upbraiding soul. [M]

(٧٤) سُورَةُ المُدَّثِّرِ

بِسْمِ اللَّهِ الرَّحْمَنِ الرَّحِيمِ

يَا أَيُّهَا الْمُدَّثِّرُ ۝

قُمْ فَأَنذِرْ ۝

وَرَبَّكَ فَكَبِّرْ ۝

وَثِيَابَكَ فَطَهِّرْ ۝

وَالرُّجْزَ فَاهْجُرْ ۝

فَإِذَا نُقِرَ فِي النَّاقُورِ ۝

فَذَلِكَ يَوْمَئِذٍ يَوْمٌ عَسِيرٌ ۝

عَلَى الْكَافِرِينَ غَيْرُ يَسِيرٍ ۝

(٧٥) سُورَةُ الْقِيَامَةِ

بِسْمِ اللَّهِ الرَّحْمَنِ الرَّحِيمِ

وَلَا أُقْسِمُ بِالنَّفْسِ اللَّوَّامَةِ ۝

Al-Insān (LXXVI)

In the Name of God, the Infinitely Good, the Ever-Merciful

5. Verily the righteous drink of a cup that is flavoured with camphor. [BC]
6. Flavoured from a fountain whereof drink the slaves of God, gushing it forth in copious draughts. [BC]
26. ...glorify Him the livelong night. [SS] [S] [L-QOS]
29. Surely this [the Revelation] is a Reminder; so let him who will, take unto his Lord a way. [NOS]
29. Verily this is a reminder, so let him who will take unto his Lord a way. [L-QOS]

Al-Mursalāt (LXXVII)

In the Name of God, the Infinitely Good, the Ever-Merciful

35. This is a day on which they speak not. [SS]
36. Nor are they permitted to proffer excuses. [SS]

(٧٦) سورة الإنسان

بسم الله الرحمن الرحيم

إِنَّ ٱلۡأَبۡرَارَ يَشۡرَبُونَ مِن كَأۡسٍ كَانَ مِزَاجُهَا كَافُورًا ۝

عَيۡنًا يَشۡرَبُ بِهَا عِبَادُ ٱللَّهِ يُفَجِّرُونَهَا تَفۡجِيرًا ۝

وَمِنَ ٱلَّيۡلِ فَٱسۡجُدۡ لَهُۥ وَسَبِّحۡهُ لَيۡلًا طَوِيلًا ۝

إِنَّ هَٰذِهِۦ تَذۡكِرَةٞ فَمَن شَآءَ ٱتَّخَذَ إِلَىٰ رَبِّهِۦ سَبِيلًا ۝

(٧٧) سورة المرسلات

بسم الله الرحمن الرحيم

هَٰذَا يَوۡمُ لَا يَنطِقُونَ ۝

وَلَا يُؤۡذَنُ لَهُمۡ فَيَعۡتَذِرُونَ ۝

An-Nabā' (LXXVIII)

In the Name of God, the Infinitely Good, the Ever-Merciful

10. We have made the night as a covering. [SS]
11. ... and the day as for livelihood. [SS]

ʿAbasa (LXXX)

In the Name of God, the Infinitely Good, the Ever-Merciful

1. He frowned and turned away. [M]
2. Because the blind man came to him. [M]
5. As to him who sufficeth unto himself. [M]
6. With him thou art engrossed. [M]
7. Yet is it no concern of thine if purified he be not. [M]
8. But as for him who cometh unto thee in eager earnestness. [M]
9. And in fear of God. [M]
10. From him thou art drawn away. [M]

(٧٨) سُورَةُ النَّبَإِ

بِسْمِ اللَّهِ الرَّحْمَنِ الرَّحِيمِ

وَجَعَلْنَا الَّيْلَ لِبَاسًا ۝

وَجَعَلْنَا النَّهَارَ مَعَاشًا ۝

(٨٠) سُورَةُ عَبَسَ

بِسْمِ اللَّهِ الرَّحْمَنِ الرَّحِيمِ

عَبَسَ وَتَوَلَّى ۝

أَن جَاءَهُ الْأَعْمَى ۝

أَمَّا مَنِ اسْتَغْنَى ۝

فَأَنتَ لَهُ تَصَدَّى ۝

وَمَا عَلَيْكَ أَلَّا يَزَّكَّى ۝

وَأَمَّا مَن جَاءَكَ يَسْعَى ۝

وَهُوَ يَخْشَى ۝

فَأَنتَ عَنْهُ تَلَهَّى ۝

Al-Muṭaffifīn (LXXXIII)

In the Name of God, the Infinitely Good, the Ever-Merciful

7. ...the iniquitous... [OS]
13. When Our Revelations are recited unto him, he saith: Tales of the men of old. [M]
14. Nay, but their earnings are even as rust over their hearts. [M]
18. ...the righteous... [OS]
21. ...those brought near to God. [OS]
25. They are given to drink of a pure wine sealed. [BC]
26. Whose seal is musk—for this let the strivers strive. [BC]
27. And its flavour cometh from Tasnīm. [BC]
28. A fountain whence drink they that are brought nigh. [BC]

Al-Burūj (LXXXV)

In the Name of God, the Infinitely Good, the Ever-Merciful

22. On a Guarded Tablet. [QACI]
22. On an inviolable tablet. [M]

(٨٣) سُورَةُ الْمُطَفِّفِينَ

بِسْمِ اللَّهِ الرَّحْمَنِ الرَّحِيمِ

كَلَّا إِنَّ كِتَابَ الْفُجَّارِ لَفِي سِجِّينٍ ۝

إِذَا تُتْلَى عَلَيْهِ ءَايَاتُنَا قَالَ أَسَاطِيرُ الْأَوَّلِينَ ۝

كَلَّا بَلْ رَانَ عَلَى قُلُوبِهِم مَّا كَانُوا يَكْسِبُونَ ۝

كَلَّا إِنَّ كِتَابَ الْأَبْرَارِ لَفِي عِلِّيِّينَ ۝

يَشْهَدُهُ الْمُقَرَّبُونَ ۝

يُسْقَوْنَ مِن رَّحِيقٍ مَّخْتُومٍ ۝

خِتَامُهُ مِسْكٌ وَفِي ذَٰلِكَ فَلْيَتَنَافَسِ الْمُتَنَافِسُونَ ۝

وَمِزَاجُهُ مِن تَسْنِيمٍ ۝

عَيْنًا يَشْرَبُ بِهَا الْمُقَرَّبُونَ ۝

(٨٥) سُورَةُ الْبُرُوجِ

بِسْمِ اللَّهِ الرَّحْمَنِ الرَّحِيمِ

فِي لَوْحٍ مَّحْفُوظٍ ۝

Aṭ-Ṭāriq (LXXXVI)
In the Name of God, the Infinitely Good, the Ever-Merciful

17. Deal gently with the disbelievers, give them respite for a while. [M]

Al-Ghāshiyah (LXXXVIII)
In the Name of God, the Infinitely Good, the Ever-Merciful

17. Will they not behold the camels, how they are created? [M] [NOS] [RS] [L-II]
18. And the firmament, how it is raised aloft? [M] [NOS] [RS] [L-II]
19. And the mountains, how they are established? [M] [NOS] [RS] [L-II]
20. And the earth, how it is spread? [M] [NOS] [RS] [L-II]

Al-Fajr (LXXXIX)
In the Name of God, the Infinitely Good, the Ever-Merciful

27. O thou soul which art at peace. [BC] [WS] [M] [NOS] [RS] [L-QD]
28. Return unto thy Lord, glad in His Gladness! [BC]
28. Return unto thy Lord with (in) gladness that is thine in Him and His in thee. [WS] [M] [RS] [L-QD]
28. Return unto thy Lord, pleased thou and whelmed in His good pleasure. [NOS]
28. Return unto thy Lord gladly and accepted in mutual gladness. [PT]
29. Enter thou among My slaves! [BC] [WS] [M] [NOS] [RS] [L-QD]
30. Enter thou My Paradise! [BC] [WS] [M] [NOS] [RS] [L-QD]

(٨٦) سُورَةُ الطَّارِقِ

بِسْمِ اللَّهِ الرَّحْمَٰنِ الرَّحِيمِ

فَمَهِّلِ ٱلْكَٰفِرِينَ أَمْهِلْهُمْ رُوَيْدًۢا ۝

(٨٨) سُورَةُ الْغَاشِيَةِ

بِسْمِ اللَّهِ الرَّحْمَٰنِ الرَّحِيمِ

أَفَلَا يَنظُرُونَ إِلَى ٱلْإِبِلِ كَيْفَ خُلِقَتْ ۝

وَإِلَى ٱلسَّمَاءِ كَيْفَ رُفِعَتْ ۝

وَإِلَى ٱلْجِبَالِ كَيْفَ نُصِبَتْ ۝

وَإِلَى ٱلْأَرْضِ كَيْفَ سُطِحَتْ ۝

(٨٩) سُورَةُ الْفَجْرِ

بِسْمِ اللَّهِ الرَّحْمَٰنِ الرَّحِيمِ

يَٰٓأَيَّتُهَا ٱلنَّفْسُ ٱلْمُطْمَئِنَّةُ ۝

ٱرْجِعِىٓ إِلَىٰ رَبِّكِ رَاضِيَةً مَّرْضِيَّةً ۝

فَٱدْخُلِى فِى عِبَٰدِى ۝

وَٱدْخُلِى جَنَّتِى ۝

Aḍ-Ḍuḥā (XCIII)

In the Name of God, the Infinitely Good, the Ever-Merciful

1. By the morning brightness. [M]
2. And by the night when it is still. [M]
3. Thy Lord hath not forsaken thee nor doth He hate thee. [M]
4. And certainly the hereafter is better for thee than the here-below. [UM]
4. And the hereafter is better for thee than this world. [UM]
4. And the last shall be better for thee than the first. [M]
5. And certainly thy Lord shall give unto thee, and thou shalt be satisfied. [UM]
5. Verily thy Lord shall give and give unto thee and thou shalt be satisfied. [WS]
5. And they Lord shall give and give unto thee, and thou shall be satisfied. [M]
6. Hath He not found thee an orphan and sheltered thee? [M]
7. And found thee astray and guided thee? [M]
8. And found thee needy and enriched thee? [M]
9. So for the orphan, oppress him not. [M]
10. And for the beggar, repel him not. [M]
11. And for the bountiful grace of thy Lord, proclaim it! [M]

(٩٣) سُورَةُ الضُّحَىٰ

بِسْمِ اللَّهِ الرَّحْمَٰنِ الرَّحِيمِ

وَالضُّحَىٰ ۝

وَاللَّيْلِ إِذَا سَجَىٰ ۝

مَا وَدَّعَكَ رَبُّكَ وَمَا قَلَىٰ ۝

وَلَلْآخِرَةُ خَيْرٌ لَّكَ مِنَ الْأُولَىٰ ۝

وَلَسَوْفَ يُعْطِيكَ رَبُّكَ فَتَرْضَىٰ ۝

أَلَمْ يَجِدْكَ يَتِيمًا فَآوَىٰ ۝

وَوَجَدَكَ ضَالًّا فَهَدَىٰ ۝

وَوَجَدَكَ عَائِلًا فَأَغْنَىٰ ۝

فَأَمَّا الْيَتِيمَ فَلَا تَقْهَرْ ۝

وَأَمَّا السَّائِلَ فَلَا تَنْهَرْ ۝

وَأَمَّا بِنِعْمَةِ رَبِّكَ فَحَدِّثْ ۝

THE HOLY QUR'ĀN: SELECTED VERSES

Ash-Sharḥ (XCIV)
In the Name of God, the Infinitely Good, the Ever-Merciful

1. Have we not expanded thy breast. [UM]
5. In truth, after difficulty cometh ease. [UM]
5. Verily with hardship cometh ease. [M]

At-Tīn (XCV)
In the Name of God, the Infinitely Good, the Ever-Merciful

1. By the fig and the olive. [UM]
2. And Mount Sinai. [UM]
3. And this safe land. [UM]
4. Verily We created man in the fairest uprightness. [UM] [ICCT] [SA]
4. Verily We created man in the fairest rectitude. [BC] [RS]
4. ...in the most perfect rectitude. [L-II]
5. Then cast We him down to be the lowest of the low. [UM] [BC] [RS] [L-II]
5. Then We reduced him to be the lowest of the low. [ICCT]
6. Yet not those that believe and that act in piety, for theirs is a meed unfailing. [UM]
6. Except for those who believe and who do the good deeds that piety demands... [RS]
7. What then shall make thee belie hereafter the reckoning? [UM]
8. Is not God the wisest of judges? [UM]

(٩٤) سورة الشرح

بسم الله الرحمن الرحيم

ألم نشرح لك صدرك ۝

فإن مع العسر يسرا ۝

(٩٥) سورة التين

بسم الله الرحمن الرحيم

والتين والزيتون ۝

وطور سينين ۝

وهذا البلد الأمين ۝

لقد خلقنا الإنسن في أحسن تقويم ۝

ثم رددنه أسفل سفلين ۝

إلا الذين ءامنوا وعملوا الصلحت فلهم أجر غير ممنون ۝

فما يكذبك بعد بالدين ۝

أليس الله بأحكم الحكمين ۝

THE HOLY QUR'ĀN: SELECTED VERSES

Al-ʿAlaq (XCVI)
In the Name of God, the Infinitely Good, the Ever-Merciful

1. Recite in the name of thy Lord who created. [M]
2. He createth man from a clot of blood. [M]
3. Recite; and thy Lord is the Most Bountiful. [M]
4. He who hath taught by the pen. [M]
5. Taught man what he knew not. [M]
19. ... prostrate thyself and draw nigh (to God). [SS] [S]
19. ... prostrate thyself and draw nigh. [OS] [NOS] [RS] [L-QOS]

Al-Qadr (XCVII)
In the Name of God, the Infinitely Good, the Ever-Merciful

1. Verily We have revealed it in the Night of Worth. [UM]
1. Verily We sent it down in the Night of Power. [BC]
1. Verily We sent it down in the *Laylati'l-Qadr*. [L-QOS]
2. And how canst thou tell the Night of Worth? [UM]
2. And how canst thou tell the Night of Power? [BC]
2. And what will tell thee what the *Laylatu'l-Qadr* is? [L-QOS]
3. The Night of Worth is better than a thousand months. [UM] [M]
3. The Night of Power is better than a thousand months. [BC] [WS]
3. The *Laylatu'l-Qadr* is better than a thousand months. [L-QOS]
4. The angels and the spirit descend therein by the leave of their Lord, from all decrees. [UM]
4. The Angels and the Spirit descend therein from the source of all decrees by the leave of their Lord. [BC]
4. The Angels and the Spirit descend... [SS]
4. The Angels and the Spirit descend therein... [OS] [WS] [L-QOS]
4. In it the angels descend, and the Spirit ... [M]
5. Peace it is until the rising of the dawn. [UM]
5. Peace it is until the break of dawn. [BC]

(٩٦) سُورَةُ العَلَقِ
بِسْمِ اللَّهِ الرَّحْمَٰنِ الرَّحِيمِ

اقْرَأْ بِاسْمِ رَبِّكَ الَّذِي خَلَقَ ۝

خَلَقَ الْإِنسَانَ مِنْ عَلَقٍ ۝

اقْرَأْ وَرَبُّكَ الْأَكْرَمُ ۝

الَّذِي عَلَّمَ بِالْقَلَمِ ۝

عَلَّمَ الْإِنسَانَ مَا لَمْ يَعْلَمْ ۝

كَلَّا لَا تُطِعْهُ وَاسْجُدْ وَاقْتَرِب ۩ ۝

(٩٧) سُورَةُ القَدْرِ
بِسْمِ اللَّهِ الرَّحْمَٰنِ الرَّحِيمِ

إِنَّا أَنزَلْنَاهُ فِي لَيْلَةِ الْقَدْرِ ۝

وَمَا أَدْرَاكَ مَا لَيْلَةُ الْقَدْرِ ۝

لَيْلَةُ الْقَدْرِ خَيْرٌ مِّنْ أَلْفِ شَهْرٍ ۝

تَنَزَّلُ الْمَلَائِكَةُ وَالرُّوحُ فِيهَا بِإِذْنِ رَبِّهِم مِّن كُلِّ أَمْرٍ ۝

سَلَامٌ هِيَ حَتَّىٰ مَطْلَعِ الْفَجْرِ ۝

Al-Qāriʿah (CI)

In the Name of God, the Infinitely Good, the Ever-Merciful

4. The day men shall be like scattered moths. [M]
5. And the mountains float like tufts of wool. [M]

Al-ʿAṣr (CIII)

In the Name of God, the Infinitely Good, the Ever-Merciful

1. By the declining day. [BC]
2. Verily mankind is in ruinous loss. [BC]
3. Except they that believe and do good works, and exhort one another unto truth and unto patience. [BC]

(١٠١) سُورَةُ الْقَارِعَةِ

بِسْمِ اللَّهِ الرَّحْمَنِ الرَّحِيمِ

يَوْمَ يَكُونُ النَّاسُ كَالْفَرَاشِ الْمَبْثُوثِ ۞

وَتَكُونُ الْجِبَالُ كَالْعِهْنِ الْمَنفُوشِ ۞

(١٠٣) سُورَةُ الْعَصْرِ

بِسْمِ اللَّهِ الرَّحْمَنِ الرَّحِيمِ

وَالْعَصْرِ ۞

إِنَّ الْإِنسَانَ لَفِي خُسْرٍ ۞

إِلَّا الَّذِينَ آمَنُوا وَعَمِلُوا الصَّالِحَاتِ وَتَوَاصَوْا بِالْحَقِّ وَتَوَاصَوْا بِالصَّبْرِ ۞

Al-Fīl (CV)

In the Name of God, the Infinitely Good, the Ever-Merciful

1. Hast thou not seen how they Lord dealt with the masters of the elephant? [UM] [M]
2. Did He not turn their plots awry? [UM] [M]
3. He sent upon them dense clouds of birds. [UM] [M]
4. That pelted them with inscribed stones. [UM] [M]
5. Thus made He them like greenery eaten down. [UM] [M]

Quraysh (CVI)

In the Name of God, the Infinitely Good, the Ever-Merciful

1. For the uniting of the Qoraish. [UM]
1. That the Quraish might be united. [BC]
2. United for the caravans of winter and summer. [BC]
2. ...the winter caravan, the summer caravan. [UM]
3. So worship they the lord of this house. [UM]
3. So let them worship the Lord of this house. [BC]
4. Who hath fed them against hunger and hath shielded them from fear. [UM]
4. Who hath fed them against hunger and shielded them from fear. [BC]

(١٠٥) سُورَةُ الْفِيلِ

بِسْمِ اللَّهِ الرَّحْمَنِ الرَّحِيمِ

أَلَمْ تَرَ كَيْفَ فَعَلَ رَبُّكَ بِأَصْحَابِ الْفِيلِ ۝١

أَلَمْ يَجْعَلْ كَيْدَهُمْ فِي تَضْلِيلٍ ۝٢

وَأَرْسَلَ عَلَيْهِمْ طَيْرًا أَبَابِيلَ ۝٣

تَرْمِيهِم بِحِجَارَةٍ مِّن سِجِّيلٍ ۝٤

فَجَعَلَهُمْ كَعَصْفٍ مَّأْكُولٍ ۝٥

(١٠٦) سُورَةُ قُرَيْشٍ

بِسْمِ اللَّهِ الرَّحْمَنِ الرَّحِيمِ

لِإِيلَافِ قُرَيْشٍ ۝١

إِيلَافِهِمْ رِحْلَةَ الشِّتَاءِ وَالصَّيْفِ ۝٢

فَلْيَعْبُدُوا رَبَّ هَذَا الْبَيْتِ ۝٣

الَّذِي أَطْعَمَهُم مِّن جُوعٍ وَآمَنَهُم مِّنْ خَوْفٍ ۝٤

Al-Kāfirūn (CIX)

In the Name of God, the Infinitely Good, the Ever-Merciful

1. Say: O disbelievers. [M]
2. I shall not worship that which ye worship. [M]
3. Nor will ye worship that which I worship. [M]
4. Nor have I worshipped that which ye worship. [M]
5. Nor have ye worshipped that which I worship. [M]
6. For you your religion and for me mine. [M]

Al-Ikhlāṣ (CXII)

In the Name of God, the Infinitely Good, the Ever-Merciful

1. Say: He, God, is One. [UM] [BC] [WS] [M]
1. ... the indivisible One-and-Only. [QACI] [SQCI]
2. God—The Eternally Sufficient unto Himself. [UM] [BC]
2. God, the Self-Sufficing in Infinite Plenitude. [SS]
2. God, the Absolute Plenitude Sufficing-unto-Himself (*Aṣ-Ṣamad*). [WS]
2. God, the Totally Sufficing unto Himself in His Infinite Perfection. [QACI] [SQCI]
2. God, the Self-Sufficient Besought of all. [M]
3. He begetteth not and He is not begotten. [UM]
3. He begetteth not, nor is begotten. [M]
4. And there is none like unto Him. [UM]
4. And none is like Him. [M]

(١٠٩) سُورَةُ الكَافِرُونَ

بِسْمِ اللَّهِ الرَّحْمَٰنِ الرَّحِيمِ

قُلْ يَٰٓأَيُّهَا ٱلْكَٰفِرُونَ ۝

لَآ أَعْبُدُ مَا تَعْبُدُونَ ۝

وَلَآ أَنتُمْ عَٰبِدُونَ مَآ أَعْبُدُ ۝

وَلَآ أَنَا۠ عَابِدٌ مَّا عَبَدتُّمْ ۝

وَلَآ أَنتُمْ عَٰبِدُونَ مَآ أَعْبُدُ ۝

لَكُمْ دِينُكُمْ وَلِىَ دِينِ ۝

(١١٢) سُورَةُ الإِخْلَاصِ

بِسْمِ اللَّهِ الرَّحْمَٰنِ الرَّحِيمِ

قُلْ هُوَ ٱللَّهُ أَحَدٌ ۝

ٱللَّهُ ٱلصَّمَدُ ۝

لَمْ يَلِدْ وَلَمْ يُولَدْ ۝

وَلَمْ يَكُن لَّهُۥ كُفُوًا أَحَدٌۢ ۝

Al-Falaq (CXIII)

In the Name of God, the Infinitely Good, the Ever-Merciful

1. Say I take refuge in the Lord of dawn. [UM]
1. Say: I take refuge in the Lord of daybreak. [M]
2. From the evil which He hath created. [UM]
2. From the evil of that which He hath created. [M]
3. And from the evil of the night when it growth dark. [UM]
3. And from the evil of dusk when it dimmeth into night. [M]
4. And from the evil of the women that blow upon the knots. [UM]
4. And from the evil of the women who breathe upon knots. [M]
5. And from the evil of the envier when he envieth. [UM] [M]

An-Nās (CXIV)

In the Name of God, the Infinitely Good, the Ever-Merciful

1. Say: I take refuge in the Lord of men. [UM] [M]
2. The King of men. [UM] [M]
3. The God of men. [UM] [M]
4. From the evil of insidious Whisper. [UM]
4. From the evil of the stealthy whisperer. [M]
5. Who whispereth in the breasts of men. [UM] [M]
6. From jinn and men. [UM] [M]

(١١٣) سُورَةُ الْفَلَقِ

بِسْمِ اللَّهِ الرَّحْمَٰنِ الرَّحِيمِ

قُلْ أَعُوذُ بِرَبِّ الْفَلَقِ ۝

مِن شَرِّ مَا خَلَقَ ۝

وَمِن شَرِّ غَاسِقٍ إِذَا وَقَبَ ۝

وَمِن شَرِّ النَّفَّاثَاتِ فِي الْعُقَدِ ۝

وَمِن شَرِّ حَاسِدٍ إِذَا حَسَدَ ۝

(١١٤) سُورَةُ النَّاسِ

بِسْمِ اللَّهِ الرَّحْمَٰنِ الرَّحِيمِ

قُلْ أَعُوذُ بِرَبِّ النَّاسِ ۝

مَلِكِ النَّاسِ ۝

إِلَٰهِ النَّاسِ ۝

مِن شَرِّ الْوَسْوَاسِ الْخَنَّاسِ ۝

الَّذِي يُوَسْوِسُ فِي صُدُورِ النَّاسِ ۝

مِنَ الْجِنَّةِ وَالنَّاسِ ۝

Appendix

The Ninety-Nine Beautiful Names of God

'God hath 99 Names. He that telleth them shall enter Paradise.' (Muslim, *Dhikr*, 2) [OS] [S]

Allāh [1]	اللّٰه	Allah, God
Ar-Raḥmān	اَلرَّحْمَٰنُ	The Infinitely Good; the Divine Beatitude; the All-Merciful
Ar-Raḥīm	اَلرَّحِيْمُ	The Boundlessly Merciful; the Bestower of Mercy
Al-Malik	اَلْمَلِكُ	The King
Al-Quddūs	اَلْقُدُّوْسُ	The All-Holy
As-Salām	اَلسَّلَامُ	Peace
Al-Mu'min	اَلْمُؤْمِنُ	The Sure; the Faithful; the Safety-Giver; the Absolutely Reliable

[1] When the Ninety-nine Beautiful Names of God are recited, it is traditional to start with: 'He is *Allāh* and there is no other god but He (*Huwa Allāhu 'lladhī lā ilāha illā Huwa*), *ar-Raḥmān, ar-Raḥīm*...'.

THE HOLY QUR'ĀN: SELECTED VERSES

Al-Muhaymin	اَلْمُهَيْمِنُ	The Guardian; the Protector
Al-ʿAzīz	اَلْعَزِيزُ	The Almighty; the Inestimably Precious; the Hard of access
Al-Jabbār	اَلْجَبَّارُ	The Irresistible; the All-Overpowering
Al-Mutakabbir	اَلْمُتَكَبِّرُ	The Proud; the Grand
Al-Khāliq	اَلْخَالِقُ	The Creator
Al-Bāri'	اَلْبَارِئُ	The Maker
Al-Muṣawwir	اَلْمُصَوِّرُ	The Former
Al-Ghaffār	اَلْغَفَّارُ	The Ever-Forgiving
Al-Qahhār	اَلْقَهَّارُ	The Ever-Compelling; the All-Compelling; the Irresistible
Al-Wahhāb	اَلْوَهَّابُ	The Ever-Giving
Ar-Razzāq	اَلرَّزَّاقُ	The Ever-Providing
Al-Fattāḥ	اَلْفَتَّاحُ	The Opener; the Victory-Giver; the Victorious
Al-ʿAlīm	اَلْعَلِيمُ	The Omniscient
Al-Qābiḍ	اَلْقَابِضُ	He Who contracts; the Straitener
Al-Bāsiṭ	اَلْبَاسِطُ	He Who expands; the Munificent
Al-Khāfiḍ	اَلْخَافِضُ	The Abaser
Ar-Rāfiʿ	اَلرَّافِعُ	The Exalter

Appendix

Al-Muʿizz	اَلْمُعِزُّ	The Honourer; the Enhancer
Al-Mudhill	اَلْمُذِلُّ	He Who humbles
As-Samīʿ	اَلسَّمِيعُ	The All-Hearing
Al-Baṣīr	اَلْبَصِيرُ	The All-Seeing
Al-Ḥakam	اَلْحَكَمُ	The Arbitrator; the Decider
Al-ʿAdl	اَلْعَدْلُ	The Just; Justice
Al-Laṭīf	اَللَّطِيفُ	The Benign; the Subtle; the All-Penetrating; the Gently All-Prevailing
Al-Khabīr	اَلْخَبِيرُ	The Aware; the All-Knowing
Al-Ḥalīm	اَلْحَلِيمُ	The Mild; the Indulgent
Al-ʿAẓīm	اَلْعَظِيمُ	The Infinite; the Immense
Al-Ghafūr	اَلْغَفُورُ	The All-Forgiving
Ash-Shakūr	اَلشَّكُورُ	The Grateful
Al-ʿAlī	اَلْعَلِيُّ	The High; the Sublime
Al-Kabīr	اَلْكَبِيرُ	The Great
Al-Ḥafīẓ	اَلْحَفِيظُ	The All-Preserver
Al-Muqīt	اَلْمُقِيتُ	The All-Nourisher; the Overseer of all; Providence
Al-Ḥasīb	اَلْحَسِيبُ	The All-Sufficient; the All-Calculating
Al-Jalīl	اَلْجَلِيلُ	The Majestic
Al-Karīm	اَلْكَرِيمُ	The Generous; the All-Bountiful; the Magnanimous

THE HOLY QUR'ĀN: SELECTED VERSES

Ar-Raqīb	اَلرَّقِيْبُ	The All-Observing; the Vigilant
Al-Mujīb	اَلْمُجِيْبُ	The All-Answering; the Responsive; the Granter of prayers; the Answerer
Al-Wāsiʿ	اَلْوَاسِعُ	The Vast; the All-Capacious
Al-Ḥakīm	اَلْحَكِيْمُ	The Wise
Al-Wadūd	اَلْوَدُوْدُ	The Loving-Kind
Al-Majīd	اَلْمَجِيْدُ	The All-Glorious
Al-Bāʿith	اَلْبَاعِثُ	The Raiser of the dead; the Sender
Ash-Shahīd	اَلشَّهِيْدُ	The All-Witnessing; the Directly Perceiving; the Witness
Al-Ḥaqq	اَلْحَقُّ	Truth; the True; the Reality
Al-Wakīl	اَلْوَكِيْلُ	The Utterly Reliable
Al-Qawī	اَلْقَوِىُّ	The Overpoweringly Strong; the Strong
Al-Matīn	اَلْمَتِيْنُ	The Steadfastly Strong; the Firm; the Strong; the Steadfast
Al-Walī	اَلْوَلِىُّ	The Patron; the Helper
Al-Ḥamīd	اَلْحَمِيْدُ	The All-Praiseworthy
Al-Muḥṣī	اَلْمُحْصِى	The Counter; the Knower of each separate thing
Al-Mubdi'	اَلْمُبْدِئُ	The Beginner; the Cause

Appendix

Al-Muʿīd	اَلْمُعِيدُ	The Bringer-Back; the Restorer; the Transformer
Al-Muḥyī	اَلْمُحْيِي	The Life-Giver
Al-Mumīt	اَلْمُمِيتُ	The Slayer
Al-Ḥayy	اَلْحَيُّ	The Living
Al-Qayyūm	اَلْقَيُّومُ	The Self-Existing; the All-Sustaining; the Absolutely Independent
Al-Wājid	اَلْوَاجِدُ	The Complete; the Finder; the All-Resourceful; the Unfailing; the Unneeding
Al-Mājid	اَلْمَاجِدُ	The Magnificent; the Glorious
Al-Wāḥid	اَلْوَاحِدُ	The One; the Sole; the Indivisible; the Immanent
As-Ṣamad	اَلصَّمَدُ	The Self-Sufficient; the Eternal; the All-Needed; the Unsurpassable
Al-Qādir	اَلْقَادِرُ	The All-Powerful; the Lord of Absolute Free Will
Al-Muqtadir	اَلْمُقْتَدِرُ	The All-Determiner
Al-Muqaddim	اَلْمُقَدِّمُ	He Who brings forward; the Promoter; He Who brings near
Al-Muʾakhkhir	اَلْمُؤَخِّرُ	The Postponer; He Who puts far away
Al-Awwal	اَلْأَوَّلُ	The First
Al-Ākhir	اَلْآخِرُ	The Last

THE HOLY QUR'ĀN: SELECTED VERSES

Aẓ-Ẓāhir	اَلظَّاهِرُ	The Outwardly Manifest
Al-Bāṭin	اَلْبَاطِنُ	The Inwardly Hidden
Al-Wālī	اَلْوَالِي	The Ruler
Al-Mutaʿālī	اَلْمُتَعَالِي	The Exalted; the Sublime; the Transcendent; the Lofty
Al-Barr	اَلْبَرُّ	The Beneficient
At-Tawwāb	اَلتَّوَّابُ	The Ever-Relenting; He Who makes repentance easy
Al-Muntaqim	اَلْمُنْتَقِمُ	The Avenger
Al-ʿAfūw	اَلْعَفُوُّ	The Effacer of sins
Ar-Ra'ūf	اَلرَّؤُوفُ	The All-Pitying
Mālik al-mulk	مَالِكُ الْمُلْكِ	The Lord of Absolute Sovereignty
Dhū'l-Jalāl wa'l-Ikrām	ذُوالْجَلَالِ وَالْاِكْرَامُ	The Lord of Majesty and Bounty
Al-Muqsiṭ	اَلْمُقْسِطُ	The Equitable; the Requiter; the Just
Al-Jāmiʿ	اَلْجَامِعُ	The Assembler; the Uniter
Al-Ghanī	اَلْغَنِيُّ	The Infinitely Rich; the Totally Independent
Al-Mughnī	اَلْمُغْنِي	The Enricher; the Availer
Al-Māniʿ	اَلْمَانِعُ	The Preventer; the Shielder; the Defender
Aḍ-Ḍārr	اَلضَّارُّ	He Who harms

Heart(s) (*cont.*)
blind hearts, 86
divided, 166
hard like rocks, 8
hardened, 164
heart knowlege, 72
hearts to be reconciled, 56
hearts united by God, 52
known by God, 52, 140
men's hearts, 70, 112
of the believers, 138
of the faithful, 138
Heaven(s), 36, 42, 68, 70, 84,
96, 98, 134, 148, 152
creation of, 62
dominion of the
Heavens, 38
Heavens and earth, 38, 40,
48, 62, 64, 74, 84, 92, 94,
108, 116, 136, 152
Heavy ones, 152
Heed, 52, 74
Heedless, 120
Heels, 22
Heights, 44
Hell, 154
Help, 2, 50, 54, 128, 170
of God, 10, 14, 52, 66
Herbs, 148
Here-below, 190
Hereafter, 4, 52, 74, 106, 114,
132, 190
Holy Monument, 12
Home, 86, 104, 166
Hope, 60, 96, 112, 116
Horizons, 132

Hosts, 54, 112
House:
at Baca, 20
Holy House, 70
of God, 86
of Peace, 60
of the Lord, 198
Household, 100
Hudā, see Guidance
Hues, 72
Humankind, 66
Humbled, 82, 166
Humility, 44, 166
Hunger, 10, 198
Huri, 156
Hurt, 22, 138
Hymn, 74

Iblis, 6, see also Satan(s)
Idolaters, 54, 168
Ignorant, 116
Illusion, 68
'Ilm, see Knowledge
Īmān, see Faith
Immortal, 56, 138
Imprecate, 20
'Imrān, 170, 172
family of, 18
Incitement:
to sin, 160
Incline, 52, 70
unto worship
and fasting, 170
Increase, 74, 76
in faith, 138
in faith and submission, 112
in knowledge, 82

Index

Give (*cont.*)
  give up, 78
  greetings of Peace, 116
Giver (The), see *al-Wahhāb*
Gladness, 188
Glance (n.), 100, 154
Glass, 92, 102
Glide, 122
Glorification, 74
Glorify, 74, 144, 182
Glory, 66, 74, 90, 100,
    122, 124
Gnat, 6
God, 14, 202
God-fearing, 4
Good, 16, 20, 28, 36, 44, 52,
    84, 98, 114, 178
  make good, 112
Goods, 10, 28, 114
Grace, 2, 26, 34, 174, 190
Grains, 148
Grant, 16, 126
Grave (n.), 56
Greenery, 148, 198
Grief, 66
Grieve, 6, 22, 34, 36, 56, 132
Ground, 70
Grow, 122, 128
  fair growing, 18
  grow dark, 202
Guidance, 4, 6, 20, 22, 54,
    100, 168
  right guidance, 78
Guide, 2, 42, 58, 60, 92, 100,
    104, 134, 174, 190
  rightly guided, 12, 100

Guilt, 138
Guilty, 152
Gush, 156
  gush forth, 8, 182

Hair, 140, 176
Ḥajj, see Pilgrimage
al-Ḥakīm:
    Infinitely Wise, 54
    Wise, 52, 56
al-Ḥamīd:
    Object of all Praise, 118
    Owner of Praise, 118
    Praiseworthy, 118
Hand, 26, 52, 138, 154
  of Allah, 138
  of God, 126, 138
  right hand, 126, 160
Ḥanīf, 108
Ḥaqq, see Truth
Hardship, 192
Harm (n.), 6
Harvesting, 10
Hate, 190
Hatred, 20
al-Ḥayy:
    Living, 82
Heads, 50, 120, 140
Hear, 16, 36, 90, 104, 160
  a wondrous recitation, 174
Hearer (The), see *as-Samīʿ*
Hearing, 72
Hearken, 120, 132
Heart(s), 50, 52, 68, 98, 102,
    128, 142, 170, 186
  at peace, 68
  at rest, 16

221

THE HOLY QUR'ĀN: SELECTED VERSES

Flee, 144
Flight, 54
Float, 196
Flood, 68
Foam, 68
Folding, 84
Folk, 40, 52, 58
  infidel, 102
Follow, 4, 6, 62, 78, 98, 132
Food, 8
  from God, 18
  lawful, 30
Forbid, 26
Force, 120
Forelock, 62, 152
Foremost, 160
Foretell, 112
Forget, 124
Forgive, 52, 56, 66, 90, 122,
  128, 138
Forgiveness, 16, 56, 120, 178
Forgiving (The), see
  al-Ghafūr
Forsake, 190
Foundation, 70
Fountains, 154, 156
Fresh, 96
Friend(s):
  Protecting Friend, 170
  protecting friends, 132
Frown, 184
Fruit, 4, 70, 124, 148, 156
  fruits of the garden, 6
  fruits of the two gardens,
    154
  two kinds, 154

Fulfil, 30, 96, 140
Fulfillment, 144

Gabriel, 170
Gains:
  of this lower life, 26
  of this world, 52
Gainsay, 78
Game, 106
Gape, 118
Garden(s), 154, see also
  Paradise
  of Immortality, 96
  of Paradise, 4, 160
  of Refuge, 146
  of Ultimate Refuge, 146
  the blissful in the Garden,
    64
  two gardens, 154, 156
  watered by flowing rivers,
    56, 138
Gaze, 44
Generations, 160
al-Ghafūr:
  All-Forgiving, 52, 98,
    128, 132
  Forgiving, 52, 54, 90, 142
al-Ghanī:
  Rich, 118, 136
Ghayb, see Unseen
Gift, 64
Give, 110
  give drink, 96, 186
  give ear, 142, 174
  give life, 72, 124
  give respite, 188
  give thanks, 98

220

Index

Exposition, 42
Extinction, 150
Extol, 68, 74
Exult, 54
Eyes, 20, 36, 62, 66, 86,
    112, 144
  coolness of, 110
  eye-sights, 86

Fabric, 158
Face, 10, 22, 26, 40, 82,
    108, 132
Face of God, 8, 38, 78
  everything perish save, 104
  is eternal, 150
Fade, 82
Fair, 28
  acceptance, 18
  example, 112
  fairest rectitude, 192
  fairest uprightness, 192
  growing, 18
  pattern, 112
  release, 114
Faith, 112, 138, 142
  former faith, 138
  have faith, 16, 34, 116
  new faith, 138
Faithful, 16, 34, 54, 138, 170
Fall, 6, 38, 46, 118
False, 76
Falter, 22
Family, 98
Farewell, 176
Fashion (n.), 108
Fashion (v.), 82
Fasting, 170

Fate, 46
Fathers, 120
Faults, 24, 26
Favour (n.), 26, 30, 74,
    100, 112
Favour (v.), 74, 76
Fear, 6, 10, 30, 34, 46, 52,
    54, 68, 76, 128, 132, 140,
    154, 198
  invoke Him in, 110
  invoke Him with, 44
  of God, 166, 184
Feast, 36
Feed, 4, 116, 198
Feet, 152
Field, 54, 84
Fig, 192
Fight, 12, 14, 26, 32, 52
  for His cause, 168
  permission to, 86
  with goods and lives, 28
Find, 26, 78, 94, 178
  peace, 60
  repose, 68
  rest, 68, 108
Finger, 50
Fire, 62, 92, 100, 150,
    152, 170
Firmament, 118, 188
First, 36, 160, 190
  generations, 160
  He is the First, 164
  sanctuary, 20
  time, 124
Flame, 150
Flavoured, 182

219

THE HOLY QUR'ĀN: SELECTED VERSES

Earth, 6, 40, 48, 52, 54,
    58, 64, 68, 72, 74, 76,
    80, 84, 92, 110, 116, 118,
    122, 134, 148, 152, 188
    boundary of, 152
    corruption upon, 44
    creation of, 62, 84, 108, 136
    darkness of, 38
    dominion of, 38
    purify with clean earth, 26
    surface of, 70
Earthenware, 150
Ease, 12, 76, 180, 192
East(s), 8, 92
    a place towards the, 80
    Lord of, 176
    two Easts, 150
Eat, 6
Eden, 56
Efface, 68
Eke, 110
Elephant, 198
Embrace, 46
Emerge, 40, 42
Encompass, 140
Encroach, 150
End, 22, 110
    Uttermost End, 146
Endure, 64, 150
    patiently, 72
Engross, 184
Enjoin, 56
Enmity, 168
Ennoble, 122
Enormous, 90
Enrich, 28, 54, 190

Enshroud, 120, 146, 176
Enter, 18, 102, 116, 140,
    170, 188
    hearts, 142
    noble entry, 26
    Paradise, 14, 22, 24, 44,
    122, 188
Entirety, 128
Entrust, 18
Envier, 202
Envy (n.), 8
Envy (v.), 202
Ephemeral, 76
Equal, 28
Establish, 20, 168, 188
    a law and a way, 32
Esteem (v.), 40, 88, 128
Eternal, 150
Eternal (The), see
    al-Qayyūm
Everlasting, 104
Evidence, 62
Evil, 20, 66, 84, 98, 138,
    160, 202
Evil-doers, 96
Example, 20, 52, 112,
    170, 172
Excellence, 156
    abodes of, 56
    foremost in, 160
Excellent, 24, 26
Exception, 28
Exhort, 196
Exhortation, 22
Expand, 14, 42, 192
Experience (n.), 78

218

Index

Curse (n.), 20

Darkness, 38, 40, 42, 122
David, 76, 84
Dawn, 194, 202
Day(s), 30, 62, 66, 82, 84,
   88, 96, 98, 104, 108, 122,
   130, 152, 176, 182, 184
  appointed days, 12
  declining day, 196
  Last Day, 4, 34, 36, 112
  of anguish, 180
  of Ḥunayn, 54
  of Judgement, 2
  of Resurrection, 46, 104
  six days, 62
Dead, 10, 22
  raised to life, 40, 42
Deal (v.), 188, 198
Death, 22, 112
Debtors, 56
Decree(s), 122, 144, 194
Deeds, 142, 170
  good deeds, 192
  of piety, 4, 34
Deem, 22, 88
Defilement, 180
Degree(s), 28, 66, 74, 154
Deliver, 28
Demon, 100
Descend, 132, 138, 166, 194
Desert, 94, 142
Deserve, 2, 142
Desire (n.), 44
Desire (v.), 96, 114
Despair, 30, 128
Devotion, 76, 176

Devout, 170
Dhikru'Llāh, see Invocation
  of God and Remembrance
  of Allah, God
Die, 22, 56
  make to die, 72
Differ, 32, 34
Difficult, 12, 192
Dignity, 90
Dim, 202
Dīn, see Religion
Disbelief, 8
Disbelievers, 30, 50, 54,
  180, 188, 200
Disbelieving, 102
Discourse (n.), 40, 116
Discriminate, 26
Disdain (v.), 6
Disguise (v.), 100
Disperse, 116
Distinction, 16
Diversion, 106
Divert, 94, 168
Divorce, 170
Doer, 64
Doubt, 4, 100, 174
Doubters, 20
Drive (v.), 86, 166
Dusk, 202
Dust, 20
Dwell, 6, 56, 138
Dwelling(s), 126, 170
  of the Prophet, 116

Eager, 44, 184
Earnings, 186

217

THE HOLY QUR'ĀN: SELECTED VERSES

Change (v.), 98, 112
Chant (v.), 176
Children, 168, 176
Chins, 120
Choice, 104
Choose, 18, 30, 46
Christians, 34, 36
Clay, 150
Clear, 20, 58, 132
  affirmation, 22
Cleft, 152
Clemency, 38
Clement (The), see
  ar-Raḥmān
Clot, 194
Clouds, 68
  of birds, 198
Combatants, 28
  non-combatants, 28
Come, 14, 18, 20, 50, 62, 76,
  86, 94, 100, 114, 116, 126,
  128, 134, 148, 150, 178, 184
  come to pass, 112
  from God, 6
  from Tasnīm, 186
  to come, 138
Command (n.), 76, 104, 124
Command (v.), 66
Communion, 26
Community, 60
  one community, 32
Companions:
  of the Left, 162
  of the Right, 160
Companionship, 26
Company, 174

Compass, 78
Conceal, 20
Confirm, 32, 68
Consecrate, 176
Consecration, 176
Consorts, 108
Constellations, 98
Consult, 22
Contend, 20
Contract (v.), 14, 42
Corruption, 4
  in land, 4
  upon earth, 44
  workers of, 4
Couches, 122
Count, 10, 22, 88, 90, 166
Court (n.), 146
Courtyard, 102
Covenant, 52, 112, 138
Covering, 184
Create, 72, 194, 202
  all the pairs, 122
  camels, 188
  Heavens and earth, 40,
    62, 84, 108, 136
  jinn, 150
  jinn and men, 144
  man, 20, 88, 96, 108, 122,
    126, 148, 150, 192, 194
  others in its likeness, 122
  what He will, 104
Createdness, 124
Creator, 132
Creature, 62, 96
Crucify, 28
Cup, 182

216

Index

Betray, 170
Beware, 90
Beyond, 74
Birds, 198
Bitter, 96
Blaze (v.), 92
Blessed, 74, 96, 98, 100,
    132, 158
  blessed place, Baca, 20
  blessed tree, 92
Blessings, 12
  upon the Prophet, 116
Blind, 86, 184
Blindfold, 120
Blindness, 66
Bliss, 110
Blissful, 62
Blood, 194
Blow (n.), 10
Blow (v.), 180, 202
Bones, 124
Book, 4, 32, 80
  Clear Book, 38
  hidden book, 162
  His Books, 16, 170, 172
  Mother of the, 68
  people of the, 8
Boundary, 152
  uttermost boundary, 146
Bounty, 54, 122, 132,
    150, 158
Bow (v.), 86, 126, 132
Branches, 70, 154
Brand (n.), 100
Brass, 152
Breadth, 54

Break, 138
  of dawn, 194
Breast, 20, 42, 44, 72, 86, 202
  contracted, 42
  expanded, 42, 192
Breathe, 72, 170, 172
  upon knots, 202
Bring:
  back unto God, 32, 34,
    88, 104
  forth, 20, 90
  home, 104
  near, 160, 186
  nigh, 160, 186
Brocade, 154
Burden (n.), 16, 82

Call, 44, 60, 82, 100
  upon God, 44, 48, 76,
    110, 130
Calumny, 28, 90
Camel(s), 86, 188
Camphor, 182
Capacity, 68
Captives, 52, 56
Caravan:
  summer, 198
  winter, 198
Case, 84, 130
Cast (v.), 28, 50, 100, 192
Cattle, 96
Cause (n.), 170
  of God, 56, 168
Cave, 56
Cease, 78
Certainty, 38, 62
Chains, 120

215

THE HOLY QUR'ĀN: SELECTED VERSES

Appoint (*cont.*)
  law, 32
  law and path, 32, 34
  law and way, 34
  middle nation, 10
Arabs, 142
Arḍ, see Earth
Arḥamu'r-Rāḥimīn:
  Most Merciful of the
    merciful, 66
Arise, 180
Ark, 122
Arrogance, 96
Arrogant, 96
Ask, 8, 12, 124
  forgiveness, 56, 178
  help of God, 66
Astray, 2, 40, 42, 58, 190
Attainment, 56
Attune, 52
Authority, 152
Avail, 54, 82, 170
Averse, 54, 168
Aversion, 74
Avoid, 26
Awe, 50, 68
al-Awwal:
  First, 164
Āyah (pl. *āyāt*), see Sign(s)
al-ʿAzīz:
  Almighty, 122
  Mighty, 52, 120, 122

Baca, 20
Ban, 170
Band, 14, 152
Banks, 68

Banquet, 36
Bar (v.), 14, 96, 102
Bare (v.), 102
Barrier, 96, 120
Bartering, 94
al-Baṣīr:
  Seer, 130, 134
al-Bāṭin:
  Inward, 164
  Inwardly Hidden, 164
'Be', 20
Bear, 116
  bear witness, 36, 46
  with patience, 176
Beatitude:
  Infinite Beatitude, 56
  of God, 56
Beds, 110, 154
Befall, 10
  evil, 20
  good, 20
Beget, 200
Beggar, 190
Behold, 74, 96, 188
Belie, 22, 148, 150, 152,
    154, 158, 192
Belief, 8
Believe, 4, 10, 14, 16, 26,
    34, 36, 54, 68, 112, 116,
    170, 172, 174, 192, 196
Believers, 28, 50, 52, 56, 90,
    108, 112, 138, 140, 144
  no believers, 4
  true believers, 22
Believing, 36, 138, 170
Bestow, 4, 80, 114, 138

214

Index

ʿ*Abd* (pl. ʿ*ibād*), see Slave(s)
Abode(s):
  abodes of excellence, 56
  of Hereafter, 106, 114
  of truthfulness, 146
Abomination, 106
Abraham, 38
  family of, 18
  religion of, 10
Abundance, 28
Acceptance, 18
Adam, 6, 18, 82
  sons of Adam, 46
  wife of, 6
ʿ*Adn*, see Eden
Adoration, 132
Adore, 2
Adornments, 114
Affairs, 22
Affection, 36
Afflict, 28
  affliction, 14
Aforetime, 4, 26
Afraid, 116
al-*Aḥad*:
  indivisible One-and-
    Only, 200
  One, 200

al-*Ākhir*:
  Last, 164
Ākhira, see Hereafter
al-*Akram*:
  Most Bountiful, 194
ʿ*Ālam* (pl. ʿ*ālamīn*), see
    World(s)
Alif-Lām-Mīm, 4
al-ʿ*Alīm*:
  All-Knowing, 8, 54, 122
  Infinitely Knowing, 8
  Knower, 92, 122
  Knowing, 56
Allāh, 40, 76
All-Merciful, see ar-*Raḥmān*
    and ar-*Raḥīm*
Almighty, see al-ʿ*Azīz*
Alms, 56, 58
Angel(s), 6, 18, 50, 68, 76,
    96, 132, 194
  help of, 170
  His Angels, 16, 116
  Noble Angel, 66
Anger (n.), 2
Answer (v.), 12, 130
Apostles, 16
Appearance, 108
Appoint, 122

213

THE HOLY QUR'ĀN: SELECTED VERSES

INSERT BY THE PUBLISHERS, BEING AN EXTRACT FROM
AL-GHAZĀLĪ ON THE NINETY-NINE BEAUTIFUL NAMES OF GOD[1]

On explaining that the names of God most high are not limited to ninety-nine so far as divine instruction is concerned

INDEED, DIVINE INSTRUCTION mentions names other than the ninety-nine, since in another version given on the authority of
Abū Hurayra—may the Lord be pleased with him—names close
to these names were substituted for some of them and even some
which are not so close. Regarding the ones close in meaning,
al-Aḥad (the One) was substituted for al-Wāḥid (the Unique), al-
Qāhir (the Conqueror) for al-Qahhār (the Dominator), al-Shākir
(the Thankful) for al-Shakūr (the Grateful). Ones not so close in
meaning were also substituted, like al-Hādī (the Guide), al-Kāfī
(the One who suffices), al-Dā'im (the Enduring), al-Baṣīr (the In-
sightful), al-Nūr al-Mubīn (the Clear Light), al-Jamīl (the Beautiful), al-Ṣādiq (the Truthful), al-Muḥīt (the Comprehending), al-
Qarīb (the Close), al-Qadīm (the Everlasting), al-Witr (the Un-
even), al-Fāṭir (the Creator), al-ʿAllām (the All-Knowing), al-Mulk
(the Sovereignty), al-Akram (the most Generous), al-Mudabbir (the
Director), al-Rafiʿ (the Elevated), Dhū'l-ṭawl (the Lord of Height),
Dhū'l-Maʿārij (the Lord of the Ascenders), Dhū'l-Faḍl (the Lord of
Benefit), and al-Khallāq (the Maker).

Furthermore, names are noted in the Qur'ān which do not
match with either of the two lists, like al-Mawlā (the Master), al-
Naṣīr (the Protector), al-Ghālib (the Victor), al-Qarīb (the Close),
al-Rabb (the Lord), and al-Nāṣir (the Deliverer). And there are
compound expressions as well, such as in the Most High's saying: *witness of retribution, receiver of repentance, forgiver of sins, merger
of night into day, merger of day into night, bringer of life from death*, and
bringer of death from life.

[1] Islamic Texts Society, Cambridge, 1995, pp. 167-168.

Appendix

An-Nāfiʿ	اَلنَّافِعُ	He Who benefits
An-Nūr	اَلنُّورُ	The Light
Al-Hādī	اَلْهَادِىُ	The Guide
Al-Badīʿ	اَلْبَدِيْعُ	The Peerless; the Marvellous; the Originator
Al-Bāqī	اَلْبَاقِى	The Permanent; the Eternal
Al-Wārith	اَلْوَارِثُ	The Heir; the Inheritor
Ar-Rashīd	اَلرَّشِيْدُ	The Infallibly Right
Aṣ-Ṣabūr	اَلصَّبُوْرُ	The All-Patient; the Long-Suffering; the Forbearing

The following are additional Divine Names for which translations were found in the writings of Dr Lings.

Al-Kāfī	اَلْكَافِىُ	The All-Sufficient
Al-Aḥad	اَلْأَحَدُ	The Transcendent One whose Oneness excludes all notion of duality
Al-Bayyin	اَلْبَيِّنُ	The Clear; the Evident; the Object of certainty
Al-Ghālib	اَلْغَالِبُ	The Conquerer
Al-Jamīl	اَلْجَمِيْلُ	The Beautiful
Al-Qarīb	اَلْقَرِيْبُ	The Near

Index

Indivisible One-and-Only (The), see *al-Aḥad*
Indulgent, 90
Infidels, 84, 102
Infirmity, 28
Inflict, 72
Inform, 32, 34
  God is informed, 26
Inherit, 80
Inheritor (The), see *al-Wārith*
Iniquitous, 186
Iniquity, 56, 106
Injuries, 14
Ink, 78, 110
Innocent, 40
Inscribe, 36
Insidious, 202
Intelligence, 142
Intercession, 82
Invite, 116
Invocation of God, 12, 68, 106, see also Remembrance of Allah, God
  absorbed in, 170, 172
  the greatest thing, 106
Invoke, 12, 76, 176
  blessings, 116
  in fear and longing, 110
  much, 112
  with fear and desire, 44
  with humility and in secret, 44
Invoker, 12
Inward (The), see *al-Bāṭin*
Irksome, 116

Irresistible, 44
Islām, 18, 30
Isthmus, 96, 150

Jahannam, see Hell
Janna (pl. *jannāt*), see Garden(s) and Paradise
Jesus, 20
  Son of Mary, 28
  the Messiah, 28
Jews, 28, 34
Jibrīl, see Gabriel
Jinn, 100, 152, 154, 158, 174
  and men, 144, 152, 202
  creation of, 150
Joyful, 122
Judgement, 84
Judges, 192
Jugular vein, 142

Kalimah (pl. *kalimāt*), see Word(s)
Keys, 38
al-Khabīr:
  Infinitely Aware, 40
Khalaqa, see Create
Khawf, see Fear
Kill, 14, 28
Kin, 98
Kindle, 92
King:
  Almighty King, 146
  of men, 202
Kingdom, 82, 130
Kinsmen, 90
Kitāb, see Book
Knots, 202

Know, 22, 38, 52, 66, 106,
   108, 110, 122, 140, 152, 178
Knower (The), see *al-ʿAlīm*
Knowledge, 20, 66, 76, 82,
   90, 92, 102, 164
  heart knowledge, 72
  His knowledge, 38
  knowledge from Our
    Knowledge, 78
Koran, see Qur'ān

Lamp, 92, 98
Land, 22, 38, 52
  corruption in, 4
  dead land, 96
  safe land, 192
Last, 162, 190
  Abode, 106
  He is the Last, 164
  Last Day, 4, 34, 36, 112
  last of us, 36
Later:
  generations, 160
  time, 160
al-Laṭīf:
  All-Pervading All-
    Prevailing, 40
Lavish, 26, 122
Lawful, 30
  made lawful, 170
Lay, 16, 114
  lay down, 148
Laylatu'l-Qadr, 194
  Night of Power, 194
  Night of Worth, 194
Lead, 2, 40, 42, 92, 106
Leaf, 38

Leave (n.), 116
  by the leave of God, 14,
    62, 70, 194
Legs, 102
Leisure, 152
Letter, 100
Lie (n.), 90
Lie (v.), 20, 70, 108, 110
Life:
  brought to life, 42
  give life, 72, 124
  Hereafter is Life, 106
  Last Abode is Life, 106
  lower life, 26, 60, 106, 108,
    114, 132
  of this world, 38
  raise to life, 42
  ways of life, 22
Light, 42, 92, 104, 134
  clear light, 28
  God, Light of Heavens and
    earth, 92
  moon, 60, 98
Lightning, 68
Likeness, 6, 122
  of a perfect man, 80
  of Adam with God, 20
  of Jesus with God, 20
Line, 70
Linger, 116
Livelihood, 184
Lives, 10, 28
Living, 10, 22
  creature, 62
  thing, 84
Living (The), see *al-Ḥayy*

Loan, 164
Loins, 46
Long (v.), 8, 44, 90, 132
  invoke Him in longing, 110
  longing, 68
Look, 112
Lord, 4, 12, 16, 18, 20, 22, 32, 34, 36, 38, 44, 46, 50, 62, 64, 70, 72, 76, 78, 80, 82, 86, 88, 96, 100, 110, 122, 126, 128, 130, 132, 146, 170, 172, 174, 176, 178, 180, 182, 188, 190, 194, 198
  boons of, 148–158
  Face of, 150
  Lord's decree, 144
  Merciful Lord, 124
  of Adam, 6
  of dawn, 202
  of daybreak, 202
  of men, 202
  of the east and the west, 176
  of the two Easts, 150
  of the two Wests, 150
  of the worlds, 2, 98, 100, 102, 162
Lords, 100
Lore, 84, 100, 102
Loss, 10, 196
Lot, 170
Love, 38, 44, 52, 104, 168
  ordaining of, 108
  to cause trouble, 20

Madman, 174
Magnify, 180
Maidens, 154

Majesty, 150, 158
Malak (pl. *malā'ikah*), see Angel(s)
Mankind, 20, 22, 46, 80, 108, 148, 196
Marks (n.), 152
Marry, 114
Martyrs, 26
Mary/Maryam, 18, 28, 80, 172
  daughter of 'Imrān, 170, 172
  offspring of, 18
Masjid, see Mosque
Master:
  masters of the elephant, 198
  of day of judgement, 2
'Me' (God), 6, 10, 12, 30, 46, 82, 110, 130
Meal, 116
Measure (n.), 72, 148, 176, 178
Measure (v.), 178
Meditate, 166
Meed, 34, 110, 114, 140, 142, 156, 174, 192
Meet, 4, 132, 150
Men, 4, 14, 20, 42, 44, 56, 68, 70, 86, 92, 96, 112, 118, 166, 186, 196, 202
  believing men, 138
  created by God, 108
  of dignity, 90
  sight of, 40
  two righteous, 170
Mention, 78, 80, 130

Merciful (The), see
  ar-Raḥmān and *ar-Raḥīm*
Mercy, 12, 44, 46, 78, 80,
  104, 178
  for the worlds, 84
  ordaining of, 108
Messenger(s), 80, 130
  angel messenger, 76
  for every community, 60
  God's messengers, 22
  His Messengers, 16
  Jesus, Son of Mary, 28
Migrate, 90
Miḥrāb, 18
Mirage, 94
Mock, 4
Monks, 36
Month, 194
  sacred month, 14
Moon, 40, 60, 98, 122,
  132, 148
Morning, 126, 190
Moses, 8, 46, 78, 82, 100
  people of, 8
Mosque:
  furthest Mosque, 74
  Holy Mosque, 14
  Inviolable Mosque, 10, 54,
  74, 140
Moths, 196
Mount Sinai, 192
Mountain, 44, 46, 116,
  166, 188, 196
Mouths, 20, 90
Muḥammad, 22, 114, see also
  The Prophet

Muḥammad (*cont.*)
  Apostle of God, 26
  pattern most fair, 112
  Messenger of Allah, 112
  Messenger of God, 14, 16,
  22, 36, 50, 54, 56, 112, 114,
  140, 142, 168
  fair example, 112
Multitude, 14, 160
Mu'min (pl. *mu'minūn*), see
  Believers
Musk, 186
Muslims, 34, 36

Nafs (pl. *anfus*), see Soul(s)
Name of God, 2, 100, 158,
  176, 194
  Beautiful Names, 48
  Most Beautiful Names, 76
Nār, see Fire
Narrow, 42
Nation, 60
  middle nation, 10
Nature:
  immense magnitude, 174
  immense nature, 174
  primordial Nature, 108
  tremendous nature, 174
  wondrous magnitude, 174
Near:
  brought near to God, 160,
  186
  God is Near, 12
  nearer to man, 142, 162
  nearest in affection, 36
  nearest of kin, 98
Necks, 120

Index

Need, 40, 124
Needy, 56, 90, 190
Niche, 92
Nigh, 14, 44, 92
  brought, 160, 186
  come, 6, 54
  draw nigh, 194
  two thirds of the night, 178
Night, 38, 74, 84, 98, 104, 122, 132, 144, 182, 184, 190, 202
  keep vigil, 76, 176, 178
  Night of Power, 194
  Night of Worth, 194
Noah, 18
  wife of, 170
Nothing, 4, 74, 94, 134
Nourishment, 18
Numbers, 54
Nūr, see Light

Oath, 138
Obeisance, 148
Obey, 16, 26
  God and His Messenger, 142
Obligation, 56
Offspring, 70, 122
Oil, 92, 152
Olive, 92, 192
Oppress, 190
Ordained, 80
Ordaining:
  of love, 108
  of mercy, 108
Ordering, 44
Original, 108

Originate, 108
Orison, 172
Orphan, 190
Ourselves, 20
Outrage, 76
Outstrip, 122
Outward (The), see *az̧-Z̧āhir*
Overcome, 14, 22, 52
Overflow, 36
Overtake, 40, 122

Pairs, 122
Palace, 102
Palm, 148, 156
  palm branch, 122
Parable, 122
Paradise, 6, 14, 22, 24, 56, 122, 132, 160, 170, 188, see also Garden(s)
  Paradises of Eden, 56
  people of, 44, 122
Pardon, 126
Party, 90
Pass, 152
  pass away, 14, 22, 150
  pass between, 154
  pass beyond, 152
  pass on, 120
  pass over, 164
  pass without, 152
Past, 138
Pastime, 106
Path, 2, 32, 34, see also Way
  ascending path, 2
  of God, 10, 14, 132
  Our paths, 106

Path (*cont.*)
  right path, 100
  straight path, 2, 120
Patience, 66, 72, 176, 196
Patient, 78
  the patient, 72
Patiently:
  endure, 72
  wait, 144
Pattern, 20
  fair pattern, 112
Peace, 26, 44, 52, 60, 160
  greetings of, 116
  hearts at, 68
  soul at peace, 188
  Spirit of Peace, 54, 138, 140
  until dawn, 194
  word from Merciful
    Lord, 124
Pearl(s), 150, 156
Peerless, 66
Pelt, 198
Pen, 110, 174, 194
Penitent, 170
People, 72, 80, 84, 120, 122
  best people, 20
  disbelieving, 102
  His people, 14
  middle people, 10
  of Abraham, 40
  of Moses, 8
  of Paradise, 44, 122
  of the Book, 8
  one People, 32, 34
  who reflect, 108
  who transgress, 170

Perceive, 10
Perchance, 76
Perfect (v.):
  Religion, 30
  Revelation, 82
Perform, 4, 82
Perish, 104
Perishable, 104
Permission, 86
Permit, 82, 182
Petition, 152
Pharaoh, 170
Phases, 122
Piety, 80, 192
  deeds of, 4, 34
Pilgrimage, 86
Pious (n.), 4, 22, 96
Place (n.), 44, 80
  blessed place, Baca, 20
  drinking place, 8
  meeting-place of two
    Seas, 78
  resting place, 122
Place (v.), 18, 28, 40, 96, 98,
  120, 176
Planet, 38, 92
Play:
  in play, 84, 136
Pleased, 82, 140, 188
Pleasure:
  good pleasure, 30, 188
Pledge, 140
Plenty, 26, 96
Pliant, 128
Plots, 198
Pomegranate, 156

Ponder, 102
Pool, 102
Poor, 56, 118, 136
  poor emigrants, 166
Portion, 62
  destined portion, 132
Possessions, 168
Poverty, 54
Power, 72, 76
Praise (n.), 2, 74, 144
Praise (v.), 68, 74
Praiseworthy (The), see
  al-Ḥamīd
Pray, 12, 56, 132
Pray-er, 12
Prayer, 4, 10, 12, 82, 172
  funeral prayer, 56
  ritual prayer, 106
Precedence, 74
Precincts, 74
Pregnant, 48
Presence, 100
Prevail, 30, 54, 152, 168
Prevent, 126
Pride, 96
Priests, 36
Proceed, 76
Proclaim, 86, 190
Proffer, 26, 182
Profit (v.), 68, 144
Promise (v.), 28, 56, 96, 112, 132
Prophet (The), 36, 52, 114, 116, 170, 174, see also Muḥammad
  Seal of the Prophets, 114

Prophet (The) (*cont.*)
  unlettered, 46
Prophets, 26, 76
Prosper, 4
Prostrate, 6, 166, 194
Prostration, 6, 86
Protection, 18
Proud, 36, 96
Psalms, 76
Punish, 54
Punishment, 72, 128
Purify, 18, 26, 58, 86, 180, 184
  the purified, 162

Qalb (pl. *qulūb*), see Heart(s)
al-Qarīb:
  Near, 12
al-Qayyūm:
  Eternal, 82
Quake, 14, 112
Quaking, 112
Question, 14, 50, 76, 78, 84, 152
Quicken, 96
Quraish/Qoraish, 198
Qur'ān/Qoran/Koran, 54, 74, 82, 104, 148, 166, 176, 178
  Wise Qur'ān, 120

Rabb, see Lord
Rabbu'l-ʿālamīn:
  Lord of the worlds, 2, 98, 100, 102, 162

ar-Raḥīm:
  All-Merciful, 6, 52, 98,
    128, 132
  Boundlessly Merciful, 2
  Ever-Merciful, 2
  Meed-Giver of Mercy, 100
  Merciful, 2, 6, 52, 54, 58,
    90, 120, 124, 142
Raḥmah, see Mercy
ar-Raḥmān:
  All-Merciful, 2, 82, 100
  Clement, 2
  God of Mercy All-
    Transcendent, 148
  Infinitely Good, 2, 76,
    80, 148
Raiment, 176
Raise, 38, 68
  aloft, 148, 188
  to life, 40, 42
Rancour, 44, 72
Ranks, 168
Rasūl (pl. *rusul*), see
  Messenger(s)
Rate, 40, 88, 128
Ravine, 86
Reach, 20, 40, 78, 82,
  100, 120
Reality, 68, 76
Reason, 74
Receive:
  a great good, 16
  sustenance, 22
  words, 6
Recital, 176
Recitation, 162, 174

Recite, 176, 178, 186, 194
Reckoning, 18, 192
Reclining, 24, 122
Recognition, 36
Recompense, 178
Rectitude, 192
Reflect, 98, 102, 108
Reformers, 4
Refuge, 58
  seek refuge, 2
  take refuge, 80, 202
Rejoice, 20, 108
Release, 114
Relent, 6, 54, 178
Relenting (The), see
  at-Tawwāb
Reliance, 176
Relief, 56
Religion, 12, 30, 52, 108, 200
  immutable Religion, 108
  is *islām*, 18
  is submission, 18
  of Abraham, 10
  of Truth, 54, 168
Remain, 68, 150
Remember, 70, 84, 96
  God, 10, 12, 24, 28, 46,
    112, 114
  God's favour, 112
Remembrance of Allah, 106,
  see also Invocation of God
Remembrance of God, 68,
  72, 82, 94, 128, 168, 176,
  see also Invocation of God
  is greater, 106
Remembrancer, 144

Remembrancing, 144
Reminder, 120, 176, 182
Remove, 44, 72
Rent asunder, 166
Repel, 190
Repent, 170
Repentance, 58, 128
Representative, 116
Reproach, 66
Requite, 52
Resolve, 22
Rest, 104, 154, 158
 in security, 68
Resurrect, 76
Return, 100
 unto God, 10, 34, 110, 122, 124, 134, 188
Reveal, 4, 16, 36, 174, 194
 the Book, 32
 unto the angels, 50
Revelation, 82, 96, 98, 120, 146, 162, 176, 182, 186
Reward, 22, 110, 142
 bountiful, 164
 inmense reward, 28, 138
 noble reward, 120
Rich (The), see *al-Ghanī*
Ride, 122
Riḍwān, 56
Rift asunder, 84
Right, 148
 Companions of the, 160
 guidance, 78
 hand, 126, 160
 path, 100
Righteous, 26, 170, 182, 186

Rightness, 174
Rise, 100
 rise up, 112
Rivers, 8
 flowing rivers, 4, 56, 138
Rock, 8
Roll up, 84
Root, 70
Rotten, 124
Ruby, 156
Rūḥ, see Spirit
Ruin (v.), 20
Rust (n.), 186

Sabaeans/Sabeans/Sabians, 34
Ṣabr, see Patience
Sacrilege, 14
Ṣadaqah (pl. *ṣadaqāt*), see Alms
Safety, 140
Saints, 26
Salām, see Peace
Ṣalāt, see Prayer
Salt, 96
Samā' (pl. *samāwāt*), see Heaven(s)
aṣ-Ṣamad:
 Absolute Plenitude Sufficing-unto-Himself, 200
 Eternally Sufficient unto Himself, 200
 Self-Sufficient Besought of all, 200
 Self-Sufficing in Infinite Plenitude, 200

as-Ṣamad (cont.)
  Totally Sufficing unto
    Himself in His Infinite
    Perfection, 200
as-Samīʿ:
  Hearer, 134
Sanctuary, 18
  first sanctuary, 20
Sandals, 82
Sap, 38
Satan, 18, 76, 82, see also Iblis
  satans, 4
Satisfied, 60, 190
Say, 4, 10, 14, 20, 26, 36, 40,
  46, 50, 52, 66, 76, 78, 82,
  86, 96, 104, 114, 124, 132,
  142, 174, 176, 200, 202
Scales, 148
Scriptures, 100, 172
Scroll, 84
Scum, 68
Sea, 38, 78, 150
  brackish salt sea, 96
  salted sea, 96
  seven seas, 110
  two Seas, 78, 96, 150
Season, 70
Seat, 100
Seclude, 80, 156
Secret:
  in secret, 44
  secretly, 110
Security, 68
Sedition, 12, 52
See, 10, 22, 36, 46, 70, 84, 96,
  100, 104, 120, 162, 166, 198

Seed, 38, 46
Seek, 26
  help, 2, 10
  His Face, 38, 78
  His favours, 104
  refuge, 2
Seer (The), see al-Baṣīr
Selling, 94
Send, 54, 84, 112, 120, 130,
  152, 168
  down, 26, 28, 36, 54, 60,
    68, 72, 76, 96, 138, 140,
    166, 194
  unto, 6, 80
  upon, 198
Senseless, 46
Sentence, 120
Separate, 28
Set, 38, 40, 42, 96, 148, 170
  free, slaves, 56
  hopes, 60, 112
Settle, 70
Seven, 74, 110
Seventy, 56
Shackles, 120
Shayṭān, see Satan(s) and Iblis
Sheaths, 148
Sheep, 84
Shield, 198
Ships, 150
Show, 16, 26, 38, 68, 82, 132
Shrink, 116
  shrink away, 110
Shun, 180
Sides, 24, 110
Sigh, 62

Sight, 40, 72, 86, 146
  of God, 88, 90, 138, 144
Sign(s), 36, 60, 72, 80, 84, 98, 108, 122, 132, 146
Silver, 154
Similitude, 70, 166
Sins, 122, 128, 152
  avoid great sins, 26
  incitement to sin, 160
Ṣirāṭ, see Path and Way
Sit, 24, 32
Six, 62
Skins, 128
Sky, 10, 60
Slaughter, 52
Slave(s), 74, 130
  of God, 12, 72, 76, 78, 128, 170, 182, 188
  set free, 56
Slay, 10, 22, 28
Smite, 14, 50
Solomon, 84, 100, 102
Son(s), 20
  most pure, 80
  of Adam, 46
Soul(s), 8, 58, 62, 66, 110, 112, 132, 138, 188
  Ever-upbraiding soul, 180
  have done wrong unto, 102
Sovereignty, 94, 126
Sovranty, 124
Span, 148
Speak, 62, 82, 90, 182
Speaking:
  idle speaking, 160
  of God, 46

Speech, 148
Sphere, 122
Spirit, 28, 72, 76, 80, 98, 170, 172, 194
  of Peace, 54, 138, 140
Splendour, 60, 92
Split asunder, 8, 166
Spoils, 26, 50, 140
Sprawl, 70
Springs, 8
Staff, 8
Stand, 24, 56, 86
  stand firm, 44
  stand over, 44
Standards, 150
Star(s), 144, 148
Station, 76
Steadfast, 10, 14, 22
Steadfastness, 10
Steadiness, 112
Stealthy, 202
Stones, 8, 198
Store:
  in store, 110, 114
  stored up, 110
Straiten, 54, 58
Strange, 112
Strength, 16, 100
Strike, 8, 50
  fear, 52
Strive, 22, 106, 186
Strivers, 186
Stumbling block, 102
Submission, 18, 42, 112
Submissive, 170
Submit, 130, 142

233

Subsistence, 18
Succeed, 98
Suffer, 72, 150
Sufficiency, 24
Summer, 198
Summon, 20
Sun, 40, 60, 122, 132, 148
Supple, 128
Support, 52
Suppress, 66
Surrender, 100, 102, 128
Sustain, 70
Sustenance, 18, 24
Swallow (v.), 118
Swear, 90
  allegiance, 138
Sweet, 96
Symbol:
  cited by God, 6, 70, 92
  of His light, 92
  of reality and illusion, 68

Tabernacle, 92
Tablet:
  Guarded Tablet, 186
  inviolable Tablet, 186
Take, 8, 74
  alms, 58
  heed, 52, 74
  refuge, 80, 202
  take away, 24, 64
  take from, 52, 122, 138, 176
  take off, 82
  take unto, 176, 182
  take upon, 90, 116
Tales, 186

Talk:
  idle talk, 40
  vain talk, 40, 160
Task, 82
at-Tawwāb:
  Ever-Relenting, 6, 58
  Relenting, 6
Teach, 78, 194
  the Qur'ān, 148
Tears, 36
Tents, 156
Term, 108
Terror, 50
Test, 112
  fair test, 32, 34
Testify, 46, 172
Thankful, 22
  be thankful, 70, 72, 104
Thirsty, 94
Thoughts, 112
Thousand:
  angels, 50
  months, 194
  years, 88
Thrill, 50, 128
Throats, 112
Throne, 62, 100, 102
Throw, 50
Thunder, 68
Tidings, 100
  glad, 4
  good, 10, 120, 132
  great, 126
  no good, 96
Tilthless, 70
Tomorrow, 78

Index

Tongue, 82, 90
Touch (v.), 80, 92, 162
Towering, 150
Townsfolk, 122
Transgress, 146, 148, 170
Transgressors, 6, 44
Travel (v.), 22
Treacherous, 52
Treachery, 52
Treasuries, 72
Tree, 6, 70, 110, 140, 148
  bad tree, 70
  blessed tree, 92
  good tree, 70
  Lote Tree, 146
  of Immortality, 82
  sacred olive tree, 92
Trespasses (n.), 138
Trifle (n.), 90
Triumph (n.), 138
Troop, 50
Trumpet, 180
Trust (n.), 116
Trust (v.), 22, 52, 72
Trustiness, 100
Truth, 20, 32, 36, 76, 108, 116, 132, 136, 172, 196
  Religion of, 54, 168
Try, 10, 84, 112
Turn, 8, 10, 22, 40, 54, 58, 108, 128, 152, 198
  turn aside, 110
  turn away, 184
Two:
  Easts, 150
  fountains, 154, 156

Two (*cont.*)
  Gardens, 154, 156
  kinds of fruit, 154
  righteous men, 170
  seas, 78, 96, 150
  second of two, 56
  thirds of the night, 178
  Wests, 150
Tyrant, 116

Unchaste, 80
Unclean, 54
Understand, 74, 106
Understanding, 84
Unite, 52
  Uniting, 198
Unmanifest, 38
Unseen, 4
Upbraiding, 66
Uprightness, 192
Uprise, 144
Uprooted, 70
Utter, 20, 28, 90
Utterance, 160, 162

Vain, 88
Valley, 68, 70
  Valley of Tuwa, 82
Vanish, 76
Vanisher, 76
Vanity, 76
Variance, 34
Vast (The), see *al-Wāsiʿ*
Vastness, 58
Veil, 120
Viceregent, 6
Victorious, 138

Victory, 86, 138, 140
Vie, 32, 34
Vigil:
  keep vigil, 76, 176, 178
Virgin maids, 170
Virginity, 170, 172
Vision, 140
Vow, 112

al-Wahhāb:
  Giver, 126
Wail, 62
Wait, 112, 144
  waiting, 116
Walk, 40, 42, 76
War, 50, 52, 54
al-Wārith:
  Inheritor, 72
Warm, 100
Warn, 98, 120, 126, 180
Warner, 96, 98
al-Wāsiʿ:
  Infinitely Vast, 8
  Vast, 8
Watcher, 32
Water, 8, 26, 62, 94, 102
  in creation, 84, 96
  scalding waters, 154
  sent down from Heaven, 68, 96
  this lower life as, 60
Waver, 112, 146
Way, 2, 10, 32, 34, see also Path
  ascending way, 60
  of God, 10, 22, 26, 28
  of Transcendence, 2

Way (cont.)
  unto his Lord, 176, 182
  ways of life, 22
Wayfarer, 56
Wealth, 58, 90
Weight, 148, 176
West(s), 8, 92
  Lord of, 176
  two Wests, 150
Whisper, 82, 202
  insidious whisper, 202
White, 66
Widows, 170
Will, 16, 18, 32, 34, 54, 60, 64, 66, 68, 78, 92, 104, 118, 134, 176, 182
  God willing, 78, 140
Wind, 112
Wine, 186
Wing, 98
Winter, 198
Wipe:
  faults, 26
  with earth, 26
Wisdom, 16
Wise, 106
Wise (The), see al-Ḥakīm
Wish, 12, 22, 32, 34, 42, 64, 124
Withdraw, 80
Withhold, 142
Witness, 36, 46, 84
Wives, 170
  of the Prophet, 114, 170
Womb, 48, 172

Women, 18, 20, 56, 202
  believing women, 138
Wont, 26, 102, 110
  of God, 58
Wool, 196
Word(s), 6, 28, 82, 124
  bad word, 70
  good word, 70
  of God, 110
  of heavy weight, 176
  of Lord, 78, 170, 172
  vain word, 160
Work(s), 122
  good works, 32, 34, 196
  work of art, 82
World, 18
  all the world, 20
  this world, 38, 52, 190
Worlds, 2, 84, 98, 100, 102, 162
  all the worlds, 18, 96
  in the worlds of creation, 150

Worship (n.), 170
Worship (v.), 2, 102, 122, 132, 144, 198, 200
Worth, 40, 88, 128, 194
Wrapped, 176, 180
Wrath, 2
Wretched, 62
Write, 110, 174
Wrong, 86, 102

Yā Sīn, 120
Yawm (pl. *ayyām*), see Day(s)
Year, 54
  thousand years, 88
Yourselves, 20, 26, 52, 100, 108, 128, 178

az-Ẓāhir:
  Outward, 164
  Outwardly Manifest, 164
Zakariya, 18
Zodiac, 98